Nutrition for Massage Therapists

By Dr. Rudy Scarfalloto

Nutrition for Massage Therapists

Rudy Scarfalloto D.C.

© Copyright 2013, Rudy Scarfalloto
All Rights Reserved.
No part of this book may be reproduced, stored in a retrieval system, or transmitted by any means, electronic, mechanical, photocopying, recording, or otherwise without written permission from the author.

ISBN: 098268326-X
ISBN 13: 978-0-9826832-6-2

Library of Congress Control Number: 2010918488

¤

¤

Serenity Press
Norross, Georgia

Readers Comments

"In a clear and intelligent manner, Dr. Scarfalloto teaches massage therapists and other bodyworkers about nutrition and food. He realizes that the mind/body connection, so inherent in our work, can be influenced by the foods we eat and the nutrients we assimilate. This book should be read by anyone who values a strong body and strong spirit. Bravo!"
 — Elaine Stillerrman, LMT, author of *Prenatal Massage*, and *Modalities For Massage and bodywork*. NYC

"I am so grateful for this book. Dr. Scarfalloto has done an excellent job researching the overwhelming amount of nutritional information on the market today, and forming a cohesive unit that makes sense and is practical in its application as well. The science of nutrition is covered, fad diets are addressed, and a guide to making good nutritional choices is included. There is a wealth of information for the massage therapist to apply personally, and hold informed conversations with clients. The presentation of the material allows the knowledge gained to be integrated immediately into lifestyle and diet. If you are a massage therapist or health professional, and you are searching for one book that covers all aspects of nutrition, this is the book for you."
 — Sasha Snyder, LMT, M.Th. Naples, Florida.

"Dr. Rudy Scarfalloto's book sheds a light of pure awareness on the connection between consciousness and the nutritional and physiological science behind the massage profession. It left me feeling motivated not only to help heal my clients from the outside in, but to heal myself from the inside out. His work is the voice of reason in a world of battling opinions on health and nutrition. It's refreshing hearing such a balanced voice!"
 — Meredith Barr, LMT, public school teacher. Atlanta, GA.

"As I think about this timely book, my first thought is that it is a great and wonderful resource--not only for massage therapists, but for anyone who may be seeking a better understanding of nutrition. Massage therapy should be viewed by our clients as a wellness practice for better health and quality of life. Dr. Scarfalloto's book provides clarity concerning what we eat and how food relates to massage therapy. I think it should be a required text for massage therapists."
 — Dante C. Tobias, LMT. Former pastor, serving the Seventh-Day Adventist Church. Lithonia GA.

"In this amazing book, Dr. Scarfalloto masterfully explains the important link between proper nutrition and the physical and emotional health of all humans. He provides an accurate and concise guide for massage therapists as well as all health care practitioners and laymen."

— Danielle J. Lefemine, LMT. Austin, TX.

"I thoroughly enjoyed this book. It is simple and clear, and especially useful as the author incorporates the little learning snippets and facts of interest, throughout the book. I do think it is exciting, and still a little "daring" to get massage therapists involved with the care of their client's nutrition as part of client treatment and wellness. In school, I remember hearing so much about things we were supposed to NOT do. It is refreshing to see a needed and welcome addition to the well being of our clients. It brings additional recognition to the fact that massage therapists are, indeed health care practitioners."

— Adam Pancake, massage therapist, psychotherapist. Atlanta, GA

"In this informative book, Dr. Scarfalloto guides the massage therapist towards a great start on the journey to healthy eating. With my perspective as both a massage therapist and the co-founder of the first farm in the Southeast to produce wheatgrass and other young greens, I fully endorse Dr. Rudy's book. Massage therapy is good medicine, and it's far more potent than most people realize. Fundamental to being effective massage therapists, we must learn n adequate self-care to support our physical, mental, and spiritual health, so that we are able to nurture and support our clients with our full potential."

— Marlene Webb, massage therapist, co-founder of Vonnie's Greens.
Decatur, GA.

"Dr. Scarfalloto has the ability to take some of the most complicated ideas and make them uncomplicated and accessible. He clears a path through the nutritional jungle and guides the reader on a journey of understanding their own body and its needs. This in turn will allow the readers to effectively help themselves and those they serve in their practices. I highly recommend this book for massage therapists or other alternative medicine practitioners, whether they are just beginning their careers or have been working for eons."

— Jeremy Taylor LMT, high school teacher. Atlanta, GA.

Acknowledgments

My thanks to Dr. Jan Ellis for providing the framework of the original nutrition course that eventually evolved into this book. I also wish to thank Karen Lyke, Dr. Brenda Hardy, Stevie Tucker, Lisa Bennett, Deborah Taylor, Jeremy Taylor, Meredith Barr, Francine Brown and Aubrey Lewis for their editorial assistance and valuable comments.

I especially wish to thank Jim Gabriel, the Founder of ASHA School of Massage, who had the vision to make ASHA the first massage school in the United States to teach nutrition as part of the core massage program. I extend the same thanks to Dr. Stan Dawson, the Owner/Executive Director of ASHA, for his continued support of nutrition education for massage therapists.

And finally, I wish to express my appreciation to the students and graduates of ASHA School of Massage. Their enthusiasm for nutrition has played a major role in motivating me to write this work.

OTHER BOOKS BY RUDY SCARFALLOTO

The Dance of Opposites

Cultivating Inner Harmony

The Edge of Time

Table of Contents

Part I: Basic Principles

Introduction 1

Chapter 1: The Foundation 5
    What is a Nutrient? 5
    Three Ways of Using Nutrients 6

Chapter 2: Macronutrients 13
    Carbohydrates, Lipids and Proteins 13

Chapter 3: Micronutrients 37
    Vitamins, Minerals and Phytonutrients 37

Chapter 4: Digestion 49
    Review of Anatomy 50
    Review of Physiology 54

Chapter 5: Cleansing & Elimination 59
    Cleaning the Large Intestine 59
    Cleaning the Liver 61
    Cleaning the Kidneys, Lungs and Skin 62

Chapter 6: The Food Groups 67
    Plant-Based Foods 67
    Animal-Based Foods 74

Chapter 7 Guidelines for Healthy Eating 83
    Food Combining 84
    Organically Grown 87

Chapter 8: Survey of Major Diets 91
    How to Evaluate Any Diet 93
    Low-Carbohydrate Diets 100
    Low-Fat Diets 106
    Vegetarian Diets 109
    Raw Food Diets 111

Chapter 9: Eating and Emotions 119
    Untangling Emotional and Nutritional Needs 121
    Eating by Instinct 125

Chapter 10: Time to Choose 129
    Choosing Your Diet 130
    What's for Breakfast? 131

What's for Lunch? 133
What's for Dinner? 134
Advising Your Client on Diet 136

Part II: Clinical Application

CHAPTER 11: NUTRITION AND YOUR MASSAGE PRACTICE 139
Dietary Stressors and Sore Muscles 140
Better Results through Better Nutrition 142
Home Remedies for Your Clients 142
Palpation and Nutrition 145

CHAPTER 12: STRESS 147

CHAPTER 13: FIBROMYALGIA AND CHRONIC FATIGUE SYNDROME 153

CHAPTER 14: BONES AND JOINTS 157
Review of Bones and Joints 157
Osteoporosis and Food 157
Arthritis and Food 159

CHAPTER 15: CARDIOVASCULAR HEALTH 163
Review of the Circulatory System 164
Edema and Inflammation 166
Reversing Cardiovascular Conditions 168

CHAPTER 16: IMMUNE SYSTEM 173
Review of Body Defenses 173
Antibiotics and Vaccinations 176
Ways of Boosting the Immune System 177

CHAPTER 17: BLOOD SUGAR 179
How Does the Body Regulate Blood Sugar? 179
Hypoglycemia and Diabetes Mellitus 180
Yeast Overgrowth 186

CHAPTER 18: COUNSELING YOUR CLIENT ON WEIGHT LOSS 189
The Stop Signal 189
Four Principles for Safe and Effective Weight Loss 191
What to Tell Your Clients 192

CHAPTER 19: DEPRESSION AND ADDICTIONS 195

APPENDIX 205
Information for Your Clients 207
Study Guide 243
References 249
Index 259

Part I
BASIC PRINCIPLES

Introduction

The Foundation

The Macronutrients

The Micronutrients

Digestion

Cleansing and Elimination

The Food Groups

Guidelines for Healthy Eating

Survey of Major Diets

Eating and Emotions

Time to Choose!

INTRODUCTION

This book is, essentially, a nutrition course designed for the massage therapist. Through reading and studying this book, you can expect to gain the following three benefits:

- Better health through good nutrition.
- Enrichment of your massage practice.
- Deeper knowledge of the "Physiology" part of the Anatomy and Physiology course you took in massage school.

Part I of this book includes information that is likely to appear in any basic nutrition book. This part of the book describes nutrients, food groups, organically grown food and a survey of the major dietary systems. This book does not endorse any specific diet, but rather provides you with the tools to evaluate each system, so you can select the one that is most appropriate for you.

Part II of this book is designed to enhance your skills as a health educator. You will be able to offer guidance to your clients who are seeking to optimize their well-being. You will also be able to provide useful information for your clients who are suffering from specific health issues that you are likely to encounter in your massage practice, such as fibromyalgia or arthritis. You will be able to clearly explain to your clients how their diet might be contributing to their chronic muscle tension, painful joints and unrestful sleep. You will be able to give them simple guidelines that will improve their health, while increasing the effectiveness of your work.

To further support you as a health educator, the appendix of this book contains a series of articles on various nutritional topics that are likely to be of interest to your clients. Feel free to give these articles to your clients.

One of the features of this book is that it provides a review of certain parts of the anatomy and physiology course that you probably took in massage school. For example, this book offers a review of nutritional biochemistry, the circulatory system, digestive system and the organs of excretion. This basic information is then specifically applied as strategies for promoting the cleansing and healing of the body. Perhaps you had an interest in these subjects while you were in massage school, but were not able to give them as much attention as you would have liked. If so, this book will provide you with an opportunity to fill in these gaps and fine-tune your grasp of human physiology, with a focus on promoting optimum health through good nutrition. In fact, since this book has more anatomy and physiology than the typical nutrition book written for the general public, it can offer a deeper level of understanding of the major nutritional issues faced by modern humans, and therefore allows the reader to more effectively navigate through the confusion and contradictions we tend to encounter in the study of nutrition.

Body and Mind

As part of your training as a massage therapist, you have probably cultivated some appreciation for the relationship between body and mind. That relationship is an integral part of this book, precisely because it is an integral part of massage, and has been from its inception in ancient China. That relationship was not lost, but rather developed "legs" when it was adapted into a Western system based on our understanding of anatomy and physiology. However, there is another reason to include the body/mind relationship in this book. As described later, the ability to properly select one's food depends on a healthy mind/body relationship. Indeed, a quick and ready way to gauge the level of integration between your body and mind is to consider your own emotional relationship to food.

Emotional comfort and eating habits are very much connected. In the world of the infant, emotional comfort and nourishment are very much connected. They are the first forms of comfort we experienced outside the womb, and are usually given at the same time, throughout infancy.

The primordial association of food and loving touch is maintained throughout childhood and into adulthood. It might explain why we tend to use food as a replacement for loving touch and emotional closeness. Likewise, that connection might explain why healing through bodywork and nutrition go so well together and actually complement each other, as explained later in this book. In particular, it might explain why many diets "don't work." Sometimes we, perhaps unconsciously, expect food to do something it was not designed to do, which is what often happens when the body/mind relationship is torn asunder.

The key word in restoring the harmony between the body and mind, whether we are working with therapeutic touch, nutrition or both, is *respect*. More specifically, respect for your body and that of your client. As you might guess, the level of respect you have for your client is a direct reflection of the respect you have for yourself.

The attitude of respect, when it is genuine, radiates silently from you. It tends to create a feeling of ease and safety for your clients, who might be searching for nutritional guidance but are leery of being judged harshly for their food choices, or of being pushed to do something that does not feel right to them. Instead, you will provide them with the breathing room to discover their own truth, including the truth of what they need nutritionally.

The most respectful attitude toward your client is the one rooted in the recognition that the innate wisdom within them knows exactly what it is doing. It is with this attitude, that I offer you this book, as a tool for enhancing your own health and enriching your practice as a massage therapist.

Chapter I
The Foundation

This chapter establishes the foundation for learning nutrition. This is where we define the terms commonly used in the study of nutrition. In addition, this chapter describes the three fundamental ways the body uses nutrients. The more precisely we describe the basics, the more clearly we can see into the world of nutrition.

Clarify and Simplify

One of the factors that complicate the learning of nutrition is the lack of clear definitions for the words we use. What is a *nutrient*? What is a *simple sugar*? What is a *complex carbohydrate*? What is *metabolism*? When we say that a food or nutrient gives us *energy*, what does that really mean? What is the difference between *food* and *medicine*? These terms have specific definitions, but popular authors often "bend" these definitions. The same word can be used in different ways by different authors. Such lack of consistency tends to confuse an already complex subject. Therefore, we will begin by providing clear definitions for the common terms used in the study of nutrition.

What is a Nutrient?

A logical first step in the study of nutrition is to define the term *nutrient*, which is not synonymous with food. Food is the stuff we eat. Nutrients are the chemicals that the body extracts from food to promote life. Most nutrients are large organic molecules. The exceptions are minerals — consist of individual elements (atoms).

Once we grasp the distinction between food and nutrients, we would not say, "wheat is a carbohydrate," because we understand that wheat is a food, while a carbohydrate is a nutrient found in wheat. Instead, we would correctly say that wheat is a rich source of carbohydrates. We would also understand that wheat contains other nutrients besides carbohydrates such as protein and fats. Similarly, we would not say, "salmon is a protein." Instead, we would say that salmon is a rich source of protein while providing other nutrients as well.

By understanding the distinction between food and nutrients, we can fully appreciate the concept of *whole food* which refers to any food that contains all the nutrients provided by Nature. For example, an orange is a whole food. On the other hand, cheese is not a whole food; it is an extract consisting of some of the nutrients (mostly protein and fat) found in milk. In other words, cheese has an unnaturally high concentration of some nutrients and is deficient in others. This is significant because the unnaturally high concentration of protein and fat could overburden the digestive system, while the lack of other nutrients essentially "robs" the body of these same nutrients. The same would apply for any extracted food, such as vegetable oil, butter or tofu. Therefore, an important concept for promoting good nutrition is to favor whole foods while avoiding or exercising moderation with any food whose nutritional profile has been altered.

Nutrients Are Used In Three Ways

The second step in our study of nutrition is an important one that is often overlooked, leading to unnecessary confusion. I am referring here to the understanding that nutrients are used by the body in one of three basic ways:

- They are burned as fuel.
- They are used as building material.
- They provide regulatory functions.

Nutrients as Fuel

Nutrients that act as fuel are simply broken down ("burned") for energy. Big molecules are broken down into smaller molecules, and in the process, energy is released. For example, glucose is burned for energy in your body cells just like gasoline is burned in your car. In fact, both gasoline and glucose, when burned efficiently and completely, will yield exactly the same waste products: carbon dioxide and water.

Since the body burns fuel continuously, *nutrients that are burned as fuel must be ingested in relatively large amounts.* Typically, nutrients used as fuel form the bulk of a person's diet. This simple concept can simplify the task of discovering your ideal diet, as described in later chapters.

Nutrients as Building Material

While fuel is broken down for energy, building material is assembled like bricks and mortar to form the flesh and bones of the body. In other words, smaller molecules are assembled into bigger molecules, and the bigger molecules are assembled into the larger aggregates that ultimately make up the cells, tissues and organs.

Nutrients used as building material are needed in lesser quantities than nutrients which are burned as fuel. This is easy to understand when we remember that fuel has to be continually replaced, while building material must be replaced to allow for growth, repair and maintenance. As an analogy, wood can be used to build and repair your house, as well as to heat your house. Ultimately, you need less wood to build and repair your house than to heat your house.

Naturally, a growing body needs more building material than one that is simply maintaining its mass. However, even when you were an infant, during which your body was engaged in its most rapid growth period, your need for building material was substantially less than that of fuel.

Nutrients as Regulatory Agents

Regulatory nutrients, as the name indicates, help to regulate the normal chemical reactions of the body. These nutrients, though very important, are typically needed in very small amounts, much less than nutrients used for fuel or building material.

Macronutrients, Micronutrients and Calories

As their respective names indicate, macronutrients are needed in relatively large amounts, while micronutrients are needed in small amounts. Below is a list of the categories of macro- and micronutrients.

Figure 1: Classification of Nutrients

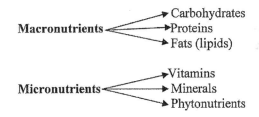

Macronutrients are needed in large amounts because they are typically burned for energy, and to a lesser extent, as building material. On the other hand, the micronutrients are needed in smaller amounts because they are typically used for their regulatory functions.

In chemistry, the energy released in a chemical reaction is measured in *calories*. In nutrition, the number of calories provided by a given food is a measure of how much energy would be released if the nutrients in the food were burned as fuel.

Though the body can burn all three macronutrients for energy, carbohydrates are the fuel of choice. Fats typically play a supporting role, but under certain conditions can have center stage. Either way, carbohydrates and fats are the dynamic duo for providing the body with energy.

What about protein? The burning of protein for energy is kept to a minimum because the excessive burning of protein can have some serious long-term consequences. This should be taken into consideration by those who want to lose weight by going on a very high protein (low fat and carbohydrate) diet. This issue will be explored more deeply later in the book.

A Closer Look at Regulatory Nutrients

Though micronutrients are the champs of regulation, this should not be interpreted as macronutrients having no regulatory functions. Carbohydrates, fats and proteins do indeed have regulatory functions, but their most obvious functions are that of fuel and building material.

Regulation of the body's physiology entails a vast number of chemical reactions. Among the many regulatory roles, three which are particularly significant are that of the antioxidants, enzymes and hormones.

Antioxidants

Antioxidants are chemicals which neutralize free radicals in the body. Free radicals are highly reactive molecules that can damage delicate proteins, lipids and even our genetic material (DNA). Free radical damage is a major cause of aging and degeneration. Conditions, such as arthritis, hardening of the arteries, loss of hair, cardiovascular disease, cancer and wrinkling of skin have been attributed to free radical damage. Many toxic chemicals are free radicals or promote the production of free radicals in the body.

The damaging effect of radiation is due to the production of free radicals. Not surprisingly, the effects of radiation can be reduced by eating foods which are rich in antioxidants. Those same antioxidants have been shown to have a protective effect against various degenerative diseases, as well as delaying the signs and symptoms of aging.[51]

Some vitamins and minerals and many phytonutrients have antioxidant activity. Among common fruits and vegetables, the highest sources by weight (in descending order) are as follows: prunes, raisins, blueberries, blackberries, kale, strawberries, spinach, raspberries, Brussels sprouts, alfalfa sprouts, plums, broccoli, beets, oranges, red grapes, red bell peppers, cherries, kiwi fruit and pink grapefruit.

Enzymes

Enzymes are proteins that speed up the chemical reactions of the body. All living organisms make their own enzymes. Regarding diet, some authors claim that enzymes found in foods are of value to us in various ways. However, food enzymes are quickly destroyed when heated beyond physiological temperatures (above 115 degrees Fahrenheit), which means that in order to benefit from food-derived enzymes, they must be consumed raw.

Hormones

Hormones are chemicals which play important regulatory roles in the body. Hormones are typically made of proteins, amino acids or fats. They often work by regulating enzymes. More specifically, hormones often influence gene expression, which in turn, determine which enzymes are made. Therefore, hormones have a profound effect on how the body develops and how it works.

The body manufactures all of its own hormones, but the overall diet can have a profound effect on hormonal levels. In addition, some plants have chemicals that have direct hormone-like effects, which may or may not be beneficial. For example, soybeans contain estrogen-like substances that could have medicinal value, but these same substances might also be harmful by disrupting the body's normal processes for regulating estrogen levels. In general, we should be cautious and conservative with products that exert a direct hormone-like effect on the body.

Metabolism

The term metabolism refers to the sum of all the chemical reactions in a living organism. The chemical reactions of the body fall into two categories: anabolism and catabolism. Anabolism refers to the building of molecules, and catabolism is the breaking down of molecules. Metabolism is regulated largely by the enzymes and hormones produced in the body, as well as the many regulatory nutrients such as ingested vitamins and minerals.

Food, Medicine and Toxins

If a nutrient is not used for fuel, building material or regulation, the only other possible effects are either that of a toxin or medicine. A toxin disrupts normal physiology, while medicine ideally helps to correct such disruption. For example, pumpkin seeds have chemical agents that kill worms, while pineapples contain the enzyme, bromelain, which helps reduce inflammation.

In order to properly distinguish between the purely nutritional effects and medicinal effects of naturally occurring substances, we must recognize that there are instances when the line between the two may be rather blurred. The term, "nutraceutical," recognizes the overlap between the nutritional and medicinal effect of various foods and nutrients. A nutraceutical refers to any food, food extract or nutrient that is promoted as having physiological benefits, beyond everyday nutrition, including the prevention and treatment of diseases.

Once we understand the distinction between the nutritive and medicinal effects, we can also understand that substances which clearly act as nutrients in the normal concentrations found in whole foods can have toxic or medicinal effects when used in larger concentrations. For example, the mineral, zinc, serves a number of normal regulatory functions, but it can quickly become toxic if taken in concentrations beyond what we encounter in whole foods. The vitamin C in foods has a number of important regulatory functions, such as participating in the production of collagen. In addition, some healthcare practitioners use very large doses of purified vitamin C, sometimes intravenously, to help overcome serious pathologies.

When we understand the distinction between the purely nutritive function of food and its possible medicinal functions, we are less likely to misuse foods and supplements. We understand that any substance that can act as medicine can also become toxic if used improperly. Therefore, when we use any substance for its medicinal value, we do so as conservatively as possible.

Individuals who unbalance themselves with food or supplements are typically trying to drug themselves, whether they are doing it for recreational (mood altering) purposes or purely medicinal purposes. Such disruption is more likely when using extracted chemicals (such as vitamins and minerals), compared to whole-foods or minimally processed supplements, because the isolated chemicals have been removed from their natural matrix and concentrated to levels the body normally does not encounter in whole foods.

Even if there are no toxic effects to speak of, when we place too much emphasis on selecting food for its medicinal value, we might be depriving ourselves of nutrients that we would normally receive when we eat to simply nourish the body. Therefore, the beginning student of nutrition is advised to first learn of the nutritive virtues of various foods, and save the medicinal exploration for later. As a rule of thumb, the more precisely we fulfill the body's purely nutritional needs, the less we have to be concerned about using medicine, natural or otherwise.

In this book, foods and their respective nutrients are explored primarily with respect to their nutritive roles, which means that we look at how they provide **fuel, building material** and **regulation.**

What about Water?

In the world of physiology and nutrition, water is the great mother. It is the matrix in which all of the macro and micronutrients are nested. Water provides the unifying presence that allows the other molecules to dance the dance of Life. Water is the solvent that allows the body to extract nutrients from food. Water carries those nutrients through the walls of the digestive tract, into the blood and into our cells. The various activities essential to life, including the contraction of muscles, the firing of nerves, and even the very thoughts and emotions that you're having right now, depend upon the molecules of life, communing with each other, as they float within the inner ocean which makes up about 65% of our body weight.

Since water is the single most abundant chemical in the body and is indispensable to life, the study of nutrition should include a thoughtful look at our water consumption with regard to quality and quantity.

To estimate the amount of water an individual needs, take his/her weight and divide by two. This will give the ounces of water required each day. For example: 128 lbs divided by 2 = 64 oz. or two quarts. Naturally, this water should be clean. Tap water is not ideal, since it is probably chlorinated, fluoridated and contains an abundance of industrial pollutants. However, water requirements vary according to a person's weight, age, occupation and activity level. Other factors to consider are diet, climate, season of the year and medication. Regarding diet, the higher our consumption of concentrated foods, or foods which have a relatively high toxic residue, the more water we should drink. Likewise, we need to drink less water if the diet includes an abundance of foods that already have a high water content and low toxic residue. For example, your need to drink water will be reduced if your diet consists entirely of fresh and raw fruits and vegetables. Both have an abundance of water that has been cleansed by the root system of the plant, which is the best filtering system we know of. The water content of most juicy fruit exceeds that of the human body, and therefore has a naturally cleansing and "flushing" effect.

It is best to drink more water in the earlier part of the day. This is when the body is most actively involved in cleansing and elimination. However, while eating, water should be minimized because it dilutes the digestive juices and tempts us to eat faster and chew less, leading to indigestion and gas. Drink water up to about 30 minutes before a meal and then wait at least one hour after a meal.

Chapter 2

Macronutrients

Carbohydrates
Lipids
Proteins

Carbohydrates

The carbohydrates we ingest are typically burned as fuel. In fact, of the three macronutrients, carbohydrates are generally burned in greatest quantities. Therefore, in most traditional diets, carbohydrates are the nutrients which provide the bulk of daily calories. In recent years, however, there has been a wave of low-carb diets that challenge the high-carb approach. Consequently, the average health seeker can become confused. Since you, as a massage therapist, have studied anatomy and physiology, you are in a position to see through that confusion simply by reviewing the basics about carbohydrates, lipids and protein.

The following chart shows the standard classification of carbohydrates used by chemists:

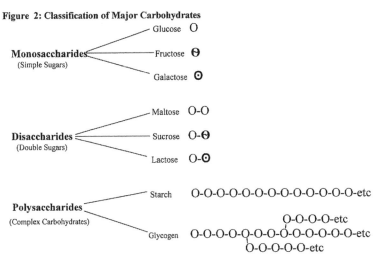

Figure 2: Classification of Major Carbohydrates

To understand how the human body handles carbohydrates, the three main terms to remember are *sugars, simple sugars* and *complex carbohydrates.*

Sugars

Any carbohydrate that tastes sweet is considered a sugar. They come in two varieties: simple sugars and double sugars.

- A **simple sugar** (monosaccharide) consists of a molecule which is small enough to easily pass from the digestive tract and into the blood without digestion.
- A **double sugar** (disaccharide) consists of two simple sugar molecules bonded together, as shown in figure 2. Unlike simple sugars, double sugars do require digestion through the action of enzymes, though they are digested rather quickly.

There are a number of simple and double sugars found in Nature. Figure 2 shows that the three major types of simple sugars are glucose, fructose and galactose.

Glucose

Glucose is our blood sugar. It is absorbed by our body cells and broken down (burned) for energy. Glucose is a simple sugar, which, again, means that it consists of relatively small molecules that can easily pass from the gut and into the blood without digestion. Glucose is abundant in fruits and, to a lesser extent, tender young vegetables.

Fructose

Fructose is similar to glucose. Like glucose, fructose is a simple sugar that passes from the gut and into the blood without the need for digestion, though it generally passes into the blood more slowly than glucose. Fructose is found in many fruits, hence its name. In other words, when you eat fruit, some of the glucose is absorbed right away to give your body an immediate source of energy, and then fructose follows later to give the cells additional energy.

Galactose

Galactose is another simple sugar. It is found in some fruits and young vegetables but less abundantly than glucose and fructose.

Maltose

Unlike the previous three, maltose is a *double sugar,* consisting of two glucose molecules bonded together, as shown in figure 2. Therefore, for the body to utilize maltose, it must first be digested down into glucose, so it can pass into the blood. This requires the presence of an enzyme called maltase. In other words, the body has to expend energy to digest maltose. Maltose is found in grains such as barley.

Sucrose

Sucrose is the sugar you buy in the supermarket. It is a double sugar consisting of a glucose and fructose molecule bonded together. Therefore, like maltose, it must first be enzymatically digested before it is absorbed into the blood.

Lactose

Lactose is the sugar found in milk. It is a double sugar consisting of two simple sugars which must be separated so they can be absorbed into the blood. The enzyme that digests lactose is called lactase. Many individuals do not have an adequate amount of lactase, which slows down lactose digestion. The undigested lactose remains in the intestines and is metabolized by microbes, resulting in the production of gas. Such individuals are said to be lactose intolerant.

Natural and Refined Sugar

Since simple sugars do not require enzymatic digestion, the body does not have to expend much energy to get them into the blood. They are, in essence, pre-digested. This is significant because digestion of large complex molecules constitutes a major energy expenditure for the body. By eating some "pre-digested" foods, the body can conserve its resources, which can then be used for other purposes, such as powering the immune system and regeneration.

The down side is that such quick absorption of simple sugars can tax the body's ability to process them, leading to blood sugar fluctuations and other issues. A simple way to avoid this problem is to get all your simple and double sugars in the form of whole foods, such as fresh fruit and young vegetables.

Sugars (and carbohydrates in general), are a problem when they are processed in a way that strips them of micronutrients and concentrates them to a level not presented by Nature. Sugars found in whole foods come with all of the vitamins, minerals and other nutrients that are necessary for the body to properly process those sugars. With refined foods, the vitamins, minerals and other nutrients have been removed. For example, refined cane sugar has nothing left except sucrose. Since all of the vitamins and minerals that occur in the sugar cane plant have been removed, the ingested sugar depletes the body of vitamins and minerals. Furthermore, because refined cane sugar is so concentrated, it has drug-like (toxic) effects that overpower the self-regulating capacity of the body. Like many drugs, refined sugar is capable of producing true addiction.

Young vegetables contain a relatively low level of sugars. Fresh fruit contains higher concentrations, but still in amounts that our digestive system can handle without difficulty. In addition, both fruits and vegetables have an abundance of fiber which slows down the passage of sugars into the blood.

Nonetheless, there is disagreement among various authors regarding how much fresh fruit we can safely consume before the sugar becomes problematic. We will address this issue in detail later. For now, the general rule is that most individuals can enjoy fresh whole fruit, either in moderate amounts or large amounts, depending on their physiology and lifestyle. On the other hand, fruit juice, dried fruit and products containing refined sugar, should be eaten sparingly or avoided entirely.

Complex Carbohydrates

A complex carbohydrate (polysaccharide) consists of many molecules of simple sugars strung together. The nutritionally significant complex carbohydrates are starch, glycogen and plant fiber.

Starch

Starch is the most common example of a complex carbohydrate. A starch molecule consists of many glucose molecules strung together into a straight or branched chain, as shown in figure 2.

If a naturally occurring plant food is sweet, it is rich in either simple or double sugars. If the plant food is not sweet, it probably has mostly complex carbohydrates, typically starch. Rich sources of starch include grains, legumes, potatoes and squash. Moderately starchy vegetables include broccoli and cauliflower. Green leafy vegetables, such as kale, spinach and collards have smaller amounts.

As previously mentioned, young plants tend to be sweeter because they have high glucose content. As the plant matures, it becomes less sweet because most of the glucose molecules are strung together into long starch molecules. For example, fresh corn on the cob is sweet, but if allowed to stay on the plant long enough, it becomes much less sweet and takes on a "starchy" quality.

When we digest starch, we break down each starch molecule into many glucose molecules. This takes quite a bit of enzyme power, which means that the body has to expend a substantial amount of its resources to digest starch.

Once the glucose gets into the blood, it makes no difference where it comes from. It is absorbed by our cells and burned for energy. Surplus glucose that is not immediately burned for energy is stored in the liver and muscles as glycogen.

Glycogen

A glycogen molecule consists of thousands of glucose molecules strung together in a branched chain, similar to starch, as shown in figure 2. In fact, glycogen is sometimes called "animal starch." In other words, we store glucose as glycogen, just like plants store glucose as starch.

However, the liver and muscles can store only a limited amount of glycogen because doing so requires a substantial amount of water. This simple fact is important in understanding why fasting or low-carb diets trigger rapid weight loss in the first few days. When we fast, or severely restrict the consumption of carbohydrates, the body quickly uses up its glycogen reserves and therefore loses the 2-6 pounds of water associated with the glycogen.

Plant Fiber

Plant fiber is an indigestible complex carbohydrate. Fiber, like starch, consists of many glucose molecules strung together. However, in the case of fiber, the glucose molecules are strung together in such a way that we cannot pry them apart with our digestive enzymes.

Virtually all plants contain fiber. All leafy vegetables are especially rich in fiber. The coarse fiber that coats grains is called *bran*. The soft fiber in fruit is called *pectin*.

A distinction is made between *soluble* and *insoluble* fiber. Soluble fiber tends to be softer and more absorbent. It includes all fruit pectin, and some forms of bran, such as those found in barley, rye and oats, as well as some legumes. Insoluble fiber is found in celery and most cereal grains such as wheat bran.

Since soluble fiber holds water, it provides quite a bit of bulk that is essential for proper cleansing of the digestive tract. Therefore, someone who starts eating more fruits and vegetables to lose weight might notice an initial "weight gain" and become discouraged, unless they understand what is actually happening.

Fabulous Fiber
Here are the main health benefits of fiber:

- Fiber decreases transit time. In other words, it causes food to pass through the digestive tract faster, rather than lingering for too long. Fiber does this in two ways: It mechanically pushes things along like a broom, scrubbing the intestinal wall. In addition, fiber stimulates contraction of the muscles in the wall of the digestive tract (peristalsis). If food remains in the digestive tract too long, some of the microbes will proliferate and produce harmful byproducts that are eventually absorbed into the blood and increase the toxic burden on the body.

- Fiber acts like a sponge that absorbs toxins so they cannot go into the blood.

- Fiber binds to excess cholesterol in the gut so it does not get absorbed into the blood.

- Fiber is a source of food for beneficial bacteria in the intestines.

- Fiber slows down the rate at which glucose and other simple sugars enter the blood, which helps to stabilize blood sugar.

- The added bulk from the fiber provides a feeling of fullness that prevents us from overeating high-calorie foods.

Refined Sugar and Sweeteners

As a way of avoiding the pitfalls of refined sugar, many individuals seek alternatives. The major commercial sweeteners are described below.

Xylitol

This is a five-carbon sugar (pentose) that looks and tastes like conventional sugar, but has about a third of the calories. It does not promote tooth decay, and does not influence blood sugar. It is found in strawberries, raspberries and plums. Its presence in strawberries might account for the claims that strawberries benefit the teeth.[1]

Stevia

This is an herbal extract. It has not been found to have any harmful side effects and is reputed to help stabilize blood sugar. If these claims are valid, it is ideal for diabetics.[2]

High Fructose Corn Syrup

This product is promoted as "natural" because fructose occurs abundantly in Nature. However, large concentrations of fructose, such as those found in virtually every packaged or processed food, activate alarm responses in the body. In addition to increasing stress, high levels of fructose promote fat production and elevation of blood fats.[3]

Saccharin

Saccharin has been used since the late 1800s. The FDA says that it is safe. However, over the years, the question of saccharin toxicity has been debated. Some studies have linked saccharin to bladder cancer in rats, but the mechanism of action is said to be unique to rats.[52] On a personal note, in the past, whenever I used products that contained saccharin, I developed canker sores.

Sorbitol

Sorbitol is the alcohol form of glucose. Since it has 2/3 the calories of glucose and is poorly absorbed, it is used as a sugar substitute. Sorbitol occurs naturally in some fruits and vegetables. Most of the sorbitol in processed foods is made from corn syrup. It has been implicated with gastrointestinal disturbances.[53]

Sucralose

Sucralose, marketed as Splenda, Sucraplus, Candys, Cukren, and Nevella, is an artificial sweetener manufactured by inserting three atoms of chlorine into the sucrose molecule. Since it cannot be burned by the cells for energy, it has zero calories. Since it is 600 times sweeter than sucrose, it can be used in very small quantities. It has been approved as safe by the FDA; however, animal studies produced shrunken thymus and enlarged livers and kidneys as short term effects.[5]

Aspartame

Aspartame is found in thousands of processed foods. It is marketed as NutraSweet, Equal, and Spoonful. It is derived from two amino acids, aspartic acid and phenylalanine. Early experiments had suggested that it might cause brain damage, but in 1981, the FDA declared that aspartame posed no significant health risk.

The FDA has approved it for use in breakfast cereals, carbonated soft drinks, chewing gum, children's vitamin supplements, and other products. Since then, studies have linked aspartame poisoning to 92 symptoms such as muscle spasms, shooting pains, numbness in the legs, vertigo, dizziness, seizures, headaches, tinnitus, joint pain, depression, anxiety attacks, slurred speech, blurred vision, blindness, brain damage, memory loss and birth defects (e.g. mental retardation). It has been linked to MS, lupus, fibromyalgia, diabetes, manic depression and brain tumors. To add insult to injury, aspartame induces a craving for carbohydrates.[6, 7, 8]

When the temperature of aspartame exceeds 86 degrees F, it converts into methanol, (wood alcohol), and then formaldehyde, and then into formic acid which causes metabolic acidosis. The methanol toxicity produces many of the symptoms of MS and lupus, and can lead to blindness and death. When people are taken off aspartame, those with systemic lupus, MS and other conditions listed above often improve.

Neotame is a variation on aspartame that contains 3-dimethylbutyl, which the Environmental Protection Agency lists as hazardous. It is 30 times sweeter than aspartame, which means that less can be used. Since the FDA does not require labels to include ingredients that comprise less than one percent of the product, neotame could be used in foods without having to be listed on the label. It might also be camouflaged under "natural flavors." It has also been approved for organic packaged food.[8]

Overcoming Sugar Addiction

When we eat food in a form other than the manner in which Nature presents it, addiction is a possibility. Our nervous system, like that of other animals, is designed to monitor and regulate the consumption of naturally occurring molecules, synergistically blended in whole foods. If a naturally occurring whole food is delicious to us, it is good food. If the food does not taste good, it is not good food. If the food has a very bitter or otherwise unpleasant taste or smell, it is probably toxic.

On the other hand, when we mix or otherwise alter foods, we will probably create situations where the yummy flavor conceals toxicity. In essence, the nervous system is deceived: We give it sweet tasting treats that give us short-term pleasure, followed by long-term suffering.

As with other addictions, total abstinence from the harmful substance can be part of the solution. However, we must also provide the body with what it actually needs. Perhaps a lack of minerals or proteinis driving the addiction. Perhaps there is a need for exercise. Perhaps the addiction is driven by non-nutritional issues. For example, there might be an unrecognized yearning for love or creative expression that we try to fill by eating strong tasting foods to excite the nervous system or numb our emotions.

In the case of sugar addiction, there is an element of grace. For most individuals, there is a simple way to mitigate or even eliminate the addiction to sugary processed foods. Every time you crave something sweet, instead of eating the usual concoctions full of refined sugar, fat and toxic non-food items, just eat some delicious fresh fruit.

The nice thing about fresh whole fruit is that the human nervous system is designed to recognize it and regulate how much we eat – as long as it has not been altered or mixed with anything else. Fresh fruit will not force itself upon you. If your body can benefit from a moderate amount of fruit, you will desire a moderate amount. If you can benefit from an abundance of fruit, you will desire an abundance.

As a point of caution, however, if you have a history of blood sugar issues, you may want to favor the lower glycemic fruits. Also, seek out high quality, organic and, ideally, tree or vine ripened fruit. Eat it slowly, in its unaltered form, and not mixed with anything else. This way, your brain has the best possible chance of giving you a good clear stop-signal when your body has had enough.

Lipids

Lipids are the macronutrients we commonly recognize as fats and oils. However, be aware that the term "fats" is frequently used loosely to mean both solid fats and liquid oils.

Lipids are strikingly different from carbohydrates, even though the two are composed of exactly the same atoms (carbon, hydrogen and oxygen). Carbohydrates are either crystalline or powder, and many of them dissolve easily in water and taste sweet. On the other hand, lipids tend repel water, they are slimy and greasy, and they do not taste sweet.

For the serious student of nutrition, a thorough knowledge of lipids is very important. For the person who just wants to eat healthy, lipids can be a major area of confusion because of the complexity of their chemistry and physiology. Add to this the economic and political agenda that has grown around lipids, and the confusion deepens. The next several pages are intended to bring some clarity and cohesion to this slippery subject.

Energy and More

Lipids serve as fuel and building material, as well as providing some important regulatory functions. More specifically:

- Fat is an important source of energy for our body cells, except for brain cells and red blood cells, which normally burn only simple sugars.
- Body fat is the ideal way to store energy because it packs twice the calories as the equivalent amount of carbohydrates or protein. Since it does not require water for storage, it can store the most fuel in the least amount of space, while being relatively light-weight.
- Body fat provides padding and thermal insulation.
- The membranes of all our body cells consist mostly of lipids.
- Lipids are especially important for maintaining a healthy nervous system. Most of the dry (non-water) weight of the brain consists of fats.
- Lipids are used in the manufacturing of hormones.

The main feature of lipids that makes them important to life is their tendency to repel water. The same feature also makes them a potential problem. To understand why, we must first be familiar with the various types of lipids found in the body. We will start by first identifying the three major categories of lipids: triglycerides, phospholipids and steroids (figure 3).

Figure 3: Classification of Lipids

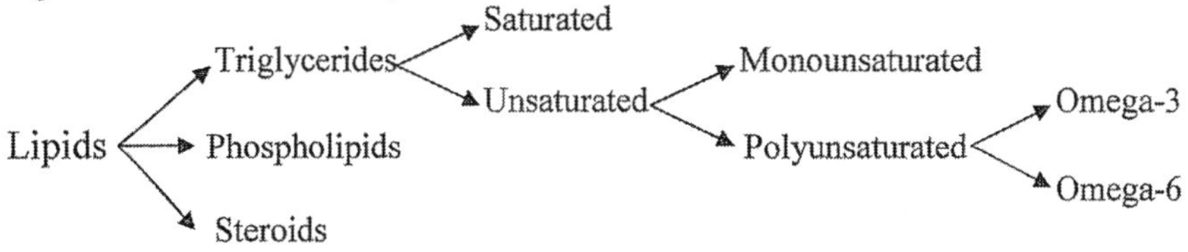

```
                    ┌─ Saturated
         Triglycerides                    ┌─ Monounsaturated
                    └─ Unsaturated                          ┌─ Omega-3
Lipids ──── Phospholipids                 └─ Polyunsaturated
                                                            └─ Omega-6
         Steroids
```

Triglycerides

Triglycerides are the most common lipids. They are the animal fats and vegetable oils we eat. Also, when we ingest more carbohydrates than we can burn for energy or store as glycogen, the extra carbohydrates are converted into triglycerides and stored as body fat. Measuring the level of blood triglycerides is important for assessing cardiovascular health.

Each triglyceride molecule consists of four smaller molecules: one glycerol molecule bonded to three fatty acid molecules, as shown in figure 4.

Figure 4: Triglyceride Molecule

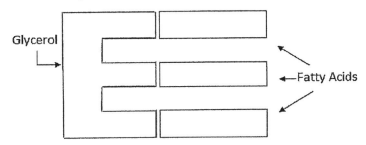

Saturated and Unsaturated Fatty Acids

The distinction between saturated and unsaturated fatty acids is rather important. To understand why this is so, let us take a closer look at the fatty acid portion of the triglyceride molecule. Figure 5, below, shows that a fatty acid molecule is essentially a chain of carbon atoms peppered with hydrogen and smaller amounts of oxygen.

Figure 5: Saturated Fatty Acid Molecule

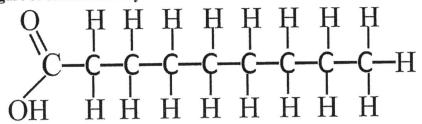

The molecule in figure 5 is said to be **saturated**, which means that it has as much hydrogen as it can hold. In contrast, an **unsaturated** fatty acid has "bare spots," where hydrogen has been removed, thus creating a pair of double bonded carbons, as in figure 6.

Figure 6: Monounsaturated Fatty Acid Molecule

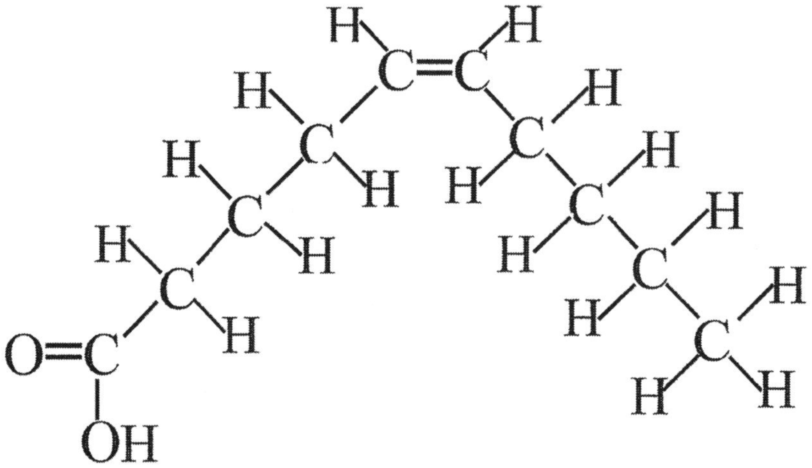

Notice the difference in shape between the saturated and unsaturated fatty acid. That difference in shape is critically important: It determines whether the fatty acids form a solid fat or liquid oil. This is because the hydrogen atoms within the molecule act like "Velcro" which clings to surrounding molecules. These bonds are weak and can only assert themselves when the neighboring fatty acid chains are straight enough to allow them to "stack up" and thereby stick together.

When the fatty acids are able to stack snuggly together, the cohesive force between them is strong enough to form a solid fat. When the fatty acid chains are "kinked," as in figure 6, they are unable to stick together as firmly, (like wrinkled Velcro), and thus form liquid oils.

Regarding unsaturated fatty acids, a further distinction is made between **monounsaturated** and **polyunsaturated** fatty acids. The fatty acid shown in figure 6 is designated as monounsaturated, meaning that it has only one set of double bonded carbons. As a result, the chain is not *too* kinked, and therefore tends to form a thick oil that can easily solidify with a relatively small drop in temperature. For example, olive oil consists largely of monounsaturated fatty acids. It is therefore fairly thick, and solidifies when the temperature drops to around 55 degrees, as when you store it in the refrigerator.

In contrast, polyunsaturated fatty acids have multiple bare spots, as shown in figure 7. Consequently, they are very kinked and therefore, produce very thin oils – that generally remain liquid in the refrigerator.

Figure 7: Polyunsaturated Fatty Acid (Alpha-linolenic acid)

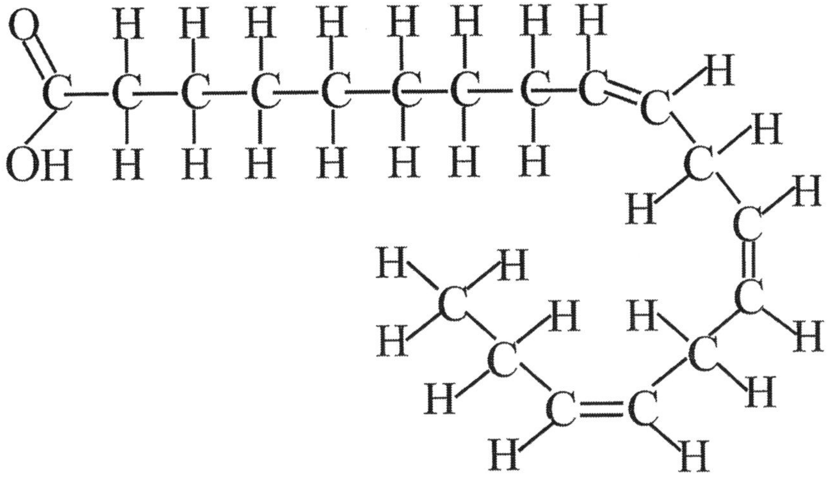

Why are these very kinky fatty acids significant for our health? To put it simply, if a fat is solid at room temperature, it is also likely to be solid at body temperature. This is entirely appropriate for some naturally occurring saturated fats, because solidness is often required to resist the dispersing and dissolving action of water. However, that same solid quality that makes saturated fats functional, can also make them problematical in large amounts. For example, an excess of saturated fats in the cell membranes results in a "stiffening" of the membranes, making them less sensitive to the hormone, insulin, thus hindering blood-sugar regulation. Not surprisingly, an increase in dietary saturated fats have been associated with diabetes.[9, 10] Other hormones can be similarly affected.

For optimum health, the body needs an ample amount of the thin polyunsaturated oils which give cell membranes the high level of fluidity required for optimum health. This is not to say that all dietary saturated fats should be avoided (which is actually impossible, because even plant-based foods have some saturated fat). Though the body can usually manufacture the needed saturated fats, small to moderate amounts of dietary saturated fats are generally well tolerated

Coconut oil and palm oil have been vilified by some nutritional authors because they are rich in saturated fats. As expected, they are solid at room temperature, but since their fatty acids are short, they quickly melt when the temperature rises above 76 degrees or so, and are nicely fluid at body temperature.

Essential Fatty Acids (EFA)

Essential fatty acids are polyunsaturated fatty acids which are important for our health, but cannot be made in the body. Deficiencies can result in a wide variety of ailments, including skin rashes, brittle nails, developmental problems (especially of the brain) in children, prostate problems, and reproductive disturbances.

Two EFAs are recognized: **Alpha linolenic acid** (shown in figure 7) and **linoleic acid**. From these two essential fatty acids, the body can manufacture other important fats.

Omega-3 and Omega-6

Alpha linolenic acid belongs to a group of unsaturated oils called omega-3. Linoleic acid belongs to another group, called omega-6. These two groups have received much attention in recent years, because the imbalance between the two contributes greatly to the major degenerative diseases in industrialized nations. Both groups are important, but must be kept in the right proportion in order for the body to maintain health.

Until recently, excess of saturated fats has been singled out as the major cause of cardiovascular problems. However, the imbalance of omega-3 and omega-6 is, arguably, just as serious, if not more so. Let's see why.

To do justice to this important topic, let's first understand why these two fats are called omega-3 and 6. "Omega" is simply the last letter in the Greek alphabet. Therefore, it is often used in science and math to designate the end of something. In this case, omega refers to the terminal carbon in any fatty acid chain. For example, if you look at the model of alpha-linolenic acid in figure 7, you will notice that the 3rd carbon from the end has a double bond. Therefore, alpha-linolenic acid is designated as an omega-3 fatty acid. On the other hand, if the last double bond is in the #6 position, we would have an omega-6 fatty acid, such as linoleic acid.

Since omega-3 and 6 are polyunsaturated, their molecules are both very kinked – but not in the same way. They have different shapes and therefore different effects on the body. With regard to diet and health, here are the essential facts about omega-3 and 6 oils:

- Omega-6 fatty acids are found abundantly in vegetable oils, peanut oil, soy bean oil, corn oil and safflower oil. They are important for a number of reasons such as growth and development, especially the brain. Deficiency can result in hair-loss, poor wound healing and behavioral problems.

- Omega-3 fatty acids are found abundantly in flax seeds, hemp seeds, chia seeds, sesame seeds, walnuts, some beans, sea vegetation, algae, grass-fed meat, egg-yokes and fish oils. Modest amounts are also found in some fruits and vegetables such as berries, kale and romaine lettuce. They are important for controlling inflammation, maintaining stable blood sugar, and keeping blood vessels soft and elastic. Inadequate levels of omega-3 oils, or too much omega-6, contribute to pain, inflammation, cardiovascular problems and other form of degeneration.

EPA and DHA

Two very important omega-3 oils are EPA (eocosapentanoic acid) and DHA (docosahexanoic acid). Both can be made in the body from alpha-linolenic acid. Our cells do this by simply lengthening the alpha-linolenic acid molecule. Therefore, EPA and DHA are called "long-chain" omega-3 fatty acids.

Some individuals seem to be able to make adequate amounts of EPA and DHA. Individuals who have problems doing so might benefit from getting these oils from food sources such as blue green algae, cold-water fish and high quality eggs with the deep orange yoke. DHA is particularly important for brain function. This is why fish has traditionally been known as "brain food."

One common way of developing a "virtual" omega-3 deficiency is with a dietary excess of omega-6. Too much omega-6 will inhibit the conversion of alpha-linolenic acid to EPA and DHA. Ideally, the consumption of omega-3 and 6 should be about equal. More specifically, the ratio of omega-6 to omega-3 should be 1–1 or 2–1, depending on the source of information. However, the typical diet provides 10 to 30 times more omega-6 than omega-3. Such massive imbalance has been associated with greater susceptibility to excessive blood clotting, cardiovascular disease, high blood pressure, autoimmune conditions, diabetes, chronic pain and inflammation, colitis, mood swings and problems with learning and concentration.[11,12,29]

Why the Gross Imbalance of Omega-3 and 6?

Given the many problems that can arise from omega-3 to omega-6 imbalance, we might ask, why are they so lopsided in modern diets? The reason is simple: The main sources of omega-6 are wheat, corn and soy, all of which are very cheap and therefore, widely used, commercially. One reason they are cheap is that they are easy to grow. However, the main reason is that both are heavily subsidized by the federal government in the USA at the present time. Their low price makes them ideal fillers in many processed foods. For the same reason, corn and soy are routinely fed to chickens and cows, which means the eggs, milk and meat are also artificially cheap and unnaturally skewed toward the omega-6 side. This is one of many reasons to minimize processed foods and emphasize whole foods.

Partially Hydrogenated Oils

Shortening and margarine are the two common examples of partially hydrogenated oils. Though they have been widely used for the past 100 years or so, they have only recently received public attention due to the ever expanding mountain of evidence which shows them to be destructive to our health. Therefore, students of nutrition should be familiar with their basic chemistry and effects on the body.

Here is how partially hydrogenated oils are made: Through an industrial process, liquid vegetable oils are solidified by introducing hydrogen into the otherwise unsaturated fatty acid chains. You can see exactly how this is done, if you look at the figure 7. Essentially, the hydrogen is inserted into the parts of the carbon chain that have the double bonds (where the kinks are). One of the two bonds is broken and is used to attach hydrogen atoms. When this happens, the chain becomes less kinked. Therefore, adjacent molecules can now stack more neatly together, which means that the liquid oil becomes a solid fat.

To make the artificially solidified oils easier to use, the food chemists developed *partially* hydrogenated oils, wherein some of the double bonds are hydrogenated, while others are left intact. Therefore, the vegetable oil solidifies, but still remains fairly soft. As an example, this is how soft ice-cream is made.

Artificial hydrogenation of vegetable oils makes them easier to use commercially because they can be stored longer without going rancid. However, our cells do not utilize them as well as the original oil because artificial hydrogenation alters the shape of the fatty acid molecules, making them less compatible with our cells.

The biological activity of organic molecules depends largely on their shape. They literally have to fit together like the pieces of a jigsaw puzzle. Thus, when we ingest artificially hydrogenated oils, we force our cells to put a square peg in a round hole. The cells are thus weakened and the entire body becomes more susceptible to a plethora of pathologies.

The effect on our health might not be so devastating if the fatty acid molecules were *completely* hydrogenated, rather than partially hydrogenated. Partially hydrogenated oils are even more toxic to the body than excessive amounts of omega-6 and naturally saturated fats. The reason is the partial hydrogenation of vegetables oils results in the formation of trans fats.

Trans Fats

As mentioned above, in the manufacturing of partially hydrogenated oil, some of the double bonds are filled in with hydrogen and some are not. The ones that are not filled with hydrogen can, none-the-less, be disrupted, causing the entire molecule to become even more distorted, as shown in figure 8.

Figure 8: Trans Fatty Acid Molecule

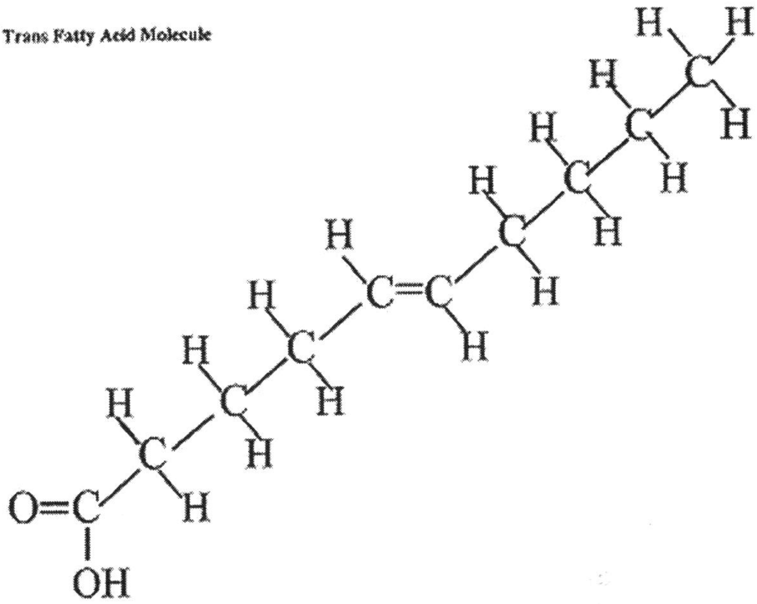

In the language of chemistry, the fatty acid in figure 6 is said to have the "cis" configuration, which is the shape of most naturally occurring unsaturated fatty acids. In contrast, the altered shape in figure 8 is called the "trans" configuration. Therefore, these manufactured mutant molecules are known as "trans fats."

A small amount of trans fats are found in meats, eggs and dairy. Cooking generates more trans fats. However, the highest concentrations, by far, are produced in the manufacturing of partially hydrogenated oils.

The Impact of Trans Fats on Health

The effects of trans fats are significant, because they are currently found in most commercially baked goods, including breads, cakes, cookies, candies and soft ice-cream. Partially hydrogenated oils, and trans fats in general, have been implicated in elevated cholesterol, cardiovascular disease, diabetes, cancer, ADD (attention deficit disorder) and ADHD (attention deficit and hyperactivity disorder).[13] This is why health authorities have unanimously recommended that trans fats be reduced to bare minimum or totally banned.

The brain is particularly vulnerable to trans fats, because it is a very fatty organ and needs an abundance of the right kinds of fats such as DHA to develop normally and work properly. The presence of trans fats in the diet disrupts our omega-3 metabolic pathways for making DHA and can thus render the brain seriously deficient in this fatty acid.

> The reduction of dietary trans fats, and increasing the omega-3 oils have been shown to help with ADD and ADHD[13] especially when refined sugar is also eliminated. The same strategy is proving to be effective with other conditions of the nervous system, such as multiple sclerosis and Parkinson's Disease.

Phospholipids

Regarding dietary fats, bear in mind that, in general, their single most important feature is their ability to repel water. This is significant because virtually all the chemical reactions in the body occur in a watery environment. How does the body reconcile its high water content with its need for the aqua-phobic fats? The answer is phospholipids.

Below is a simplified model of a phospholipids molecule. Notice the difference between this molecule and the triglyceride molecule in figure 4.

Figure 9: Phospholipid Molecule

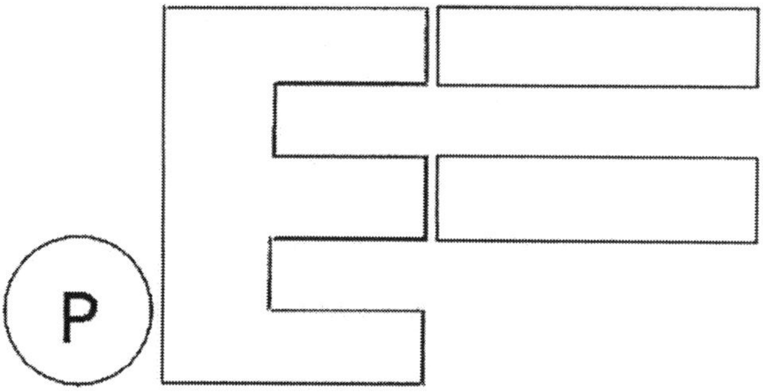

The difference is that phospholipids have two, instead of three, fatty acids. The third fatty acid has been replaced with another organic molecule that contains phosphate. The phosphate portion of the molecule mingles easily with water, while the other end behaves like a typical lipid, which means that it repels water and is drawn to other fatty molecules.

Phospholipids are critically important to life because their dual nature allows them to act like the diplomats of the biochemical world. Specifically, they have a detergent action which allows water and lipids to interact. In fact, some laundry detergents work through the action of phosphate-rich organic molecules, similar to phospholipids.

In the body, phospholipids form the bulk of the cell membranes. The fatty acid part of the molecules makes for an effective barrier, while the phosphate parts allow for a stable and harmonious interphase with the watery environment within and around the cells.

Another function of phospholipids is to help keep other fatty substances freely suspended in the body's watery fluids rather than clumping and depositing on and in the walls of arteries. This is especially important in the case of fats that are highly water-repellent and solid at body temperature, such as saturated fats and cholesterol — which brings us to the thirds major category of fats — steroids

Steroids

Steroids are a class of lipids having a complex ring structure. The most common steroid in the body is cholesterol. It is made by the liver and has three major functions:

- It is converted into hormones, such as cortisol.
- It is converted into Vitamin D.
- It helps to stabilize cell membranes. Without cholesterol, cell membranes would be too fluid and flimsy.

However, the same highly insoluble nature of cholesterol that makes it useful in the cell membranes also makes it more likely to deposit in places where we do not want it to do so. Therefore, the cholesterol which circulates in the blood is combined with phospholipids as well as water-soluble protein molecules. In this form, the cholesterol molecules are less likely to aggregate and cause trouble. These lipid-protein complexes exist in two major forms:

- **Low density lipoproteins** (LDL), having a lower protein content, are more likely to accumulate in the arterial walls and can thus contribute to clogging of the arteries and heart disease.
- **High-density lipoproteins** (HDL), having a higher protein content, are more likely to stay safely suspended in the body fluids.

In measuring the cholesterol levels in the blood, we are interested in the relative amounts of the low and high density forms. Though both play a role in maintaining health, we want more of the high density and less of the low density lipoproteins.

Cholesterol Medication

For those who are contemplating taking cholesterol medication, it is important to note that the major cholesterol-lowering drugs cause liver damage, as well as other health issues. One study on pregnant women showed a 50% higher incidence of birth defects when the individual takes a statin drug.[14]

Oils and Oxidation

Oils are subject to oxidation (going rancid) from exposure to heat, light and oxygen. This is especially true of oils rich in polyunsaturated fatty acids. Individuals who take supplemental omega-3 oils should bear in mind that such oils tend to be even more unsaturated than omega-6, and therefore more vulnerable to oxidation.

EPA and DHA are the most unsaturated and therefore, the most vulnerable. In fact, DHA has 6 *pair* of double bonded carbons, which makes it the most highly unsaturated omega-3 oil. This is very useful for cold water fish, because the high degree of unsaturation allows the oils to retain their fluidity in cold temperatures. This same quality makes it useful for brain function. However, all those double bonded carbons also make the DHA molecule *extremely* sensitive to oxidation.

The "fishy" smell of fish is due to the presence of oxidized omega-3 oils. This is why fresh fish do not smell too bad, but the longer they sit, the fishier they smell due to the accumulation of rancid omega-3 oils (mostly DHA) – which are toxic. For this reason, fish oil supplements are somewhat a double-edged sword. If the fish oils have undergone a considerable amount of oxidation (a very real possibility) they might do more harm than good.

The EPA and DHA made in the body are naturally protected by antioxidants. The same applies for the oils found in fresh and raw whole foods. However, when these oils are extracted from food sources, they are separated from their natural antioxidants, subjected to heat and light, and sit for a long time in a warehouse or brightly lit store. Therefore, some oxidation is likely to occur, even when steps are taken to maximize freshness.

Guidelines for Eating Fats

- Limit the consumption of saturated fats. Favor plant foods and lean meats.
- Eliminate partially hydrogenated vegetable oils (trans fats). Read the label.

- ¤ Balance the omega-6 and omega-3 oils. The ideal ratio is 1:1 or 2:1. The typical diet that is high in grains, vegetables oils and grain-fed meat might be around 20:1 or 30:1 in favor of omega-6. A healthier ratio is provided by a diet that features generous portions of unprocessed fruits and vegetables, the appropriate amount fresh fish and grass-fed meats, nuts and seeds.
- ¤ Favor whole-food fats over extracted oils. Rather than using large amounts of extracted oils to make your salad dressing, use ground-up or blended nuts and seeds or an avocado.
- ¤ If you do buy extracted oils, make sure they are reasonably fresh. Keep them refrigerated, use them raw, as in homemade salad dressings, or add them to foods *after* cooking. Purchase only the amount that you will use quickly. For added protection, you can throw in some Vitamin E oil to inhibit oxidation. This is especially beneficial with liquid DHA supplements.
- ¤ Favor foods that provide fats in the raw form. Cook the fatty foods when you need to; eat them raw when you can.
- ¤ If you are going to cook or bake with oil, your best options are coconut oil, palm oil and olive oil — in moderation. Coconut and palm oil are saturated, and olive oil is monounsaturated, therefore they are less reactive under heat, compared to polyunsaturated oils, like safflower oil.

Proteins

Proteins make up about 20% of the body-weight. Excluding water, the body is mostly protein. Our cells can burn protein for energy, but prefer to use it primarily as building material or for making regulatory substances. When protein is used as building material, it is called *structural* protein. When it serves regulatory functions, it is called *functional* protein.

- ¤ **Structural proteins** are the "brick and mortar" of the body. They are tough, do not dissolve in water, and are not very sensitive to changes in temperature or pH. The main structural protein in the body is collagen which is a key ingredient of bone, muscles, fibrous connective tissues (tendons, ligaments, and deep fascia), skin and blood vessels. If you look at a chart of the skeletal or muscular system, all the white stuff you see is fibrous connective tissues. It looks white because that is the color of collagen. Healthy collagen is important, not just for musculoskeletal health, but also the rest of the body, especially blood vessels. *Failure to maintain the integrity of the collagen of the blood vessels (perhaps due to vitamin C deficiency) is a major contributing factor in vascular disease.*

◘ **Functional proteins** include a vast variety of different substances that carry out specific regulatory functions in the body. Among them are enzymes, hormones and neurotransmitters.

The Shapes of Proteins

Since the activity of organic molecules, such as our enzymes and hormones, depends largely on their shape, any disruption of their delicate three-dimensional shape is a serious matter. To understand how such disruption can happen, let us first look more closely at the composition of protein molecules.

A protein molecule consists of many smaller molecules, called amino acids, strung together. A typical protein molecule consists of 50-300 amino acid molecules strung together. Each amino acid is composed of carbon (C), hydrogen (H), oxygen (O), nitrogen (N), and sometimes sulfur (S).

There are 20 different amino acids used to make proteins. From these twenty amino acids, the body can make thousands of different proteins. What distinguishes one protein from another is the sequence of amino acids, which is determined by the information encoded in the DNA molecules.

The amino acid sequence is critically important because the specific sequence of the amino acids causes the entire chain to fold into its unique three dimensional shape — which, in turn, determines protein's function. The bonds that maintain the three dimensional shape are often very delicate. Changes in pH and temperature can disrupt the shape. If the pH and temperature changes are drastic enough, the protein is permanently altered (denatured), as in a hard-boiled egg. This is one of the reasons that the pH of the body has to be carefully regulated.

Dietary Protein

When we eat proteins, our digestive system breaks them down to their constituent amino acids. These free amino acids are eventually absorbed into our cells, where the amino acids are reassembled to form our own unique proteins.

In order to make the proteins we need, all of the necessary amino acids must be present in the right proportion. Some of these amino acids can be manufactured in the body. Those which cannot be manufactured in the body must be ingested from the foods we eat, and are therefore called *essential amino acids*.

Essential Amino Acids

Phenylalanine	Methionine
Valine	Histidine (infants)
Threonine	Arginine (infants)
Tryptophan	Leuciene
Isoleucine	Lysine

Non-essential Amino Acids

Alanine	Glutamine
Asparagine	Glycine
Aspartate	Proline
Cysteine	Serine
Glutamic acid	Tyrosine

With regard to nutrition, a high-quality protein (sometimes called a complete protein) is one that has all the essential amino acids in proper proportion required by us. For example, meat, eggs and dairy are considered to be sources of high-quality protein. In contrast, plant protein may be deficient in one or more essential amino acids.

To get all the essential amino acids from plant foods, variety is the key, though the different protein sources do not have to be eaten in the same meal, or even the same day. None-the-less, traditional diets frequently combine two specific plant foods whose proteins complement one another. In other words, the amino acids deficient in one food are abundant in the other. The typical way to do this is to combine a grain with a legume, such as rice and beans.

Many plant foods do contain all the essential amino acids. For example:

- *Fruits:* bananas, tomatoes, dates.
- *Vegetables:* alfalfa sprouts, bean sprouts, seaweed, carrots, sweet potatoes, broccoli, cabbage, corn, okra, squashes.
- *Nuts and seeds:* almonds, coconuts, filberts, sunflower seeds, walnuts, Brazil nuts, Pecans.

However, though all eight amino acids are technically present, they do not necessarily occur in the ideal *ratio* found in eggs and other animal protein. Here again, variety is the key.

Protein Requirements

According to official estimates, the average adult male needs to ingest about 56 grams of protein a day to replace the amino acids lost though normal metabolic activity, and an adult female needs about 44 grams This generally translates into 10-15% of daily calories. Pregnant women need about 30 additional grams, and lactating women need about 20 extra. However, realistically, these numbers can vary according to the quality and overall digestibility of the protein, as well as the individual's ability to digest and absorb it.

Inadequate protein intake can result in lowered immunity, growth retardation, poor wound healing, irritability, low endurance and muscle weakness.

Conversely, chronic over-consumption of protein can overtax the liver, damage the kidneys and has been associated with various degenerative diseases, such as osteoporosis, cancer, Alzheimer's disease and cardiovascular disease.

Protein Toxicity

Studies show that animal protein promotes growth and repair more efficiently than plant based protein.[20] This is not surprising, because animal protein has an amino acid profile that more closely resembles our own. However, this does not necessarily mean that any given individual should favor animal source protein. The same "high quality" that is ideal for growth and repair also makes it ideal for promoting the growth of tumors when consumed in quantities that exceed the person's requirements.

Another issue with protein in general (animal and plant source) has to do with the toxicity associated with the breakdown of its constituent amino acids. The amino acids not used for building and regulation cannot simply be stored (like carbohydrates and fats). Excess amino acids are burned for energy or converted into glucose. Either way, the result is production of ammonia, a substance that is so toxic that the liver must convert it into urea and uric acid. Furthermore, some amino acids contain sulfur, which has a strong acidifying effect on the blood. To neutralize the extra acid, the body pulls calcium out of the bones and teeth, resulting in weaker teeth, osteoporosis and increased hip fractures. In contrast, the complete breakdown of carbohydrates and fats by our cells produces only carbon dioxide and water as waste products, both non-toxic.

In addition to tumor growth and osteoporosis, overconsumption of protein has been associated with damage to the internal organs, especially the kidneys, and accelerated aging of the body. Therefore, the ideal diet should include adequate protein, but not too much. Obviously, the same applies for any nutrient, but it is especially important in this case. We should get sufficient protein to provide the amino acids we need to promote growth, repair and maintenance, but not so much as to force the body to burn too many amino acids.

Chapter 3

Micronutrients

Vitamins
Minerals
Phytonutrients

Vitamins

The criteria for designating a nutrient as a vitamin are somewhat nebulous. In general, vitamins are a group of nutrients which play a wide variety of regulatory roles such as acting as enzymes helpers (co-enzymes).

Here is a list of the officially recognized vitamins:

- Vitamin A – retinol
- Vitamin B1 – thiamine
- Vitamin B2 – riboflavin
- Vitamin B3 – niacin
- Vitamin B5 – pantothenic acid
- Vitamin B6 – pyridoxine
- Vitamin B12 – cobolamin (methylcobolamin or cyanocobolamin)
- Folate
- Vitamin C – ascorbic acid
- Vitamin D – calciferol
- Vitamin E – tocopherol

Water soluble vitamins include the B vitamins and vitamin C. They are measured in milligrams. Fat soluble vitamins include vitamins A, D, E and K. They are measured in international units (IU). Fat soluble vitamins are stored in body fat and the liver and can be toxic in large amounts. All vitamins are vitally important to our health and can easily be lost through any sort of processing such as cooking and refining, or simply storage.

Vitamin Trivia

The term "vitamin" is actually a misnomer; a relic from the early days of vitamin research. Since all the vitamins are generally present in any diet that has a variety of fresh whole foods, our ancestors (including the early food scientists and health professionals) did not have a clue about the existence of vitamins until the processing of food had progressed to the point of seriously depleting the availability of these nutrients. The result was the emergence of mysterious and previously unknown diseases. One of the first clues to the existence of vitamins was probably the death of many sailors from scurvy, a disease later found to be caused by a severe vitamin C deficiency.

The clue that finally alerted scientists to the existence of vitamins came in the nineteenth century with the introduction of polished rice to the Asian diet. Polished rice has no bran, which makes it more appealing and easier to cook. However, this practice was followed by a dramatic rise in the death rate from a disease called beriberi.

A closer examination of the discarded bran revealed chemicals that were apparently "vital" for our health. The chemicals that seemed directly linked to beriberi appeared to be *amines*, a class of nitrogen containing organic molecules. Since these chemicals were essential to life, they were called "vitamines," by combining the words "vital" and "amines." However, further refinement revealed the presence of other essential nutrients, besides the amines. Sadly, the name, "vitamines," was no longer accurate. So, to make the misnomer less obvious, and to avoid confusion, the chemists of the day changed the name from vit*amines* to vit*amins*. The ones that were linked to beriberi were eventually identified as the B vitamins — which really are amines. All the others are not amines — though they are still vital.

Vitamin A

Vitamin A benefits the eyes, especially night vision. It also promotes healthy membranes and skin. It is available in two forms:

- **Retinol.** It is fat-soluble and may be found abundantly in fish liver oil.

- **Beta-Carotene.** It is water-soluble and found abundantly in yellow and green leafy vegetables. The liver converts beta-carotene to vitamin A, as needed.

The RDI (recommended daily intake) is 5,000 IU. Therapeutic doses of 100,000 IU have been used. A diet that is rich in fruits and vegetables can easily provide beta-carotene in amounts that are 5-10 times greater than the RDI, and sometimes more. However, caution should be used with externally derived retinol because high doses can be toxic. It is interesting to note that the toxic reactions to vitamin A overdose resemble the symptoms of deficiency:

Deficiency	*Overdose*
Night blindness	Eye disorders
Skin disorders	Dry skin
Respiratory infections	Altered mucous membrane
Loss of appetite	Loss of appetite

B Vitamins

B vitamins help the cells burn carbohydrates for energy. They are also important for the nervous system, skin, hair, eyes, mouth, muscle tone in the gastrointestinal tract, and liver integrity. Symptoms of deficiency include fatigue, depression, lack of muscle tone, constipation, gray hair, acne, cracks in the corner of the mouth and anemia. B vitamins are found in whole grains, brewer's yeast, fruits and vegetables. Some are produced by intestinal bacteria.

Vitamin B_{12} is of special interest because it is the only B vitamin that is not readily available in commonly available plant foods. It is produced by bacteria which live in the top part of the soil, float in the air and stick to the surface of plants. B_{12} is plentiful in animal products because herbivores consume the B_{12} and bacteria that stick to the plants. Small amounts are also found in mushrooms and some sea vegetation. It is necessary for production of hemoglobin, vascular health and proper development of the nervous system.

B_{12} deficiency in industrialized nations is common, even in individuals who consume large amounts of animal products.. Here are the reasons:

- Factory farming destroys the soil organisms that produce B_{12}.
- The practice of vigorously washing and scrubbing fruits and vegetables eliminates the beneficial bacteria and B vitamins adhering to the outside of the plant. This is particularly significant in vegan diets, which do not use any animal products.
- Food allergies and overeating grains inhibit B_{12} absorption.
- Large amounts of fat in the diet can slow down the absorption of all water-soluble vitamins, as well as inhibiting the secretion of a substance called *intrinsic factor*, which is necessary for the proper absorption of B_{12}.

- Vitamin B_{12} is heat-sensitive and can therefore be destroyed by prolonged or high-temperature cooking, as in broiling and frying.

Improper absorption is a major contributing factor to B_{12} deficiency. Vegans tend to be especially vulnerable to B_{12} deficiency when they eat a lot of grains and vigorously wash their fruits and vegetables. However, individuals who eat a great deal of factory farmed meat, such as grain-fed beef, can also become deficient in B_{12}.

- If you do not eat organically produced animal products (and even if you do), here are some ways of enhancing your B_{12} levels:
- Take B_{12} supplements. Methyl cobolamin is preferable. The other form, cyanocobolamin, is the cheaper, but also releases tiny amounts of cyanide into the body.
- Consume organically grown green leafy vegetables and floral vegetables (broccoli and cauliflower) which have a large surface area for the bacteria that make B_{12}. If you have a reliable source of reasonably clean organic vegetables and are not so fastidious about washing them, you can get B_{12} that way.
- Be moderate with the consumption of grains and high-fat foods.
- B_{12} might be provided by intestinal bacteria, if the gut is healthy and well populated by the right organisms, but this source is questionable.[59]
- A modest amount of active B_{12} is provided by mushrooms, especially raw.[80]
- B_{12} has been found in sea vegetation, blue green algae and the organisms in fermented food. However, some of these sources may also contain the inactive forms of B_{12} that can interfere with absorption of the active form. Analysis of nori (the sea vegetable used to make sushi) suggests that it provides active B_{12}.[60]

Vitamin C

Vitamin C consists of a molecule called ascorbic acid. In its natural form, ascorbic acid is combined with other substances, including flavonoids, rutin and hesperidin. Together, they make up *C complex*. Food sources include virtually all fruits and vegetables. Here are some of the functions of vitamin C:

- Is a component of collagen, therefore, it is vital in wound healing, regeneration and tissue maintenance. For example adequate vitamin C is essential for maintaining the integrity of the inner lining of blood vessels.
- Aids in the formation of red blood cells.

- Prevents hemorrhaging and bruising by strengthening vascular walls.
- Fights infections and viruses, such as the common cold.
- Reduces allergies (assists adrenal function).
- Is a major anti-oxidant. One of its functions is to restore the antioxidant capacity of vitamin E.
- Symptoms of deficiency include:
- Bruising and bleeding, especially of the gums.
- Slow wound healing
- Cardiovascular disease
- Lowered immunity

The RDA has been set at 75mg for females, 90mg for males. For optimum health, these numbers are probably way too low! In addition to human studies, a look at the rest of the animal kingdom suggests a much higher need for this vitamin.[81] Most animals make their own vitamin C. Humans are among the few animals who must get vitamin C from food. Animals in the wild who get their vitamin C from food, such as the monkeys and apes, do so in amounts that are 10-20 times the RDI for humans.[81] Likewise, animals capable of making their own vitamin C produce at least ten times the RDI that is set for humans.[82]

Vitamin C Supplementation

The need for vitamin C increases with any kind of stress, especially infection and increased toxic burden. Under such circumstances, the right kind of supplementation can be beneficial, though studies suggest that vitamin C tends to be more effective when obtained from whole foods.[73] For optimum health, some health authorities, suggest around 1000 mg of vitamin C per day, although the studies cited above indicate that even higher levels may be appropriate. In the absence of supplementation, these high levels can be achieved with one to two pounds of high-vitamin C fruits (such as citrus, kiwi, pineapple, papaya, mango and strawberries) and two pounds of green vegetables (such as kale, spinach, romaine lettuce, broccoli and chard).

If you are not getting enough vitamin C from food, supplementation is best done in smaller doses, since absorption of vitamin C supplements is limited. 250mg, 1-4 times a day would provide fairly good absorption.

Vitamin D

Vitamin D seems more like a hormone than a vitamin. Like our true hormones (and unlike other vitamins) it is produced in the body. Ultraviolet light from the sun striking the skin triggers the conversion of cholesterol in the skin into vitamin D. For this reason, vitamin D is sometimes called the 'sunshine vitamin.'

Like many of our hormones, vitamin D has a broad range of functions. It is needed for absorption of calcium, bone formation, thyroid function, immune system function, brain development in babies, and blood sugar regulation. Also, like our hormones, vitamin D has been shown to influence gene expression.

RDI is 400 IU. Deficiency results in demineralization of bone, poor immune function, depression and increased risk of several specific cancers, especially in women.

Vitamin E

Vitamin E is a major anti-oxidant. Since it is fat soluble, it is important in preventing the oxidation of LDL cholesterol. It also dilates blood vessels, prevents clot formation and supports the reproductive system. Deficiency can contribute to heart and menstrual problems.

Goods sources of vitamin E include unrefined vegetable oils, raw seeds and nuts and soybeans. RDI is 15 IU, but this might be too low if our goal is optimum health. 100 IU might be more beneficial.

Vitamin K

Vitamin K is important for blood clotting, liver function, and proper utilization of calcium. Deficiency results in poor blood clotting (hemorrhaging), decreased bone density, and greater tendency of calcium to deposit on arterial walls. Vitamin K is manufactured in the intestines by the fermentative bacteria. It is also found in green vegetables.

Minerals

Minerals are elements which are nutritionally important in relatively small amounts. The human body is composed of 4-5% minerals. After we ingest minerals, most of them become ions (electrically charged particles). Therefore, such minerals are also called *electrolytes*. Our body fluids contain a wealth of minerals in the form of ions; they play an important role in our overall physiology. Working together with vitamins and enzymes, minerals are involved in muscle contraction and relaxation, nerve impulses, digestion, hormone production, water balance, pH, and antibody formation.

Macro-minerals are those present in the greatest amount in the body. They include calcium, phosphorus, magnesium, sodium and potassium. *Micro-minerals*, or trace minerals, are required in very tiny amounts.

Calcium

Calcium is the most abundant mineral in the body. 99% of it is located in the bones and teeth. The rest is dissolved in the body fluids as calcium ions. In addition to building and maintaining bones and teeth, calcium is a pH buffer, regulates heartbeat, and is needed for muscle contraction.

It is found in dairy, dark leafy greens, figs, olives, oranges, sesame seeds, and fish with tiny edible bones. RDA is 1000mg. Proper calcium absorption requires adequate HCl (hydrochloric acid) in the stomach, sunlight for production of Vitamin D, and exercise. Deficiency can result in muscle cramps, osteoporosis, heart palpitations, insomnia, and irritability.

Magnesium

Magnesium is needed for carbohydrate and protein metabolism, pH regulation and for countering the stimulatory effect of calcium, in regard to heart function. RDI is 300 to 500mg daily. Deficiency can show up as insomnia, rapid pulse, heart problems, irritability, nervousness and muscle twitches. It is found in green vegetables, fruits, seeds and nuts.

Sodium

Sodium is found predominantly outside of the body cells. It functions as a pH buffer with potassium and participates in muscle contraction and nerve stimulation. Excess sodium, which is fairly common, causes a loss of potassium. It is found in all greens, seafood, meat, poultry, beets, carrots and kelp.

Potassium

Potassium is important for regulating water balance (with sodium), relaxation of heart muscle and nerve impulses. Deficiency, usually due to excess sodium intake, can result in insomnia, nervousness and irregular heartbeat. It is found in virtually all fruits and vegetables.

Phosphorus

Phosphorus is the second most abundant mineral with 80% located in the bones. It is present in every cell and is heavily involved in cellular metabolism. Phosphorus serves as a pH buffer. Deficiency results in poor bone and teeth structure, nervousness and irregular breathing. RDI is 800mg. It is found in animal products, grains, seed and, nuts.

Microminerals

Name	FUNCTION	SOURCE
Chromium	glucose metabolism	Brewer's Yeast
Cobalt	B12 component	organ meats, green vegetables
Copper	formation of hemoglobin and red blood cells	seafood, nuts, molasses
Iodine	function of thyroid gland	Seaweed
Iron	component of hemoglobin	liver, eggs, molasses, (aids red blood cells tin carrying oxygen), raisins, greens, beets
Manganese	integrity of tendons and ligaments	whole grains, nuts, leafy green veggies
Molybdenum	integrity of tendons and ligaments	legumes, whole grains, dark green veggies
Nickel	enzyme component	dried peas and beans, whole grains and nuts
Selenium	fertility, anti-oxidant	Brewer's Yeast, whole grains, Brazil nuts
Sulfur	detoxification, healthy hair, nails and skin	animal protein, garlic, onions
Zinc	prostate function, wound healing	seafood, soybeans, sunflower seeds

Minerals and Acid /Alkaline Balance

One of the ways ingested minerals profoundly affect our health is their influence over the acid/alkaline balance of the body. An acid is any chemical that releases hydrogen ions when dissolved in water. A base or alkaline substance is any chemical that releases hydroxide ions when dissolved in water. The pH scale is used to measure acidity and alkalinity.

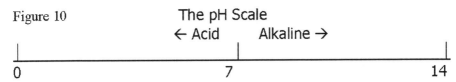

Figure 10 — The pH Scale

A substance that has a pH of 1 is highly acidic. A substance with a pH of 14 is highly alkaline. A substance that has a pH of 7 is neutral. The pH of the stomach ranges from 1 to 3, which is very acidic, while the neighboring duodenum is just a hair over 7, which makes it slightly alkaline. The pH of the blood should be between 7.35 and 7.45.

For our present purpose, we will simply say that maintenance of proper pH in the body is extremely important for our health and longevity. If the pH of the blood strays beyond that range, all sorts of things can go wrong. Not surprisingly, the body has a number of ways of assuring that the pH does not stray beyond the ideal range.

In the above list of minerals, notice that sodium is alkalizing, while chloride is acid-forming. This presents an interesting situation, because we tend to ingest sodium in the form of sodium chloride (NaCl). So, is NaCl acid forming or alkalizing? As it turns out, it is acid forming because the effect of the chloride seems to outweigh sodium. In other words, when we ingest too much sodium chloride, in addition to suffering the ill effects of too much sodium, we have the added burden of the acidifying presence of too much chloride.

Diet and pH

The mineral content is the primary dietary factor which determines whether a food is acidifying or alkalizing in the body. Some minerals tend to have an acid reaction when they enter the blood, while others tend to have an alkaline reaction.

- **Acid forming minerals** include sulfur, phosphorous, iodine and chlorine.
- **Alkaline forming minerals** include sodium, potassium, magnesium and iron.

In other words, just because a food is acidic in the mouth does not necessarily mean that it has an acidic reaction when its constituent nutrients enter the blood. For example, a lemon is quite acidic to the taste (sour), but once it is metabolized, its reaction in the blood is alkaline.

For optimum health, it is recommended that we eat a diet consisting of about 80% alkaline forming foods and 20% acid forming foods. Most fruits and vegetables tend to be alkalizing, while animal products, grains, nuts and seeds tend to be acidifying.

> **Minerals and Massage**
> An excess of acid-forming foods, which is very common, is associated with toxicity, muscle spasms, and chronic pain. Obviously, this can influence the results you get in your massage practice. If, through your suggestion, some of your clients apply the 80%-20% principle, they might respond more favorably to your work.

Phytonutrients

The term, phytonutrients, includes a broad category of nutrients derived from plants. Fruits and vegetables that have a high phytonutrient content are typically colorful: red, orange, yellow, purple and deep green. They are also found in lesser quantities in grains and seeds. Phytonutrients serve a wide variety of functions. For example, many of them are powerful antioxidants. Phytonutrients also contribute to the flavor or aroma of the food. Two of the best known categories of phytonutrients are flavonoids and carotenoids.

Flavonoids

Flavonoids, also called *bioflavonoids*, are a group of water-soluble nutrients that include hesperidins, rutin, tangeritin and quercetin. They are closely associated with vitamin C. Not surprisingly, they are found in all the same foods that provide vitamin C. For example, they are abundant in the white part of lemons, limes, oranges and grape fruit.

Flavonoids enhance the action of Vitamin C and protect it from oxidation. The combination of vitamin C and flavonoids is important for reducing inflammation, fighting infections and building collagen. Flavonoids also affect the permeability of capillaries; therefore, they have been called "Vitamin P." In addition, some flavonoids seem to have a beneficial effect on brain chemistry, promoting positive mental and emotional states.[98]

Carotenoids

Carotenoids consist of about 600 chemicals. They include the *carotenes*, of which the best known is **beta carotene**, which converts into Vitamin A. Carotenes, in general, are potent antioxidants, enhance the immune response and protect the skin against UV radiation. They promote detoxification and help to conserve glutathione, which is very beneficial for the liver because glutathione is a powerful and important detoxifier which cannot be gotten from foods.

Carotenoids are found in yellow, orange and red plants, such as tomatoes, parsley, squash, oranges, papaya, pink grapefruit and spinach. They give egg yolk its yellow/orange color. The orange color of carrots is due to the abundance of beta-carotene.

Chapter 4
Digestion

Digestion is the part of our physiology that can be most obviously and powerfully influenced by diet. To understand how we can positively impact digestion, let us first review the digestive system.

Figure 11: Digestive System

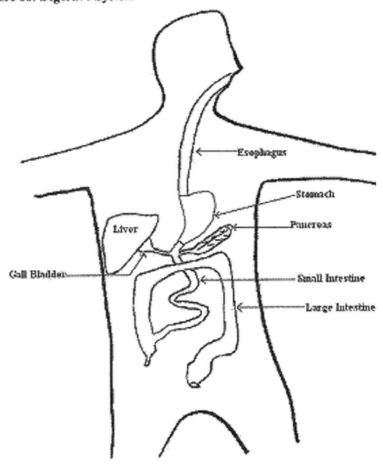

Review of Anatomy

The digestive system consists of the alimentary canal and the accessory organs. The alimentary canal, also known as the digestive tract, is a tube approximately 30 feet long, beginning at the mouth and continuing as the pharynx (throat), esophagus, stomach, small intestine and large intestine, which terminates as the anus. The accessory organs are the teeth, tongue, salivary glands, pancreas, liver and gall bladder. Although, food does not pass through them, each one helps in its own way in the process of digestion.

Mouth

The mouth contains salivary glands which produce saliva, a fluid consisting mostly of water with some other dissolved chemicals. One of these chemicals is **amylase,** an enzyme that begins the digestion of starch. If starchy foods are thoroughly chewed, a substantial amount of starch is digested in the mouth. Starch tastes sweeter the longer you chew it because it breaks down into maltose (a double sugar). This reduces the digestive burden further on down. Therefore, it is good to thoroughly chew each mouthful of starchy food.

Stomach

The stomach is situated within the dome of the diaphragm, on the left side of the upper abdominal cavity, protected by the ribs. In humans, its capacity seems to be around 1.5 quarts, and, when empty, it can shrink down to the size of a fist. However, it can be "trained" to hold more. It has a natural elasticity that can, potentially, allow it to expand to hold about one gallon. This is consistent with what we find in Nature where animals often consume volumes of food that far exceed the typical human diet.

The human stomach has shrunk because we tend to eat foods which are low in fiber, dehydrated and calorically very concentrated. Unfortunately, those same foods promote constipation and intestinal toxicity which can contribute to the onset of degenerative diseases; such as cancer, cardiovascular, diabetes and arthritis.

Apparently, the human stomach has retained its natural elasticity, as seen in individuals who significantly increase their consumption of raw fruits and vegetables (high in fiber and water and low in calories). Their stomachs quickly adapt to hold larger volumes of food.

The upper portion of the stomach is called the fundus, the middle portion is called the body, and the lower portion is called the pylorus. The entrance into the stomach is guarded by the cardiac sphincter, a ring of muscle between the esophagus and stomach. The exit is guarded by the pyloric sphincter, a ring of muscle between the end of the stomach and the beginning of the small intestine. Within the mucosa of the stomach are millions of tiny glands that secrete gastric juice.

To understand the digestive role of the stomach, let us consider the three major components of gastric juice: pepsin, hydrochloric acid and mucus.

- **Pepsin** – an enzyme that begins protein digestion.
- **Hydrochloric acid** (HCl) – activates the pepsin and destroys microbes. HCl is our first line of defense against ingested pathogens. HCl is also important for mineral absorption. The chronic use of antacids can interfere with digestion of protein and absorption of minerals, as well as contributing to gastrointestinal disbiosis.
- **Mucus** – protects the inner lining of the stomach from the acid and pepsin. Too much acid or not enough mucus can result in a gastric ulcer. However, what is termed "acid indigestion" is typically not due to excess HCl production. In fact, most adults have insufficient HCl output due to years of eating concentrated and highly processed food.

> **Acid Reflux and Hiatal Hernia**
>
> A common cause of acid indigestion or "heartburn" is acid reflux which is the seepage of a gastric juice up into the esophagus. A number of factors can trigger acid reflux. One very common factor is the hiatal hernia: the protrusion of the upper part of the stomach through the opening in the diaphragm that normally provides passage for the esophagus. A severe hiatal hernia is treated medically with surgery. Milder cases, which are quite common, are simply treated with antacids to relieve the burning sensation. However, the hiatal hernia can often be reduced through a manual correction, typically done by some osteopaths and chiropractors. This procedure can also be easily done by a massage therapist.

Small Intestine

The small intestine is a tube about 20 feet long and 1 inch wide. It is divided into three parts: *duodenum, jejunum,* and *ileum.* The lining of the small intestine has numerous glands which secrete intestinal juice that includes a variety of digestive enzymes. Chemical digestion is completed in the small intestine, and the nutrients pass into the blood. To facilitate absorption, the inner lining of the small intestine has villi and microvilli, finger-like projections that greatly increase surface area. The actual surface area for absorption has been estimated to be equivalent to that of a tennis court.

Large Intestine

The large intestine is about 5 feet long and 2-3 inches wide. Its three parts are the cecum, colon and rectum. The cecum is the first 3-4 inches, which merges with the small intestine. The opening between the end of the small intestine and the beginning of the large intestine is guarded by the ileo-cecal valve. The very tip of the cecum has a squiggly little tube called the vermiform appendix.

The colon forms the bulk of the large intestine. It is divided into four parts: the ascending colon, the transverse colon, the descending colon and the sigmoid colon.

The last 5-6 inches of the large intestine, the rectum, is an expanded pouch which opens to the outside via the anal canal. The external opening of the anal canal is called the anus, which is guarded by two rings of muscles: the internal sphincter (smooth muscle) and the external sphincter (skeletal muscle). The latter is formed by the levator ani, which provides us with voluntary control of bowel function. As you may recall, the levator ani is the main muscle that forms the pelvic floor. Inflammation and enlargement of the veins in the anal canal are called hemorrhoids.

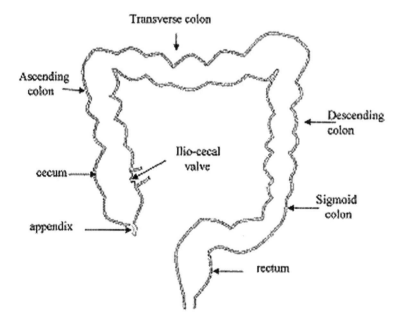

Figure 12: Large Intestine

Pancreas

The pancreas is a six-inch long carrot-like organ situated just below the stomach. Its wide medial end is tucked inside the "C" of the duodenum, and the pointed lateral end touches the spleen. The lateral end of the pancreas secretes the hormones which regulate blood glucose. The rest of the pancreas secretes pancreatic juice, which consists of water, salts (such as sodium bicarbonate), and enzymes. The enzymes include pancreatic amylase (which is the same as salivary amylase), pancreatic lipase which digests fats, and three enzymes for protein digestion called trypsin, chymotrypsin and carboxypeptidase. Pancreatic juice is channeled through the pancreatic duct into the duodenum.

Liver and Gallbladder

The liver is tucked under the diaphragm on the right side of the abdominal cavity. It does about 500 different things, most notably:

- Detoxifies the blood
- Prepares nutrients to be utilized by the body cells
- Produces most of the plasma proteins in the blood
- Stores glycogen
- Destroys old blood cells
- Produces cholesterol
- Changes some of the cholesterol into bile salts
- Makes bile, a greenish mixture consisting of water, cholesterol, bile salts and a number of waste products extracted from the blood. Some of the bile is excreted into the duodenum, and the rest of it is stored in the gall bladder.

The gall bladder is a sac about the size of a fist and tucked under the liver. Its function is to store and concentrate the bile produced by the liver. After a meal (especially a fatty meal), the gall bladder contracts, squeezing a generous helping of bile into the duodenum, where the bile salts (acting like soap) emulsify the fats and fat-soluble nutrients, making them easier to digest and absorb.

If the flow of bile into the duodenum is obstructed, the excess bile is absorbed into the blood and results in a yellow coloration of the skin and eyes, a condition known as jaundice. The two major disorders of the gall bladder that could possibly result in jaundice are cholecystitis (inflammation of gall bladder), and cholelithiasis (gall stones).

The Hepatic Portal System

The hepatic portal system consists of a group of veins which channel blood from the digestive tract to the liver where the nutrients and toxins absorbed from the gut are immediately processed.

The veins that carry blood out of the stomach, small intestine and large intestine collect into a single vein called the hepatic portal vein. This vein continues to the liver, where the vein branches once again into a succession of smaller veins that distribute the blood to the capillaries of the liver. The capillaries of the liver collect into a succession of larger veins, and come together into a single hepatic vein that merges with the inferior vena cava, which carries the blood back to the heart.

Liver congestion can result in increased blood pressure in the hepatic portal system which can contribute to hemorrhoids. In fact, liver congestion might be the direct cause or a major contributor for many hemorrhoid cases.

Review of Physiology

Digestion involves both mechanical and chemical breakdown of food.

- **Mechanical digestion** may be likened to the action of a blender. It involves grinding up large chunks of food and mixing it with digestive juices. Mechanical digestion starts with the chewing. Then, the food is gradually propelled along the entire alimentary by peristalsis, the rhythmic contraction of the smooth muscles. The presence of solids or liquids in the esophagus initiates the peristalsis that pushes the food into the stomach. Peristalsis is also exhibited by the walls of the stomach, small intestine and large intestine. Reversal of peristalsis in the stomach and esophagus results in vomiting.
- **Chemical digestion** involves the breakdown of large food molecules into smaller molecules that readily pass through the wall of the alimentary canal and into the blood. Chemical digestion is needed for protein, lipids and carbohydrates (except simple sugars). Salts (minerals) and vitamins are readily absorbed into the blood with little or no chemical digestion.

Protein Digestion

A protein molecule consists of many smaller molecules called amino acids strung together into one or more chains. Chemical digestion of protein involves the breakdown of these chains into individual amino acids, through the action of enzymes.

Carbohydrate Digestion

There are three main forms of carbohydrates: monosaccharides, disaccharides and polysaccharides. Digestion of carbohydrates is simple: reduce all disaccharides and polysaccharides into monosaccharides. This is done through the action of enzymes.

Lipid Digestion

The lipids which are most commonly ingested as food are the triglycerides. Each triglyceride molecule consists of one molecule of glycerol (glycerin) and three fatty acid molecules as shown in figure 4. Lipid digestion involves the breakdown of triglycerides into glycerol and fatty acids. Since lipids are highly insoluble in water, their digestion is not easy because the molecules tend to clump together and therefore become inaccessible to the enzymes. To make things easier, we have bile salts that emulsify the lipids (they cut the grease), breaking the large clumps of fat into tiny clumps of fat, so that the enzymes can get to them more easily.

Figure 13
summary of chemical digestion

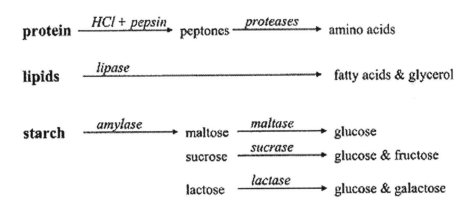

Chemical Digestion, Level by Level

Mouth

The only chemical digestion in the mouth is the breakdown of starch molecules into maltose, through the action of salivary amylase. If the starch stays in the mouth long enough, it would be broken down completely into maltose (it would taste sweet), but we usually swallow it long before that happens.

Stomach

In the stomach of adults, only protein molecules are actively digested by gastric juice. Specifically, protein molecules are chopped up into smaller chains called peptones. This is accomplished by the combined efforts of pepsin and hydrochloric acid. Another enzyme, called rennin, causes milk protein (casein) to precipitate (curdle). The curd is then digested by pepsin. A third enzyme, lipase, is supposed to digest fat. However, in adults, the highly acidic environment inhibits rennin and lipase.

Small Intestine

Chemical digestion is completed in the small intestine through the action of pancreatic and intestinal enzymes and bile salts. However, these enzymes operate best at a neutral pH, whereas the sludge that pours into the small intestine from the stomach is seething in acid. Therefore, in order for chemical digestion to commence in the small intestine, the acid must be neutralized. This is accomplished by the presence of buffers in the intestinal and pancreatic juice. Too much acid pouring into the intestine from the stomach (or a lack of buffers) can burn a hole into the wall of the duodenum. This is called a *duodenal ulcer*. Absorption of nutrients into the blood occurs mostly through the wall of the small intestine.

Large Intestine

The large intestine does not secrete digestive enzymes, but two important processes happen here:

- The water, minerals and enzymes that were poured into the alimentary canal as part of the digestive juices are absorbed into the blood.
- Intestinal bacteria break down the organic residue, producing various byproducts, including some gases such as hydrogen, methane, carbon dioxide and hydrogen sulfide.

The material eventually expelled is called feces. It consists of undigested matter (plant fiber and animal collagen), decomposed food, bacteria and their byproducts, mucus, bile pigments and just enough water to allow the matter to pass out without too much grunting.

Intestinal Bacteria

There are approximately 100 trillion bacteria (2-3 pounds) in the intestines. The vast majority are located in the large intestine. They include about 500 different species; however, for the purpose of understanding digestive health, we place them into two broad categories:

- **Putrefactive bacteria.** These include Escherichea Coli, Salmonella and Clostridia. They tend to break down undigested protein and bile salts, and produce potentially toxic byproducts.
- **Fermentative bacteria** (lactic acid bacteria). These include lactobacillus acidophilus and bifidophilis bulgaris. They break down plant fiber and other carbohydrates, producing a number of useful byproducts, such as vitamins, lactic acid and enzymes.

A favorable balance of intestinal bacteria, consisting of about 85% fermentative and 15% putrefactive, is extremely important to our overall health.

Health Benefits Provided by Fermentative Bacteria

- They produce vitamin K and B vitamins, especially folic acid, biotin, and vitamin B_{12}.[59]
- They promote mineral absorption.
- They support protein and carbohydrate digestion through the production of enzymes.
- They help maintain proper bowel transit time.
- The lactic acid produced by fermentative bacteria discourages the growth of the putrefactive bacteria, as well as yeast, protozoans and worms.
- They support the immune system and the normal inflammatory response.

Probiotic Supplements

Probiotic supplements consist of beneficial bacteria. This is particularly helpful after having taken antibiotics. In the absence of supplementation, we can promote the healthy balance of intestinal bacteria simply by getting plenty of dietary fiber, especially from raw fruits and vegetables.

A sluggish large intestine means that bacteria have more time to produce chemical irritants. In addition, these irritants have more time to pass through the wall of the large intestine and into the blood, creating more work for the liver, and eventually bathing the cells of the body. A vast number of degenerative diseases have been linked to a sluggish large intestine.

Chapter 5
Cleansing & Elimination

The elimination portals through which the body expels waste products are the large intestine, kidneys, lungs and skin. In addition, the liver and lymphatic system are also important, although they do not expel waste products directly into the external environment.

Large Intestine

The ideal transit time from mouth to anus is about 24 hrs. However, because of years of stress, including the consumption of constipating foods, many individuals' transit time is 2-3 days or longer. The resultant toxicity is believed to contribute to a wide variety of degenerative conditions. Therefore, the proper cleansing of the large intestine is important for health.

During its extended sojourn in the large intestine, the food-residue provides a fertile breeding ground for putrefactive bacteria and other microbes whose toxic byproducts continuously seep into the blood and bathe the cells of the body. Some of these toxins are potent carcinogens. In addition, some of the residue can become caked onto the wall of the large intestine, where larger parasites (worms) can more easily proliferate. The general guideline for cleansing the large intestine is to have a bowel movement at least once a day (preferably more), and that the odor is not too bad.

How to Promote Cleansing of the Large Intestine

The simplest, safest, cheapest and most natural way to cleanse the large intestine is to simply allow it to cleanse itself. This is done by reducing the concentrated and highly processed foods, while increasing the foods which promote cleansing, namely, fresh and raw fruits and vegetables that are rich in fiber and water. Concentrated and processed foods, such as products that contain meat, dairy, eggs, grains, legumes, nuts and seeds, tend to leave more toxic residue than fruits and vegetables.

If you do not want to totally eliminate the heavier cooked foods (and even if you do) here are some other ways of cleansing the large intestine:

- **Drink ample water.**
- **Use bulking agents**, such as powdered psylium and flax seeds. The usual dose is one teaspoon to one tablespoon in 8-10 oz of water. Shake it up and drink it quickly because it gels up fast. Psylium can also be taken in capsules.
- **Take antimicrobial/antiparasitic products** to eliminate putrefactive bacteria, yeast, protozoa and worms from the small and large intestine. Raw garlic is one of the most potent and inexpensive antimicrobial agents. Others include olive leaf extract, black walnut hulls, wormwood, fennel seeds, carrot juice and citrus extract.
- **Take probiotics** or **fermented foods**, such as sauerkraut and yogurt to help promote a robust population of beneficial bacteria. This is especially important if you take the antimicrobial agents mentioned above, or, for that matter, if you have taken antibiotics.
- **Take a high enema**, which is done with 1-2 quarts of warm clean water, gradually introduced into the rectum. There is disagreement among various schools of thought regarding the benefits and safety of doing enemas. The benefits are that it can rapidly eliminate a log-jam of putrefying debris. The draw backs are that it will cause the body to lose some minerals, as well as beneficial bacteria and their byproducts. Furthermore, some of that extra water that is introduced into the large intestine will seep into the blood, carrying toxins with it, especially if the body is already dehydrated. As most individuals would agree, it is best to just eliminate the offending matter from the large intestine by "pushing" it out from above, through an increase in the consumption of raw fruits and vegetables, or even taking some specialized colon cleansing preparations, as mentioned above. However, if the large intestine becomes so congested and devitalized that it is obviously having a hard time moving things out on its own, a little washing from the other end, done judiciously and conservatively, can do some good.
- **Get a colonic irrigation.** The colonic irrigation can clean the large intestine more thoroughly than several flushes with a conventional enema bag. However, just as the benefits of the enema are amplified with the colonic, so are the possible draw-backs. There is going to be substantially more water and toxins entering the blood and more minerals flushed out of the body.

The colonic irrigation is performed by a trained colon hydrotherapist. Home colonic units are also available, but when a trained technician does the procedure, you can relax more completely. Furthermore, the technician will quite often massage the colon to encourage thorough cleansing. In fact, many colon hydrotherapists are massage therapists, or, at least, have some massage training.

Liver

When the colon is fairly clean, the next organ to consider is the liver. As you may recall, the liver receives blood directly from the GI tract through the hepatic portal system. That blood is rich in nutrients and toxins. The liver breaks down or alters some waste products and prepares the nutrients to be utilized by the body cells.

How to Promote Liver Cleansing

One of the most important things to do to promote liver cleansing is to first clean the large intestine. After the large intestine has been cleansed, continue to eat an abundance of raw fruits and vegetables to keep the GI tract clean, while, perhaps, taking specific steps to promote liver cleansing:

- Consume dark green leafy vegetables rich in phytonutrients, such as fresh dandelion and spinach.
- Consume cruciferous vegetables such as kale, broccoli and Brussels sprouts.
- Drink apple juice (Use organic. Commercially grown apples are heavily sprayed).
- Drink carrot juice and beet juice (about 6 parts carrot to 1 part beet)
- Take milk thistle, an herb that has been shown to promote live detoxification.
- Drink lemon juice (½-1 lemon in warm water every morning).

The Liver Flush

The liver flush, like the enema and colonic irrigation, has received mixed reviews. Many have reported noticeable benefits in both body and mind, including relief from abdominal pain and headaches, elimination of bloating and gas, improvement of eye-sight and improvement in mood. Others, perhaps unaware or skeptical of the positive reports, have dismissed the possibility of potential benefits and warn that it could be dangerous.

In the past, I have experienced positive results and no harmful effects of which I was aware from the liver flush. I have also spoken with many individuals over the years who have reported only positive results from the liver flush, or, at the least, no negative reactions, other than temporary nausea. However, I would not categorically say everyone can benefit from this procedure. Neither would I dismiss the possibility that this procedure could do more harm than good.

Instructions on doing the liver flush are readily available on the internet. However, if you feel inclined to try a liver flush, I would recommend that you first consult with a health care provider who is familiar with this procedure, as well as being familiar with your specific situation.

As a rule of thumb, I would recommend procedures which support the liver in cleansing itself with ease and grace. Before doing anything as invasive as a liver flush, the individual might be able to promote substantial liver-cleansing by just eating (exclusively or mostly) raw fruits and vegetables for a while.

Kidneys

The kidneys are located on the posterior wall of the abdominal cavity, partially covered by the last two ribs (the floating ribs). They are, essentially, filters that remove metabolic waste from the blood. In that regard, they are similar to the liver. However, the liver has the ca-pacity to remove large molecules and worn out red blood cells, where-as the kidneys remove relatively small molecules dissolved in the body fluids. The mixture of waste products and water, collected by the kid-neys, is called urine.

The main metabolic waste in urine is urea, with lesser (much less-er, hopefully) amounts of uric acid. This is how the body disposes of most of its excess nitrogen, which comes from the breakdown of ami-no acids and, to a lesser extent, nucleic acids. When our body cells break down amino acids, they produce ammonia as waste product. As you may recall, ammonia is so highly toxic that the body literally can-not get rid of it fast enough! It is toxic to all life. This is why it is used commercially as a disinfectant. The body deals with ammonia by con-verting it into urea. This occurs in the liver. The nitrogen in nucleic acids is converted into uric acid.

Figure 14: Formation of Urea

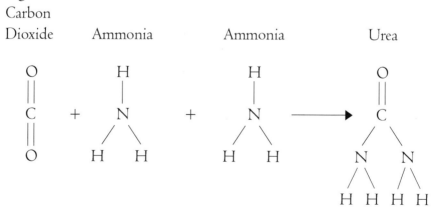

In some animals, the pathways for making urea and acid acids are related, but do not appear to be related in humans. Either way, ideally, it is preferable to dispose of most of excess nitrogen in the form of urea, rather than uric acid, because the latter is not very water-soluble. Therefore, if the uric acid becomes too concentrated in the body fluids, it can precipitate into crystals. These crystals have jagged edges which irritate tissues. A common place for uric acid crystals to accumulate is in joints resulting in irritation and pain. Such individuals often find their way to a massage therapist because the pain probably is not traced to the diet. If the irritation from uric acid is severe enough, it is called gout. This condition is characterized by severe pain, swelling and redness of joints. The uric acid crystals can also build up in the kidneys, irritating and damaging the microscopic blood vessels as well as the nephrons (the microscopic tubules that filter waste products from the blood).

If the concentration of uric acid is high enough, it can precipitate into kidney stones. When kidney stones grow large enough, they can trigger low back pain and nausea so severe as to send the person to the emergency room. However, even if stones do not develop, the delicate nephrons and microscopic blood vessels of the kidneys can still be gradually broken down over the years through constant irritation by uric acid and other chemicals. The result is a gradual, shrinking, aging and loss of function of the kidneys, which means they become progressively less efficient in removing waste products from the blood. In fact, between the ages of 20 and 80, kidneys shrink by about 33%. Consequently, blood flow through the kidney drops by about 50%.

How to Promote Kidney Cleansing

- Take diuretics, such as watermelon and cucumbers.
- Increase your intake of magnesium and B vitamins, especially vitamin B6, which can help prevent and dissolve stones.
- Avoid over-consuming protein. Overconsumption of protein can stress the kidneys.

Lungs

We take in oxygen and expel carbon dioxide and other waste products through the lungs. An easy and safe way to cleanse the lungs is deep (diaphragmatic) breathing, as when we exercise vigorously. Beneficial herbs for the lungs include fenugreek, marshmallow and mullein.

Skin

We breathe through the skin, taking in oxygen and expelling carbon dioxide. We also expel other metabolic wastes through the skin. In fact, the skin is often described as the "third kidney" because the content of sweat is similar to urine. One pound of waste may be discharged from the skin each day.

For massage therapists, it is good to know that if the skin is extremely sensitive to touch, it may indicate substantial toxicity. Doing things that promote efficient excretion through the skin is good for the body as a whole, but in particular, it reduces the burden on the kidneys.

Cleansing the Skin

- Induce sweating through exercise or sauna.
- Dry skin brushing. Use a lufa, coarse brush or rough towel.
- Hot (3 minutes) and cold (30 seconds) showers to stimulate circulation through the skin (not for individuals who have a heart condition).

The Lymphatic System

The lymphatic system is part of the circulatory system. The lymphatic system acts as a vast collection of sewer pipes that conduct waste products away from the body cells for later removal by the elimination organs. Lymph vessels carry byproducts away from our cells, and collect into a succession of larger vessels, much like many small creeks collecting into larger creeks, which collect into major rivers. All lymph vessels in the body collect into two main lymphatic vessels in the chest where they dump lymph into the left and right subclavian veins, close to the heart.

Lymph nodes are pea-size pellets situated along the course of the lymph vessels. Their function is to filter the lymph. Lymph flow is dependent on the activity of surrounding skeletal muscles.

How to Promote Lymphatic Cleansing

- Walking or other forms of exercise.
- Exercise on a rebounder (a mini trampoline).
- Dry skin brush - toward the heart.
- Lymph-cleansing supplements: proteolitic enzymes, herbs, homeopathics.
- Massage, such as effleurage and lymphatic drainage massage.

Water Revisited

One of the most important things we can do to promote body cleansing is to drink clean water. For that reason, avoidance of municipal water is probably a good idea. Let us take a closer look at the three major forms of pollution typically found in municipal water. They are chlorine, fluoride and industrial pollutants.

Industrial Pollutants

The EPA allows measurable amounts of numerous contaminants, including lead, aluminum and arsenic, in drinking water. Hundreds more are not regulated or tested and are known to cause cancer and birth defects.

Chlorine

Chlorine is linked to high blood pressure, anemia, diabetes, increased cholesterol and coronaries. When it reacts with organic chemicals, chlorine forms other toxic substances such as chloroform. Chloroform belongs to a category of chemicals called trihalomethanes. Trihalomethanes have an adverse effect on the nervous system and muscles.

Fluoride

Fluoride, we are told, is added to the water to decrease dental cavities. The fluoridation of municipal water has been a controversial topic since it was started in the 1950s. The main reasons for opposing it are as follows:

- ¤ The research suggesting that fluoridated water promotes strong teeth has been seriously questioned and shows signs of deception and fraud.[35]
- ¤ The sodium fluoride used to treat municipal water is, in fact, a highly toxic byproduct of the aluminum industry. It interferes with enzyme function and mineral balance and is carcinogenic.

Mercury

Mercury poisoning has been associated with MS, epilepsy, suicidal tendencies, fatigue, high or low blood pressure, tachycardia, arthritis, lupus, scleroderma, cancer (especially Leukemia and Hodgkin's Disease), mono and allergies.

"Silver" dental fillings are the main source mercury exposure for most humans. Such fillings are 50% mercury with smaller amounts of silver, copper, tin and zinc. Since mercury is a poisonous heavy metal, it must be handled and disposed of with extreme care as a hazardous material by dentists. In light of this scientific data and a growing body of evidence linking mercury fillings to a wide variety of diseases, serious doubt is thrown into the American Dental Association's claim that mercury fillings are safe.

The official stand is that mercury is stable once it is mixed with other metals. However, when a 10-15 year old filling is removed and analyzed, the mercury content can be as low as 5%. Research also indicates that mercury is discharged into the body with eating, drinking and gum chewing. It can be stored in the liver and other tissues, causing various health problems. Its poisonous effects are cumulative.

Non-amalgam fillings are available. They are made of composite resin (plastic material that matches tooth color), ceramic/porcelain or gold. In addition, some dentists specialize in the safe removal of mercury fillings. During the course of mercury filling removal, specific nutritional products can aid the body so the mercury will go out of the system and not redeposit in another area.

Other Sources of Mercury:

- Fish, especially larger fish, such as tuna and swordfish.
- Vaccinations
- Cleaning products such as Ajax, Comet, dishwashing liquids and Dove soap.
- Ophthalmic products and contact lens solutions
- Nasal sprays
- Topical anti-microbials and disinfectants (e.g., Merthiolate, tincture of Merthiolate)
- Diuretics
- Eye cosmetics

Chapter 6
The Food Groups

The ideal way to obtain nutrients is in the form of whole foods. A whole food is one which contains all the nutrients Nature puts into it. Any whole food has a wide variety of macronutrients and micronutrients. However, for our nutritional needs, a given food may be a rich source of some nutrients, while being deficient in others. We can conceivably get the necessary macronutrients (carbohydrates, lipids and proteins) from just a few sources, but variety is important if we want to get all the micronutrients (vitamins, minerals and phytonutrients) we need.

For convenience, we will place foods into two broad categories: plant-based foods and animal-based foods.

Plant-Based Foods

Plant foods include grains, legumes, fruits, vegetables, nuts and seeds.

Grains

Grains are the seeds of plants we commonly refer to as grasses. They include wheat, barley, rye, corn, rice, oats and millet. Grains form the basis of diets in most parts of the world. They are commonly eaten as cold or hot breakfast cereals. For lunch and dinner, we typically eat grains in the form of cooked rice, bread or pasta.

The tough outer covering of the grain is made of a coarse fiber called bran. Bran also has vitamins and minerals. For example, rice bran is used as a source of B vitamins. White bread and pasta are made of wheat that has been refined, which means that the bran (and most of the vitamins and minerals) has been removed.

The inside of the grain is rich in starch. Most grains also have a significant amount of protein. The major protein found in grains is called *gluten*. Different grains have different forms of gluten.

Grains have a number of issues that might necessitate moderation, or for some individuals, elimination from the diet:

- Grains have protease inhibitors.
- They contain phytic acid which pulls minerals from the body.
- They are high in calories, mostly in the form of starch, which effectively increases with cooking. The high caloric content, in and of itself, is no reason to eliminate grains, but rather necessitates moderation.
- Since the caloric content is high, a diet that provides the bulk of calories from grains can easily become deficient in vitamins, minerals and phytonutrients. This becomes even more problematical if the grains are refined as in wheat and rice.
- Since cooked grains tend to be bland, flavor enhancers and fats are generally added, which tends to promote overconsumption and reduction of fruits and vegetables. The typical results are weight gain, nutritional deficiencies, increase in the toxic load on the body, and overstimulation of the adrenal glands.
- Wheat, rye and barley have high levels of gluten, a protein which can trigger allergic reactions in some individuals. In general, non-hybridized grains are easier to digest and are less allergenic than heavily hybridized grains.

Tips For Healthy Grain Eating

- Eat them in moderation.
- Favor whole grain products.
- Favor organically grown grains.
- Look for bread made with sourdough instead of yeast. Unlike yeast bread, sourdough bread relies on bacteria to make the bread rise – the same sort of bacteria that populate our intestines. These bacteria produce a number of beneficial byproducts, including B vitamins, amino acids and lactic acid. The latter discourages the growth of harmful organisms in the digestive tract. In other words, sourdough bread tends to be more nutritious than yeast bread. When you buy sourdough bread, read the label and make sure that one of the ingredients is *sourdough starter*. Some commercial forms are called "sourdough bread" but are actually yeast bread with other chemicals thrown in to make it taste like sourdough.
- Look for breads made from **sprouted grains**. Sprouting reduces the allergenic qualities of grains and makes them more nutritious and digestible. A popular form of sprouted grain bread is *Ezekiel 4:9 bread*. It is high protein bread made from sprouted whole wheat, lentils and other

seeds. You can find it in the frozen food section of health food stores and some supermarkets.

Legumes

Legumes include beans, peas and peanuts. Since legumes are seeds, they are a good source of macronutrients. Specifically, they contain significant amounts of protein, carbohydrates and some lipids. If they are organically grown, they are also a good source of minerals. The gas that is often associated with legumes is attributed to difficulty in digesting the carbohydrates. Soaking and sprouting, as done in some traditional diets, reduces the gassiness, as does cooking.

Some individuals digest legumes better than others. For those who can digest legumes well, these foods are an excellent source of plant-based protein, as well as soluble fiber, minerals and phytonutrients. However, there are two common legumes that should be closely examined before they are liberally included in the diet: peanuts and soybeans.

Peanuts

Like other legumes, peanuts are high in protein. They are also very high in fat (peanut oil). One of the issues with peanuts is their tendency to trigger allergic reactions. The other issue is the presence of carcinogenic substances, called aflatoxins that accumulate on the surface, mostly due to prolonged storage inside the shell. In light of these two issues, I would advise the health seeker to eat peanuts in moderation or avoid them altogether.

Soybeans

Soy has the highest protein content of any legume. Because it is cheap and versatile, it is widely used. However, there is much controversy about soy in the nutrition world. Below are the main points to consider about soy.

Fermented Soy

The most beneficial forms of soy are the traditional fermented products, such as miso, shoyu (traditional soy sauce), tempeh and natto. Much of the reliable evidence that links soy to reduction in cancer and heart disease came from Japan, where soy has been traditionally consumed in the form of fermented soy products.

Fermentation makes soy more digestible. For example, fermentation, along with soaking and cooking, reduces the level of the gas-producing carbohydrates. Fermentation reduces the antinutrients (see below) found in soy beans and creates beneficial substances, including vitamins, antioxidants and enzymes. For example, one of the enzymes found in natto is called nattokinase, which has been found to break down blood clots and lower blood pressure.

Toxins and Antinutrients

Soy beans that have not been soaked, well-cooked, sprouted or fermented contain several substances which are the focal point of controversy:

- *Allergens.* Soy protein is one of the top eight allergens.
- *Saponins.* Saponins can lower cholesterol, but can also irritate the lining of the intestines.
- *Protease inhibitors.* Like all seeds, soybeans contain protease inhibitors, which interfere with protein digestion. On the other hand, some authorities claim that these protease inhibitors might actually be beneficial in treating AIDS and reducing infection and inflammation.
- *Isoflavones.* Isoflavones are naturally occurring phytoestrogens (plant estrogens). The most popular form is called *genistein.* Some studies suggest that isoflavones inhibit certain cancers, while other studies suggest that the same chemicals *cause* cancer, as well as contributing to reproductive problems, brain degeneration and the production of fibrin — a sticky protein in the blood that is responsible for making blood clots, fibroid tumors and scar tissue. In contrast, natto (fermented soy) contains nattokinase, which breaks down fibrin.
- *Phytate* (phytic acid or IP6). This substance pulls minerals, such as calcium, zinc and iodine out of the body, resulting in a number of problems, such as enlargement and malfunctioning of the thyroid gland. On the other hand, the same phytate seems to be useful for pulling toxic metals out of the body, as well as fighting heart disease and certain cancers. Phytate is found in all seeds, but is especially high in soybeans.

Tofu and Other Soy Products

Although traditional tofu is a fairly clean food, we should bear in mind that it is not a *whole* food. Like cheese, it is a concentrated protein extract. Digesting tofu is not unlike digesting pasteurized cheese or cooked meat, requiring a large output of enzymes.

Other processed unfermented soy products include *soy flour, soy lecithin* and *textured vegetable protein (TVP).* The latter is largely MSG (monosodium-glutamate). Some of the health problems encountered by modern vegetarians and vegans may be attributed to the over-consumption of highly processed soy products. In contrast, vegetarian or near vegetarian societies that show good health and longevity, typically consume an abundance of fresh fruits and vegetables (when available), along with whole grains, legumes and starchy vegetables.

Furthermore, much of the commercially produced soybeans in the U.S. are genetically modified and sprayed heavily with pesticide and herbicide. In fact, the genetically engineered soy beans have been specifically modified to tolerate larger doses of herbicide, which means that when you eat those beans, you get the double whammy of genetic modification and higher levels of herbicide residue.

Bottom Line on Soy

If you decide to use soy as food, you may want to favor the traditional fermented soy products made from organically grown soybeans. Such soy is nutritious and has real health promoting benefits. If tofu is appealing to you, eat it in moderation, as you would any other concentrated food, and combine it with a liberal amount of vegetables and a good source of trace minerals such as sea vegetation as done in traditional Asian diets.

Fruits

A fruit is the fleshy covering around a seed. Fruits tend to be rich in simple sugars, vitamins, minerals and antioxidants. Compared to other food fruits, they tend to be lowest in fat and protein. They also have the least toxic residue of the all the food groups, and often provide carbohydrates, protein and fat in a predigested form. They tend to have high water content and are also rich in pectin. Therefore, most fruits are cleansing for the digestive system and the body in general.

For nutritional purposes, fruits are divided into three categories: acid, sub-acid and sweet.

- *Acid* fruits include oranges, lemons, grapefruit, limes and pineapple.
- *Subacid* fruits include apples, pears, grapes, apricots, strawberries and cherries.
- *Sweet* fruits include bananas, dates, figs and persimmons.

Some Fruits of Interest

- **Apples:** Contain malic acid, which stimulates cleansing of the liver and has been shown to be beneficial for individuals with fibromyalgia.
- **Bananas:** Very rich in potassium. Contain several factors which calm the emotions and lift depression. Fully ripe bananas contain a chemical which inhibits tumor growth, inhibits viral replication and enhances the immune system.
- **Blueberries:** High in antioxidants, good for heart, brain and eyes.
- **Strawberries:** High in antioxidants. Rich in xylitol, which may account for strawberries having a reputation for being good for teeth and gums.

- **Red or purple grapes:** High in antioxidants, especially resveretrol, have been shown to promote vascular health and activate two so-called "anti-aging genes, which seem to have a protective effect on DNA.
- **Prunes:** Highest antioxidant content of any common fruit or vegetable.
- **Pineapples:** Contain bromelain, an enzyme which digests protein and has been shown to have anti-inflammatory effects.
- **Papaya:** Contain papain, a protein-digesting enzyme.
- **Watermelon:** Promotes cleansing of the intestines, liver and kidneys. Rich in lycopene. Reputed to be beneficial for individuals with psoriasis, arthritis and kidney stones.
- **Figs:** High in calcium and iron. Very cleansing, especially mucus.
- **Pomegranates:** Very rich in antioxidants. Good for cardiovascular health. Helps to lower blood pressure. Has been shown in human and animal studies to <u>reverse</u> arterial plaquing.[65]
- **Kiwi Fruit:** Very rich in enzymes, Vitamin C and lutein. Also rich in Vitamin E, folic acid and potassium.

Vegetables

The term "vegetables" typically refers to edible roots, stems and leaves. Some vegetables, such as cucumbers, are fruits, technically. In the language of botany, the fruit is simply the soft covering around the seeds. To a botanist, cucumbers, tomatoes, bell peppers and okra are fruits, but from a dietary standpoint, we use them with other vegetables. Fleshy vegetables, such as potatoes and squash, are rich in starch.

Green leafy vegetables tend to be rich in minerals and phytonutrients, which make them good for alkalizing and cleansing the blood and liver and protecting against aging and degeneration through their antioxidant action. Yellow and orange vegetables are rich in beta carotene, which the body converts into vitamin A.

Some Vegetables of Interest

- **Carrots** are rich in beta carotene, which, among other benefits, promotes eye health. They also contain oils that help to eliminate intestinal parasites. Promotes cleansing of the liver.
- **Beets** are rich in iron. Promotes cleansing of the liver.
- **Dandelion greens** promote cleansing of the liver.
- **Celery** is an excellent source of minerals. Soothing for the nervous system. Helps to lower blood pressure.

- **Broccoli** has essential oils that have anticancer properties. Rich in Vitamin K. Rich in sulfur-containing oils, which help detoxify the liver.
- **Kale** has the highest antioxidant content of any vegetable. Good source of calcium and iron. Like other dark green leafy vegetables, it promotes cleansing of the liver and blood. Like broccoli, it is rich in sulfur-containing oils.
- **Spinach,** like other dark green leafy vegetables, promotes cleansing of the liver and blood. Rich in antioxidants. Good source of iron.
- **Bitter Melon** is rich in iron, calcium and potassium. Good source of Vitamins C, B1, B2, B3 and beta carotene. Helps lower blood sugar. It has been shown to be helpful for individuals with diabetes mellitus.

Nuts and Seeds

From a nutritional standpoint, the foods that we classify as nuts and seeds can generally be eaten raw, though roasting is a common practice. They tend to be high in proteins and fats. Many nuts are excellent sources of trace minerals.

Since nuts and seeds tend to be rich in fats, they are best eaten in moderation. Also, their rough texture can irritate the stomach and intestines if eaten in large amounts. They are most nutritious when eaten raw, soaked and maybe sprouted. They can also be soaked 4-12 hours, depending on their size. After draining the water, you can sprout them for 1-3 days.

Some Nuts and Seeds of Interest

- **Walnuts** contain about 60 chemicals that are beneficial for the brain.
- **Flax seeds** are good for intestines and an excellent source of omega-3 fatty acids, fiber and various other beneficial phytonutrients. Promote intestinal motility and beneficial bacteria.
- **Pumpkin seeds** are rich in zinc. Excellent for the reproductive organs, especially the prostate. They also contain oils that help eliminate intestinal worms.
- **Sesame seeds are an excellent source** of trace minerals. The lignins in sesame seeds have many health benefits, such as protecting against free radical damage of DNA and other forms of free radical damage. They also help to lower cholesterol and reduce inflammation.
- **Almonds** are relatively low in oils and high in protein (compared to other nuts and seeds). According to some sources, they have anticancer properties.
- **Sunflower seeds** are highly nutritious, easy to sprout and inexpensive.
- **Brazil nuts** are rich in protein. Very rich in selenium.

Animal-Based Foods

Animal products include all foods derived from the bodies of animals, as well as their eggs, milk and milk products. The term "flesh foods" refers to any edible part of land animals, birds or fish. The term "meat" generally refers to the muscles of land animals, which might include poultry, depending on who you ask. The term, "organ meat" includes liver, kidneys and pancreas. "Red meat" generally refers to the muscles of hoofed animals, most notably beef.

Animal products are rich in protein and fat. A quarter of a pound (four ounces) of beef, chicken or fish provides 30-35 grams of protein. The protein in animal products is considered to be of high quality because it closely resembles our own proteins in terms of amino acid profile. By weight, the fat content is typically less than the protein, but in terms of calories, the fat content can actually be higher, since a given amount of fat has twice the caloric value as the same amount of protein. Animal-based foods also contain certain critical nutrients that tend to be lacking or more difficult to get in plant foods, especially DHA, vitamin B_{12}, vitamin D3, selenium and zinc.

Here are the reasons to be moderate with animal-based foods:

- The fat portion includes a substantial amount of saturated fat, as well as trans-fats.
- The toxic residue tends to be substantially higher compared to plant-based foods. For example, red meat is associated with iron toxicity, which increases the oxidative stress on the body and has been associated with increased cancer rates and oxidation of cholesterol. Flesh food, especially red meat, is high in uric acid, which, among other things, stimulates the adrenal glands, similar to caffeine.
- Animal products are also subject to contamination, which largely has to do with dirty farming practices that usually occur on a mass production scale. One-third of all inspected poultry was found to be contaminated with salmonella. The routine use of antibiotics in cattle results in the breeding of virulent strains of E. coli. Therefore, if you eat meat on a regular basis, buy organic.

The Good News

The above facts are no reason to totally exclude animal products, but rather to exercise moderation, as with grains and soy products. The good news is that the specific nutrients provided by animal products are so concentrated that we do not have to consume very large amounts of these foods to get the nutritional benefits.

Fish

Fish is the most easily digestible and nutritionally complete of flesh foods, especially if it is eaten raw as in sushi. In addition to being a good source of protein, fish are high in omega-3 oils and minerals.

Though fish (wild fish, at least) are not subject to the antibiotics and other chemicals used in growing livestock, fish from polluted waters obviously pose a problem. The major concern with fish is the mercury content. In general, big fish that live a long time, such as tuna, have higher mercury content than small fish that have a shorter life cycle. Below is a guide for minimizing mercury exposure from fish, based on government and academic sources:

- *Lowest mercury content:* Salmon, sardines, sole, freshwater catfish, shrimp
- *Limit to once per week*: Orange roughy, sea bass, *red snapper, *flounder, *fresh water bass, *halibut, *grouper trout, *fresh tuna
- *Limit to once per month:* *Swordfish, *shark, tilefish, *king mackerel, *marlin

*These fish were found to occasionally have unsafe levels of mercury. The biggest and oldest fish consistently had the highest levels.

Pork, Beef, Poultry and Eggs

Pork leaves the largest toxic residue of the flesh foods and can harbor a swarm of parasitic infections, most notably trichinosis. Pork is also not easy to digest. By thoroughly cooking it at high temperatures (which is necessary to eliminate the parasites), it becomes even more difficult to digest.

Beef tends to be cleaner than pork, because the traditional food of cows (grass) is cleaner than the food consumed by pigs. Grass-fed beef is available in some supermarkets, as well as some farmers markets.

Poultry tends to be more digestible than beef and has less saturated fat. Commercially raised chicken is loaded with toxic residue, but free-range chicken and turkey are readily available in some supermarkets, farmers markets and health food stores.

Eggs are an excellent source of protein, omega-3 oils and fat-soluble vitamins. However, commercial eggs come from factory raised chickens, which have been raised under extremely unsanitary conditions, are loaded with antibiotics, and are subject to salmonella. Organic eggs are available in health food stores and some supermarkets. They contain higher levels important fatty acids, especially DHA. The really good organic eggs will have a rich orange yolk and are generally tastier than commercial eggs.

Milk Products

Milk is a mixture of nutrients designed to support the growing mammalian infant. It contains protein (mostly casein), sugar (lactose) and lipids (butter fat). It is also loaded with vitamins and minerals. It is especially rich in calcium. The protein part of milk is used to make cheese. The fat part is used to make butter.

Some individuals handle dairy fairly well. Many do not. They might have an allergy to the milk protein, or they may lack the enzyme to digest the lactose. In fact, about 70% of humans are lactose intolerant to a certain degree.

For those who do not handle cow's milk very well, goat's milk might be an excellent alternative. Here are some advantages of goat's milk:

- In general, goat's milk is more like human milk than cow's milk.
- Goat's milk is digested much more quickly than cow's milk.
- Because the protein of goat's milk is more easily digested, it is less likely to produce allergic reactions and is less mucus forming.
- It has less lactose and is therefore less likely to cause bloating and gas.
- The fat in goat's milk is more easily digested and includes a higher proportion of medium chain fatty acids which benefit the immune system and inhibits the growth of yeast.
- Compared to cow's milk, goat's milk has about 13% more calcium, 25% more Vitamin B-6, 47% more vitamin A, 134% more potassium, 350% more niacin and 35% more selenium.

Raw Milk

If you feed pasteurized milk to a calf, it will die in about six weeks. Pasteurization oxidizes the milk fat and alters the milk protein so that it is more difficult to digest. Pasteurization destroys the enzymes that allow us to utilize the nutrients. Heat makes the calcium in milk less compatible for the body, causing it to form arterial deposits.

Raw milk is significantly more nutritious and easier to utilize than pasteurized milk. However, it is illegal to sell raw milk for human consumption in most states in the United Sates. You can often buy raw goat's or cow's milk directly from certain farmers, if you earnestly explain that you are getting it for your cat.

If you do want to drink the pasteurized milk that is commercially available, buy organic milk, especially organic goat's milk, and use it sparingly.

What about Butter?

Butter, just like any extracted oil, is not a whole food. It is a concentrated fatty extract, high in cholesterol and saturated fat. On the positive side, it is a rich source of fat soluble vitamins and beneficial short-chain fatty acids. If you feel inclined to eat butter, do so in small amounts— as with other non-whole foods. The best is raw butter or, at least, organic butter. Commercial butter is made from pasteurized milk, which means that it contains some oxidized cholesterol and all of the fat-soluble chemicals used in raising the cows. However, commercial butter is still preferable to margarine.

Fermented Foods

Fermentation is a process in which the food is partially broken down by bacteria or fungus, producing a wealth of beneficial byproducts, such as vitamins, amino acids, lactic acid and enzymes. Fermented foods are an excellent way of getting some of the nutrients that are missing in the diet due to the lack of fresh and raw foods. Fermentation also increases the digestibility of foods that otherwise might be problematic, such as dairy and soy. When buying fermented foods, read the label to make sure the product really is fermented and really does contain a significant amount of live cultures and their byproducts.

Examples of Fermented Foods

- **Sauerkraut:** Fermented cabbage.
- **Pickles:** Fermented cucumbers.
- **Miso, tempeh, natto, soy sauce:** Fermented soy products.
- **Fermented milk products:** Milk is fermented by infusing it with bacteria that convert the milk sugar (lactose) into lactic acid. The acid causes the milk protein to solidify (curdle). Depending on the bacteria that are used, the milk will initially turn into buttermilk, yogurt or kefir. If the solid curd is allowed to separate from the liquid part of the milk (the whey), the curd forms cheese. Like other fermented foods, fermented milk products provide beneficial bacteria and their byproducts. Since most of the lactose has been converted into lactic acid, fermented dairy is better tolerated by individuals with lactose intolerance. Furthermore, some of the enzymes produced by the bacteria assist in digesting the milk protein and fat. Fermented milk products are especially beneficial when made from raw milk. Even in places where it is not legal to sell raw milk, raw cheese is still available. Raw cheeses are readily obtainable in health food stores and farmers markets.

Replacement Foods

The bottom line for healthy eating is to favor whole foods which have had minimal processing. However, for those individuals who are used to the convenience, taste and texture of fast foods, here are some alternatives:

Non-Dairy Milk

Non-dairy milk can be used by individuals who want to avoid dairy but still would like to have something that resembles milk for drinking or pouring on cereal. The four major alternatives are soymilk, rice milk, nut/seed milk and coconut milk. As dairy alternatives, all four can vary greatly in quality. Read the label. Look for organic ingredients and a minimum amount (zero, preferably) of added sugar. Also, the milk alternatives that are not refrigerated come in cartons that are typically lined with aluminum, which could possibly leach into the milk.

- *Soymilk* is readily available and relatively inexpensive. Since soy is a legume, the protein complements the whole grain cereal that you place it on. However, it is not as nutritionally complete as dairy milk, and, like other unfermented soy products, soymilk is not that easy to digest and contains substances (such as phytoestrogens) that could be detrimental for some individuals, especially if consumed in large amounts. Therefore, as with dairy milk, do not depend on it as a major protein source, and use it in moderation.

- *Rice milk* is hypoallergenic and easier to digest than soymilk. However, as with soymilk, it is still not as nutritionally complete as dairy milk. Therefore, do not rely on it as a staple, but use it when you feel like having some "milk" as a quick beverage or to put on your cereal.

- *Nut/seed milk* is the most nutritionally complete of the milk substitutes. For example, it provides a significant amount of protein and is rich in beneficial fats. Many nuts and seeds provide omega-3 oils, while soy is very high in omega-6. If the milk is made from raw (and organic, preferably) nuts and seeds, it is also rich in vitamins, minerals and phytonutrients. The most readily available nut/seed milk on the market is almond milk. Nut/seed milk is also relatively easy to make at home. The quickest and easiest way is to grind the nuts/seeds of your choice in a coffee grinder and throw them in a blender with some water.

- *Coconut milk.* The liquid part of the coconut, though pleasantly sweet, is generally too watery to serve as a milk substitute for most people. However, when the water from a young ("green") coconut is blended with some of the coconut meat, the two combine into a delicious and satisfying drink that, for many individuals, replaces the flavor, texture and satisfying quality of dairy milk.

Soy Burgers and Soy Franks

These products are highly processed and often contain toxic substances from the industrial processing. The toxicity issue is compounded if the products are made from commercially grown (and genetically modified) soybeans.

Are they better than fast-food beef-burgers and hot dogs? That depends. If your primary consideration is to eat healthier, the choice between meat-based and soy-based fast foods might be a bit like the choice between fried pork skins and potato chips. Actually, the soy might win out when we consider what goes into fast-food burgers and franks. However, choosing the lesser of two evils is not the same as choosing for optimum health. The soy analogues of burgers and franks are not the sort of food that you would eat several times a week as "health foods."

Non-Dairy Cheese

The main choices are almond, rice and soy cheese. These cheese-like products tend to be highly processed. If you specifically want to try them as a way of reducing your dairy, be aware that many "non-dairy" cheeses do have casein (milk protein) as one of the ingredients.

Non-Dairy Ice Cream

If you really like ice cream, nothing replaces it. However, non-dairy frozen treats can offer a tasty alternative when you feel like having a dessert that resembles ice cream, in texture and sweetness, but want to avoid dairy. You can also make some surprisingly tasty and satisfying raw "ice cream" from blended frozen fruits, such as bananas, with, perhaps, some nuts and seeds for a creamier texture.

Supplements & Specialty Foods

The ideal way to get our micronutrients is to eat a wide variety of organically grown whole foods, especially fresh and raw vegetables and fruits that are vine or tree ripened. Micronutrients are lost through factory farming, picking food before it is ripe, extended storage, processing and cooking. We can obtain some of the key nutrients that are lacking in the diet from laboratory-formulated supplements, extracts from whole-foods and herbal products. Synthetic vitamins are chemically reproduced without the synergistic factors that occur in nature, while whole food supplements are more complete.

Digestive Enzyme Supplements

Digestive enzyme supplements may be taken to promote good digestion. Furthermore, cooked food requires more "clean up" than raw food, thus increasing the requirement for enzymes. In addition to improving digestion and possibly reducing food allergies, supplemental enzymes allow the body to conserve the resources that are needed to produce enzymes. Those same resources can then be used to produce enzymes which help the body detoxify, overcome and prevent infectious diseases and cancers and promote healing and regeneration.

Powdered Greens and Blue Green Algae

This is a quick and easy way to get the benefits of eating greens. In general, the freeze dried juice of young grasses, such as barley and wheat, tend to be the most nutrient dense.

Algae are primitive green plants that typically consist of single cells. They are harvested from the oceans as well as some lakes. Like all greens, they are rich in vitamins, chlorophyll and phytonutrients. In addition, they are rich in protein, minerals and omega-3 oils. The main forms of nutritional algae are spirulina, chlorella and AFA (Aphanizomenon Flos Aquae). All three are available in powder, capsules and tablets.

Medicinal Plants

There are a vast number of plants which have healing properties. The ones described below have been used traditionally to promote cleansing and healing and are readily available in health food stores and on line.

Aloe Vera

Aloe vera is perhaps the best known of the healing plants. It has been shown to be beneficial for just about everything from cancer to minor cuts. It is healing for the digestive system, as well as having significant antimicrobial activity. The ideal way to get the healing benefits of aloe is to harvest the leaves from a live plant and eat the slimy innards right away. The next best alternative is to get stabilized aloe, which tends to be very expensive.

Echinacea

Echinacea, is usually sold in the form of tinctures and capsules. It is popular for supporting the immune system during cold and flu season.

Noni

Noni is a fruit that grows in Tahiti and Hawaii. It has strong anti-inflammatory, anti-oxidant and analgesic properties. It has been used to relieve arthritis pain. It strengthens the immune system, while modulating an overactive immune system — which means that noni might be helpful with a broad range of autoimmune conditions, such as rheumatoid arthritis, asthma, colitis, blood sugar issues and fibromyalgia. By helping to regulate hormones and neurotransmitters, noni can help with memory, depression and recovery from addiction.

Goji Berries

Goji berries are rich in Vitamin C, B vitamins, Vitamin E, iron, omega-3, minerals, beta carotene and 18 amino acids (including the eight essential amino acids). The anti-oxidant content of goji berries is very high. Goji berries are used extensively in traditional Chinese herbal formulas, especially for depression, eye conditions, improved sleep and rejuvenation. They have also been used for memory, glandular health, kidney and liver issues, fatigue, impotence and immune system issues.

Chapter 7
Guidelines for Healthy Eating

To gain some perspective on healthy eating, let us consider animals in the wild. They are exposed only to raw and unprocessed whole foods, usually consumed as a mono-meal. Their nervous system is designed for such foods. The human nervous system is fundamentally the same. It is designed for raw food, one item at time. Under these conditions, whatever tastes good is also good for you. The brain can easily discern when you have eaten enough, at which point you feel satiated and therefore stop eating.

On the other hand, the cooking, refining and mixing of foods expose us to chemicals and combinations of chemicals our nervous system is not designed to handle. Therefore, the food can taste and smell yummy, but is not necessarily beneficial. For example, in the wild, a whole food which tastes sweet, such as fruit, contains nutrients in concentrations and proportions we can easily handle. However, if we extract the sugar from that fruit and use it to sweeten things that are normally bad-tasting or bland, such as partially hydrogenated vegetable oil (shortening) and refined wheat flour, we trick our nervous system; we feel pleasure as we consume large amounts of a mixture that is nutritionally unbalanced while leaving a substantial toxic residue. This does not mean that we should totally abstain from all food except for that which is raw, unprocessed and unmixed. That would not be realistic for most people. The point is this: To the extent that we eat food in a manner other than how Nature presents it, our eating instincts will have a harder time guiding us. Therefore, for most of us civilized folks, healthy food choice is a combination of two things:

- ¤ Instinct (taste and intuition)
- ¤ Educated common sense. Though the study of nutrition is rather complicated, we do have some simple guidelines.

General Guidelines

- For better digestion, avoid eating food that is too hot or too cold. Very hot foods debilitate the stomach, and very cold foods take vitality from the system, inhibiting digestion.
- Minimize or eliminate fluids with meals. Ideally, do not drink for one-half hour before the meal, and for two hours after.
- If you tend to feel "stuffed" after you eat, eat more slowly so your brain has a chance to catch up with your stomach. Another trick is to stop eating when you feel about 80% full – which is easier to accomplish if you eat slowly. In fact, if you just put your attention on eating more slowly, you might find that you automatically eat about 20% less.
- Eat your last meal of the day 2-3 hours before you go to bed. The stomach needs to rest and regenerate at night. However, if you have blood sugar issues, a light snack before bedtime might be beneficial.

Food Combining

In the natural world, foods that tend to be high in fat also tend to be high in protein, and proportionately lower in carbohydrates. For example, beef provides all of its calories in the form of fat and protein, having virtually no carbohydrates. On the other hand, fruits, vegetables, legumes and grains tend to provide most of the calories from carbohydrates with relatively small contributions from fat and protein. Grains and legumes do have significant levels of protein, but carbohydrates still dominate.

The combination of macronutrients that typically does NOT occur in Nature is one that is simultaneously high in carbohydrates *and* fats. None-the-less, that combination is very common in our own culinary creations: cookies, cakes, ice-cream, pizza, ham sandwiches with mayo, potato chips, French fries, etc. Here are the main issues that arise with this combination:

- **Overeating.** When a meal has both concentrated fats *and* concentrated carbohydrates, it is easy to over-consume calories. *This is a major contributor to unwanted weight gain.*
- **Digestive disturbance.** Carbohydrates digest relatively fast, while fats and proteins require more time. It is, therefore, not surprising that digestion is best when we do not mix large amounts of high-carb food with large amounts of high fat and protein foods. When the three are all mixed in large amounts, the fat and protein (especially the fat) slow down the digestion of carbohydrates, which, in turn, provide food for gas-producing bacteria and yeast.
- **Blood sugar issues.** High levels of fat in the blood interfere with the body's ability to move the glucose into the cells.

Likewise, the proper combination of foods can greatly assist digestion. The general principle is to avoid combining foods that differ widely with regard to time spent in the stomach. Food requiring a short transit time, such as fruit, will be "stalled" in the stomach and rot if it has to wait on another food that has a longer transit time (like meat, dairy or fatty plant foods. Based on this principle, here are some general guidelines for food combining:

- ¤ Vegetables combine well with flesh foods, fatty foods and grains.
- ¤ In general, keep high protein/fat foods separate from high carbohydrate foods.
- ¤ Eat fruits separate from other foods.
- ¤ Acid fruits combine fairly well with subacid. Subacids combine fairly well with sweet fruit. Acid fruits do not combine well with sweet fruits.
- ¤ Eat melons separate from other fruits.

How Important is Food Combining?

Does everyone need to practice food combining? Do you have to follow these guidelines to the letter? The answer is "no" to both questions. Most people could probably benefit from minimizing the consumption of sugary fruits while eating foods that require an extended sojourn in the stomach. Beyond that, food combining may or may not be necessary for a given individual. In general, the more sensitive or "slow" your digestive system, the more you are likely to benefit from practicing food combining. And, of course, the best sort of food combining is to include with each meal a generous helping of blessings and thanksgiving.

Food Preparation — Raw and Cooked

There are two major options in food preparation: cooked or raw.
Here are some suggestions for raw food preparation:

- ¤ Soak or sprout nuts and seeds.
- ¤ In addition to just cutting up vegetables and making a salad, you can shred or grind them for easier chewing and variety of flavor and texture.
- ¤ Vegetables that are relatively soft and fleshy, such as zucchini, yellow squash and cucumbers can be quickly shredded. You can then throw them on a salad or serve as a side dish, seasoned to your taste.
- ¤ Using a simple gadget called the spiral slicer, you can turn various vegetables into something that looks like spaghetti. Zucchini spaghetti has its own subtle flavor and texture, which you can then embellish with the topping of your choice, including raw or cooked tomato sauce.

- Coarser vegetables such as carrots, celery, and beets can be finely ground with a grater or other simple kitchen tools. Finely ground carrots have a delightful flavor and texture.
- Re-discover the natural flavor of unprocessed foods. Experiment with very simple meals such as a fruit mono-meal.

Regarding cooked food, first of all, replace aluminum and Teflon cookware with stainless steel, porcelain or glass. The aluminum does get into the food. The longer you cook the food, the higher the aluminum content. This is especially true with acidic foods that naturally react with metals, such as tomato sauce. If you cook a tomato-rich meal in an aluminum container and then let it sit for several hours, it can absorb dangerous levels of aluminum. Individuals who eat such leftovers can get so ill they have to be rushed to the hospital. However, even if you do not allow such extremely high levels of aluminum to accumulate, the low levels that are added to the food every time you use aluminum cookware can still accumulate in the body over time – especially the brain.

What is wrong with Teflon? For starters, small pets, such as birds, have died from the fumes that are emitted from Teflon cookware. Furthermore, the manufacturing of Teflon releases the same chemical (perfluorooctanoic acid or PFRA), which has been found in wells far removed from the factory. That chemical has been detected in humans throughout the world. PFRA has been linked to various ailments in animals, including cancer, liver damage, birth defects and immune system suppression. It has also been linked to birth defects and other ailments in humans. Every time you cook with Teflon cookware, PFRA gets into the food you eat and the air you breathe.

Cooking Methods

Having selected the proper pot, the options for cooking are steaming, boiling, baking, frying and microwaving. For best nutritional results, the rule of thumb is to minimize time and temperature of exposure.

- *Steaming* is best for preserving the nutrient content, especially the vitamins.
- *Baking* and *boiling* are a toss-up. Baking generally exposes the food to higher temperatures than boiling, while boiling can result in the loss of water-soluble vitamins and minerals – unless you drink the cooking water.
- *Frying.* The high temperatures and oxidation of oils that occur during frying result in the production of all manner of abominations (that taste good). Prolonged frying can be saved for special occasions. For day-to-day cooking, favor the quick stir-fry method, using oils that are less vulnerable to oxidation, such as olive oil or coconut oil. To minimize frying time, you can steam the vegetables to soften them and then do a quick stir-fry to give them that special flavor.

◘ *Microwaving* has just about all the disadvantages of frying and none of the advantages. In other words, microwaving alters the chemical make-up of the food and produces toxic byproducts, but does not provide that yummy flavor and feeling of contentment that makes fried food appealing. Microwaving disrupts the natural shape of nutrient molecules more so than conventional cooking. Furthermore, the plastic containers used in microwave ovens release toxic chemicals into the food.

> **The Price of Convenience**
> In addition to the effects of the microwaves on food, leakage from microwave ovens has been shown to have adverse affects on the people in the vicinity. In the U.S., by law, a certain amount of radiation leakage is permitted from microwave ovens. Furthermore, the leakage increases with age, which means that older microwave ovens exceed the "safe" limit. In Russia, where the original microwave research was conducted, microwave ovens have been banned. Here are some of the effects of microwaves on living organisms:
>
> ◘ Breakdown of red blood cells
> ◘ Changes in cell metabolism (similar to cancer)
> ◘ Disruption of hormonal cycles

Organically Grown

To understand the significance of the term "organically grown," let us start by pointing out that the human body is made of the same molecules that make up the plants, animals and microbes all around us. Microbes produce the soil which allows for the growth of plants, which are then eaten by animals. When animals and plants die, they are broken down by other microbes whose byproducts enrich the soil, allowing more plants to grow.

When we eat artificial foods and dump toxic chemicals into the environments, we disrupt the cycles and rhythms of Nature. Ultimately, what we do to the environment, we do to ourselves, because we are part of the cycles of Nature. One of the most basic ways to harmonize with Nature is to eat organically grown whole foods.

What Does "Organic" Mean?

The nutritional usage of the word organic refers to how food is grown. According to the current federal organic standards, food is considered organic if it is grown without insecticides, herbicides, antibiotics or other synthetic chemicals, and free of genetic engineering. The term organically grown also implies the soil itself is kept in good condition – rich in minerals, decayed plant matter, microbes, worms and their excrements; the blacker the better.

Reasons for Buying Organic

- Organic produce contains an average of 63% more calcium, 59% more iron and 60% more zinc, and is much richer in trace minerals.[54]
- Organic farming preserves the soil organisms which produce vitamins, such as Vitamin B_{12}. These vitamins are either absorbed by the plants or adhere to the outside, along with the associated bacteria, thus providing an important source of vitamins.
- Organic food tastes better. Gourmet chefs use organic foods in their recipes because they taste better.
- Organic food contains significantly less toxic residue than conventional foods. Most of the conventionally grown foods have detectable levels of pesticides, while most of the organically grown foods are free of pesticides. The EPA says that 60% of all herbicides, 90% of all fungicides, and 30% of all insecticides are potentially carcinogenic.
- Organic farming protects air and water. Pesticides can get into wells and reservoirs. They can evaporate into the air and drift for miles. They are detectable in the fog, snowflakes and rainwater. It is common to find pesticides in municipal drinking water. The EPA estimates that pesticides contaminate the ground, polluting the primary source of drinking water for more than half of the country's population.[55]
- Organic farming protects children. It is estimated that the average child receives four times more exposure than an adult to widely used cancer-causing pesticides in food. Babies and young children do not have the biological defenses which normally protect adults. A "safe" level for adults can be far more damaging for children. For example, the blood brain barrier does not develop until the baby is six months old. This is of particular concern when we consider that many pesticides are neurotoxins.
- Organic farming protects unborn babies. Pesticides get through the placenta easily.
- Organic farming promotes public health. Conventional farmers have the highest rates of certain cancers, as do their children. Other studies suggest a link between pesticides and birth defects in areas close to agricultural fields. Still other studies suggest that women who grew up in agricultural areas are more likely to have children with birth defects.[47]

- Organic farming protects topsoil. Conventional farming erodes topsoil. The soil that does remain is continuously depleted of minerals. Organic farming builds soil. Organic farming maintains a rich supply of humus in the soil, which holds water, thus protecting the soil from drought, flooding and erosion.
- Organic farming supports a sustainable economy. Organic foods seem to cost more, but conventional foods contain many hidden costs, including:
  - Billions of dollars in federal farm subsidies.
  - The expense of regulating and testing chemicals.
  - The cost of disposal and clean-up of hazardous waste.

The really great news is that organic food is becoming more popular, and organic farms are on the increase. Every time you buy organic food, you become part of the massive grassroots movement that is creating a demand for organic farms and sustainable agriculture.

Chapter 8
Survey of Major Diets

There are currently a number of different diets promoted by various authors who are often at odds with each other. Why so many different diets? The primary reasons are as follows:

- More and more people are becoming aware of the impact of diet on health, hence there is a big market for diet books.
- Limitations in the availability of various foods.
- Diversity of preferences.
- Constitutional variations among individuals. This point is especially important. Some individuals seem to process some foods better than others. Furthermore, nutritional needs can change within the same person as time passes.

The above four points have created fertile ground for the emergence of many dietary systems — and much disagreement among them. The proponents of Diet "A" warn us of the dangers of Diet "B" and vice versa. What's more, both parties might sound pretty convincing. When we also consider the strong emotional connection we tend to have with food, we can see how the disagreement can become rather heated.

The more emotional charge we have on the various dietary choices, the less objective we tend to be. This certainly applies to the individuals that teach a particular dietary system. No matter how intelligent and sincere the teachers happen to be, they will probably be less than totally objective about their diet. To complicate matters, in addition to the emotional bias, there might also be a substantial financial investment. When money pressures demand that we "sell" our product, objectivity can easily fall by the way side.

Therefore, those who advocate a particular diet might (perhaps unconsciously) emphasize the strong points and minimize or censor the weak points. I certainly find myself tempted to do this — even though I personally *do not* have financial ties to any one given system. I can only imagine how much more difficult it is for someone who does have such financial ties.

How does the health-seeking individual navigate through all that? The answer is to just get both sides of the story on any dietary issue. If any of the diets described in this chapter seriously speak to you, learn as much as you can from its teachers and advocates, and then listen to what the critics have to say. It is that simple. However, "simple" is not the same as "easy." In this case, the simple solution also requires that you have enough self-awareness and mental discipline to maintain a measure of objectivity.

Do Not Marry Your Diet

Since objectivity is important in the study of nutrition, and since being objective is not necessarily as easy as we might think, let us give it some attention here. As with the teachers of a given diet, any individual who is "sold" on a given diet, and stays on it long enough can become emotionally attached to it. Any of us can become so emotionally identified with our diet of choice, as to be in denial about its potential issues. Eventually, we are no longer students of nutrition, but rather defenders of the faith.

Granted, it is appropriate for an individual to change from being a simple explorer of nutrition to an advocate of a given system. However, such change should be made intentionally and thoughtfully — and only after being thoroughly convinced the diet is beneficial and sustainable. Without such mindfulness, the sincere student of nutrition might drift into the role of the crusader, motivated by emotionally-based factors that he or she is barely aware of.

A given diet probably works well (at least in the short-term) for the individuals who promote it, therefore, they will, more than likely say only good things about it. The fundamental question is, how will that diet work for *you*? That is a question only personal experience can answer. The student of nutrition is, therefore, advised to regard each diet with an open mind, tempered with healthy skepticism.

Remember that your primary responsibility is to your body, which means that your primary loyalty is to the truth — the truth of what your body needs here and now. In my opinion, the process of discovering that truth is, to a large extent, an inside job. In other words, you and you alone are responsible for choosing which foods are allowed to enter your body.

The more we claim that responsibility, the more objective we become. When we remain fairly objective, we are likely to discover that most dietary systems have something of value to offer. In addition, though the study of nutrition can be complicated, we discover that the basics are actually quite simple, as described below.

How to Evaluate Any Diet

How do dietitians and nutritional researchers begin the task of evaluating a given diet? We can answer that question with just one word: Calories!

As you may recall, the nutrients found in foods are used by the body in three ways:

- They are burned for energy, which is measured in calories.
- They provide building material for the body.
- They have regulatory functions.

All three functions are important to life, but for the purpose of analyzing a given diet, the calories provide the foundation for rationally considering everything else. The nutrients that provide calories are carbohydrates, fats and protein (the macronutrients). When food scientists and dietitians analyze any diet, or when doctors and science-based nutritional counselors examine an individual's diet, one of the first items they consider is the ratio of calories provided by the macronutrients in the diet. Therefore, let us consider the caloric analysis of various foods, as shown in the table below.

Caloric Analysis of Common Foods

Name	%Carbohydrate	%Fat	%Protein
Fruits	90	5	5
Vegetables	70	15	15
Whole wheat	80	5	15
Walnuts	8	84	8
Ground beef	0	65	35
Lamb	0	75	25
Chicken	0	55	45
Pork	0	51	49
Fish	1	52	47
Whole Milk	30	49	21
Mozzarella Cheese	3	66	31

A brief examination of the above table reveals a pattern: In generally, naturally occurring foods that tend to be higher in fat also tend to be higher in protein, and proportionately lower in carbohydrates. For example, in the above table, we can see how animal products, nuts and seeds provide calories mostly from fat, secondarily from protein, and little, if any, from carbohydrates. On the other hand, fruits, vegetables and whole grains tend to be high in carbohydrates and relatively low in fat and protein. Whole milk is a special case because it is specifically formulated to support the growth of a rapidly growing mammalian infant.

In other words, *any whole food, in its natural form, typically features either carbohydrates or fats as the dominant source of calories.* The two have an inverse relationship. As one goes up, the other goes down — like a see saw[62]. This provides us with the key to understanding how the various diets differ from one another.

The Key

The fundamental way that various diets differ from one another is in the ratio of carbohydrates to fat. Yes, it is that simple. Fats and carbohydrates are typically the main providers of calories. If we increase one, we must decrease the other. Once we understand this, the other important considerations, such as the quality of the food can be properly addressed.

What about protein? From one diet to the next, protein does not fluctuate nearly as much as the other two macronutrients. This reflects the fact that the body tends to burn carbohydrates as the primary fuel, with fats serving as second banana. The burning of protein is, normally, kept to a minimum. Here are the reasons:

- Burning protein creates toxicity.
- Protein is too valuable to burn. In the natural world, protein is more difficult to get than fat or carbohydrates, and is needed for growth and repair — most of the dry weight of the body is protein!
- Living organisms are alive because they are efficient and exceedingly conservative with their expenditure of energy. Burning protein is inherently inefficient and downright wasteful. This is a major reason why high-protein diets tend to produce rapid weight loss. In other words, the higher the percent of protein in diet, the more calories the body will have to burn in order to process the extra protein that is ingested.

How We Go Off Track

Here is how most individuals go off track nutritionally: *They over-consume calories.* More specifically, the individual either over-consumes carbohydrates, fats or both. Whatever the case, the typical modern diet tends to be rich in macronutrients (too many calories) and deficient in micronutrients (not enough vitamins, minerals and phytonutrients). The result is an increase in weight and a decline in health. *Virtually all the degenerative diseases that we face today can be linked to an over consumption of macronutrients and an under consumption of micronutrients.*

Much has been written about the problems which arise from not having adequate levels of vitamins, minerals and phytonutrients. However, the issue of toxicity from too many macronutrients is of equal importance. Below is a description of what can happen when we over-consume protein, fats, and carbohydrates.

Too Much Carbohydrate

- An excess of sugar in the body provides food for yeast and other types of fungi.
- If carbohydrates (in the form of glucose) flood the blood stream in concentrations that exceed the body's ability to move the glucose into the cells, the result is excessive elevation (spiking) of the blood sugar. The body responds by producing high levels of insulin, which has been associated with cardiovascular disease, Alzheimer's disease and rapid aging of the tissues.
- If the total ingested calories exceed the body's daily requirements, the extra carbohydrates are converted into fat, which is then transported through the blood. The result is elevation of blood triglycerides, and eventually, cholesterol. In other words, excess carbohydrate consumption will result in some of the same harmful effects as excess fat consumption.
- If the carbohydrates happen to be in the form of unnaturally high levels of fructose, as in high-fructose corn syrup, the conversion into fats is further accelerated.
- If the main source of carbohydrates are grains and starchy vegetables (especially highly processed and heavily spiced grains), the individual can easily over-consume calories, while being deficient in vitamins, minerals and phytonutrients. Furthermore, grains, like other seeds, tend to have enzyme inhibitors and anti-nutrients which block the proper digestion and absorption.

Too Much Fat

The main issue with fat is that it does not dissolve in water. Our cells, tissues and organs require a watery environment, and can essentially get "clogged up" in the presence of too much fat. Excess fat, especially saturated fat and trans-fats, contributes to plaquing of arteries. High levels of fat in the blood are also associated with decreased oxygenation of cells and Type II Diabetes.

Furthermore, foods that are naturally high in fat also tend to be high in protein. Therefore, the toxicity that comes from excess fat is likely to be accompanied by the toxicity of too much protein, as described below.

Too Much Protein

To understand the seriousness of protein toxicity, let us review how the body handles this, otherwise, vital nutrient. The protein we eat is first digested into its constituent amino acids, which are then absorbed into the blood and transported to the body cells. Our cells use amino acids primarily as building material to manufacture the various proteins that make up our muscles, bones, tendons and ligaments, as well as making regulatory substances, such as enzymes, hormones and neurotransmitters.

If the protein we ingest exceeds the amount we actually need for building material and regulation, the excess is simply burned for energy. As you may recall, when the cells break down amino acids, ammonia is produced. The liver converts this toxic chemical into urea and uric acid. Furthermore, as soon as the animal is slaughtered, urea and uric acid and other waste products begin to accumulate in the meat, even when frozen.

If the protein consumption is high enough, the amount of ammonia produced by the cells can actually exceed the liver's ability to detoxify it, producing nausea. To avoid this, most diets guide the individual away from eating the very high levels of protein that have been shown to precipitate such an episode. However, long before we reach the point of nausea from liver toxicity, the body can still be subjected to higher levels of irritants and metabolic poisons. For example, the extra uric acid from a high protein diet can easily form microscopic crystals that produce a constant low-grade irritation of tissues, most notably, joints and kidneys. If the uric acid levels are high enough, the joint irritation can result in gout, and the crystals in the kidneys can grow into painful stones.

Such overt signs of protein excess might actually be a blessing, because they compel us to stop stressing the body with excessive amounts of protein. In the absence of these obvious signs, the subclinical (hidden) irritation can continue year after year, contributing to the degradation and rapid aging of the kidneys and other vital organs.

Here is an excerpt from an article by Owen Parrett MD:

"Beefsteak contains about 14 grains of uric acid per pound. ...The uric acid accounts for the quick pick up a steak seems to give, much like a cup of coffee gives. Uric acid, or trioxypurin, closely resembles caffeine... The late Dr. L. H. Newburg, of the University of Michigan, called attention to the fact that when meat formed 25 percent of a rat's diet, the rat became bigger and more active than rats on a normal diet. But after a few months, the kidneys of the meat-eating rat became badly damaged."[15]

In light of the above considerations, we can understand why our body cells tend to burn mostly carbohydrates and fats for energy. Our cells burn amino acids (from protein) only when they have to.

Balance

Based on the above considerations, the National Institute of Health (NIH) recommends that 55-60% of your daily calories come from carbohydrates, no more than 30% from fats, and 10-15% from protein. The World Health Organization (WHO) offers similar numbers, only slightly lower on the fat and protein. Though some dietary teachers deviate from these proportions, the NIH and WHO numbers still provide a useful reference point for evaluating and comparing various diets, as shown in the table below.

Name	% of Carbohydrate	% of Fat	% of Protein
NIH	55-60	< 30	10-15
Low-Fat Diets	60-80	10-20	10-15
Low-Carb Diets	10-40	30-70	20-35

In the above table, you will notice that diets deviate from NIH by either reducing the fat or carbohydrates. Therefore, a low-carb diet has to be a high-fat diet. Likewise, a low-fat diet has to, realistically, be a high-carb diet. The only way that a diet can simultaneously be low in both fat *and* carbohydrates is to have dangerously high levels of protein.

Furthermore, low-carb (high-fat) diets tend to have a substantial amount of animal products. Likewise, low-fat (high-carb) diets have little or no animal products.

In other words, whether you are aware of it or not, your ideal diet will, first and foremost, get you into your personal sweet spot, where your body is getting the ratio of carbohydrates, fats and protein that is right for you. That ratio, in my opinion, can vary from person to person, and does not necessarily have to be super precise for a given individual. It can even vary with the seasons. None-the-less, most nutritional authors agree there is an ideal "zone" in which your body wants to get its calories. Granted, there is some disagreement as to where to place the borders of that zone, but, when you go beyond your ideal zone (wherever it happens to be), your body will experience predictable problems — sooner or later. What does this mean to you as a health seeker? It means that if you are experiencing problems with your diet, and wonder what is wrong, the first place to look is the source of calories. If you proceed from there, you will probably get meaningful answers.

My point here is not to favor low-carb or low-fat diets, but rather to emphasize that the proportion of carbohydrates, fats and protein is the scientific foundation for understanding *any* diet. When this foundation has been established, we can make sense of the other considerations. Without this foundational knowledge, confusion reigns, or we have to blindly trust the creators of a given diet — which is what most individuals tend to do.

Do I Really Have to "Count Calories?"

The simple answer is no, provided that you have enough access to your eating instincts. In fact, your instincts, with minimal help from the educated mind, should be able to guide you to your ideal foods. On the other hand, if you want to provide science-based nutritional guidance, knowledge of calories is essential, even if you never mention calories to your clients.

Knowledge of calories simply gives you a road map that helps you find your way to your ideal diet. Once you reach your destination, you can put the map away. The only reason we even need a map is that our food instincts (especially the sense of taste) are exposed to foods not found in Nature. Our food instincts seem to work best with foods that are whole, fresh, raw, unadulterated and eaten one at a time. The more we alter and mix foods, the tougher it is for our sense of taste to distinguish nutrients from toxins, or to determine if the body is getting the right amounts of the required nutrients. This is where a map can be very useful.

The main purpose of this chapter is to show the reader how to "read the map" that allows us to navigate though the world of diets. As you examine the diets described below, you will quickly learn that the names of the diets are not that important. Any specific diet can fall out of fashion and become forgotten, only to be "reborn" again years later — by a different name! For example, the Atkins Diet started what appeared to be a new trend. It was introduced to the public in the form of a book called, *Dr. Atkin's Diet Revolution*. It was not a "revolution" at all. That same concept had been tried many years earlier.

By learning how to rationally analyze any new diet, we can avoid having to "reinvent the wheel." We can easily recognize a diet's "signature," regardless of its name or how it is marketed. On that note, let us begin our examination of the major diets that are currently in use.

The Blood Type Diet

The Blood Type Diet is unique among the others, because it does not present a signal formula for all humans. This diet, developed by Peter D'Adamo, N.D., uses the ABO blood groups as the primary factor for determining the diet of an individual. Therefore, the percentage of carbohydrates, fats and proteins can vary considerably from one individual to the next.

The dietary guidelines are based on the presence of chemicals in foods, called lectins. Different foods have different lectins. The lectins in a given food can react differently depending on the blood type of the individual. Based on these reactions, every food is categorized as being "beneficial", "neutral" or "avoid" for a given blood type.[42, 43] For example:

- If you are blood type "O," you are said to be relatively well-adapted to red-meat and most vegetables and fruits, but should avoid dairy and most grains and legumes. The developer for the blood-type diet suggests that the dietary preference of blood type "O" came about during the hunter/gather period of our ancestors.
- If you are blood Type "A," you can chow down on virtually all grains, most legumes and most types of vegetables and fruits, while exercising moderation with animal products, avoiding red-meat altogether. Blood Type A is said to be an adaptation to the development of agriculture that followed the hunter-gatherer period of our ancestors.
- Blood types B" and "AB" are said to be, somewhat, in between A and O.

Strong Points

- There are enough positive results from this diet that some naturopathic schools teach it in their programs.
- The diet encourages whole organic foods.

Weak Points and Criticisms

- Some critics claim that the positive results from this diet are due to a general improvement in diet, rather than blood-type considerations.
- The theoretical basis for this diet, as presented by Dr. D'Adamo, has been widely criticized. Part of it has to do with Dr. D'Adamo's assertion that the blood types originated as a consequence of the changing diet of our ancestors, rather than simply suggesting that the evolution of the ABO blood groups were *influenced* by diet.

¤ Though some correlations have been found between physiological tendencies and the ABO blood groups, they are not necessarily consistent with Dr. D'Adamo's dietary guidelines.

My Opinion

The basic theory behind the blood type diet does seem somewhat flawed to me. For example, the ABO blood groups exist in anthropoid apes[97]. However, "flawed" is not the same as totally false. Over the last fifteen years, I have seen enough (potential) association between blood type and food reaction (in myself and my students and patients) that I would not totally dismiss the entire concept at this time. I have noted some patterns with the ABO blood groups, even if the patterns don't quite conform to Dr. D'Adamo's specifications. My observations include specific positive results which I would be hard-pressed to explain in terms of "general improvement" in food choices, as suggested by some critics of this diet. Therefore, I suspect that the blood-type might, indeed, be a piece of the nutrition puzzle, even if it is not the most important piece, and even if Dr. D'Adamo's interpretation of it is in need of revision.

The Bigger Picture

Even if future research shows no significant correlation between blood type and diet, we are still left with the possibility that humans might vary significantly in their dietary needs. These differences may not fall neatly into categories defined by blood type or other population subgroups, but simply reflect individual differences.

Some general principles for healthy eating are certainly emerging, and may actually be found in a number of divergent dietary systems, as explained below. However, in my opinion, the health-seeking public would be better served if the authors and advocates of the various diets remained open to the possibility that good nutrition is not necessarily "one size fits all."

Low-Carb Diets

The low-carbohydrate diets are typically, though not necessarily, high in fat. Most of them rely on animal products for the bulk of daily calories.

On the positive side, low-carb diets do away with the over-consumption of refined grains and sugar, and tend to produce rapid weight loss. The potential problem with this dietary approach is that it can easily result in the over-consumption of protein and fat, and deficiency of nutrients that are found in plant-based foods (most vitamins, minerals and phytonutrients).

Eating substantially more protein and fat than the body needs can predispose the individual to certain degenerative conditions. The question is, how much is too much? Obviously, those who promote low-carb diets believe that the average person can safely consume more protein and fat than recommended by the NIH and WHO. Likewise, those who promote low-fat diets generally set the tolerance levels much lower.

Regarding fat, we have another point to consider. The studies linking high-fat diets with degenerative diseases typically focus on the *quantity*, not the *quality*, of the fat. Proponents of low-carb diets assert that quality makes big difference. More data is needed before we can say anything definitive on this issue. However, it is reasonable to suggest a high-fat diet featuring a good balance of fats is healthier than one that does not. For example, a low-carb (high-fat) diet rich in whole foods that provides an abundance of omega-3 and omega-6 oils in the right proportions is going to be easier on the body than one that is high in saturated fats, trans fats and extracted oils. This is precisely what some low-carb diets attempt to do.

The Atkins Diet

The Aktins Diet was the first of the modern low-carb diets. This diet advises us to consume all the meat and dairy we desire, while avoiding grains, starchy vegetables and fruit.

Caloric Ratio: Carbs 5-20%   Fats 60-75%,   Protein 25-30%.

Strong Points

- It is doable for the average person. All foods are readily available.
- There have been many reports of benefits, such as weight loss and even improvement in blood pressure, blood lipids and blood sugar.

Weak Points and Criticisms

- There are numerous reports of people becoming ill on this diet, including lawsuits.
- The improvement in blood pressure and blood lipids is sometimes followed by a worsening of both.[16]
- As shown above in the caloric ratio, the extremely low level of carbohydrates necessitates very high levels of protein and fat that can stress the kidneys and liver.
- The diet has nothing to say about the *quality* of the food. It makes no distinction between broiled salmon and KFC nuggets. It even recommends the use of artificial sweeteners.

Some of the issues associated with this diet are addressed simply by selecting higher quality food, reducing the animal products and replacing them with generous servings of vegetables and fruit, as in the two low-carb diets described below.

The Westin A. Price Diet

This diet is said to be based on research done by Dr. Weston A. Price in the 1930s. He traveled the world and noticed people were significantly healthier when they lived on traditional diets consisting of locally grown or wild-gathered foods. Though the cultures studied by Dr. Price varied widely in their diets, the creators of this diet believe there is enough of a pattern to use Dr. Price's findings to promote their dietary recommendations which may be summarized as follows: A liberal amount of flesh foods, dairy, eggs, vegetables, fermented products, and a modest amount of whole grains, legumes and fruit. Advocates the use of high-quality fermented foods.

Caloric Ratio: Carbs 10-35%   Fats 45-60%,   Protein 20-30%.

Strong Points

- Offers a wide variety of foods and is therefore very doable.
- Provides ample fat-soluble nutrients, such as DHA and EPA.
- Advocates locally grown foods and sustainable agriculture, such as organic and biodynamic farming.[103]
- The use of animal products includes raw milk, pasture raised animals, free-range poultry and their eggs.
- Discourages the overconsumption of refined sugar and grains, especially refined white flour.
- Discourages the consumption of foods that come from animals raised in conventional (unsanitary and in-humane) factory farms.
- Encourages the use of the whole animal, including organ meats and soup stocks made from bone and bone-marrow.

Weak Points and Criticisms

- Dr. Price did not track the subjects of his study for an extended period of time, and as a dentist, focused mainly on teeth and dental arches. He gave little attention to the rest of the body, nor did he give much consideration to longevity.

- Some critics of this diet claim the cultures studied by Dr. Price varied too widely in their diets to justify using his name to describe this particular dietary system.
- Some critics claim that the actual diet recommended by Dr. Price was lower in fat and protein and used animal products more conservatively, contrary to the recommendations of the modern Westin A. Price Diet.[17]

The Paleolithic Diet

Like the Westin A. Price Diet, the Paleo Diet provides a substantial amount of calories from animal products. The main difference is the Paleo Diet advocates less fat (especially less saturated fat).

Caloric Ratio: Carbs 22-40%   Fats 28-47%,   Protein 20-35%.

This diet establishes its essential features by using lean meats and an abundance of low-starch vegetables and fruits, especially the lower-glycemic fruits, such as berries. Eggs are permitted in moderation. Dairy, grains, legumes and potatoes are excluded.

The diet is based on theories regarding our prehistoric ancestors. Proponents of this diet point out that our ancestors appear to have been hunter/gathers much longer than they were farmers. Therefore, it is reasonable to suggest that our bodies are better adapted to eat flesh foods, vegetables and fruit, as compared to grains, legumes and dairy.[18]

A variation on this diet is the **Primal Diet**, which features 55-60% fat, does not restrict saturated fats and limits fruit. It also allows small amounts of dairy.[20]

Strong Points

- As with the previous diet, this one uses common foods which are fairly easy to get.
- Although you can prepare elaborate dishes and be creative, meals can be very simple —meat and vegetables, with fruits and nuts as snacks or dessert.
- It discourages the use of salt, MSG, artificial sweeteners, processed meats and factory raised animals.
- It eliminates common allergens such as wheat, soy, peanuts and dairy.
- This diet is arguably the most "natural" of the low-carb diets. In its purest form, it consists essentially of meat, vegetables and fruit — just like our paleolithic ancestors.

- Since some vegetables and virtually all fruit do not require cooking, the diet can include a large amount of raw food, as well as small amounts of raw animal products, such as sushi. In general, the diet emphasizes foods that have had a minimum amount of processing, and encourages organically grown plant foods, grass-fed beef, wild caught fish and free-range poultry, as well as supporting sustainable agriculture.

Weak Points and Criticisms

- Most nutritional authorities consider 35% protein to be excessive.
- The actual diet eaten by our pre-agricultural ancestors is open to debate. Recent studies suggest their diet was more diverse than the modern Paleolithic Diet.[91]
- The originator of this diet points out that humans have been cultivating grains and legumes for only 10,000 years or so, and therefore, he asserts that we have not had the time to biologically adapt to these foods. However, population studies suggest that some adaptation has occurred. For example, Northern Europeans seem to handle dairy much better than Africans.[19] Furthermore, recent analysis of paleolithic fossils suggest that our ancestors started consuming starchy vegetables and even grains long before they settled down into agricultural communities.
- The diet of our paleolithic ancestors was not necessarily the diet for optimum health; it was simply the diet that allowed them to survive and reproduce, even though their ancestral food (fruit) was no longer readily available. Their diet changed, but their nutritional needs, according to some authors, stayed basically the same as their primate predisesors.[92,93,94] The Paleolithic period, though longer than the agricultural period, was still relatively brief compared to the preceding 60 million years of primate evolution. In other words, one of the fundamental flaws with the Paleo Diet is that it simply may not be "paleo" enough.

The Zone Diet

The Zone Diet, developed by Barry Sears, Ph.D., attempts to balance hormones to control hunger on fewer calories, while still getting the proper amount of micronutrients.

Caloric Ratio: Carbs 40%   Fats 30%,   Protein 30%.

Strong Points

- ¤ It is said to be effective for managing blood sugar and promoting weight loss.
- ¤ It is doable for the average person. For example, when eating at home, the ideal high-protein foods are chicken, turkey, salmon, sardines, mackerel and beans. To this, add twice the amount of high fiber veggies and an appropriate amount of whole grain products.

Weak Points and Criticisms

- ¤ Though the developer of The Zone Diet describes it as a moderate-carbohydrate, moderate-protein, moderate-fat diet, it has been criticized by others for not having enough carbs and too much protein, resulting in deficiencies of vitamins, minerals, and loss of calcium.

High-Protein Diets

High protein diets are low in carbohydrates. However, unlike the other low-carb diets, this one is also low in fat. This is typically accomplished by using processed foods, such as soy powder, milk protein and egg-white.

The purpose of the high protein intake is rapid weight loss. However, you pay the price in the form of tissues degeneration and rapid aging of vital organs.[21] The fact that this diet relies on processed protein isolates, rather than whole foods, should be reason enough for concern. This sort of diet, at best, should be done only for a limited time. The protein in this diet can easily exceed 40% of daily calories, and can be as high as 60%. At such high levels, protein toxicity might actually be high enough to become noticeable as weakness, nausea and diarrhea.[22]

I first encountered protein toxicity early on in my practice as a chiropractor. One of my patients came in with a flair-up of low back pain, and also complained of nausea and generally not feeling well. When she mentioned having recently started a diet consisting of massive amounts of animal products, I explained that such a diet can be stressful to the liver and kidneys, which would explain her symptoms, including the low back pain. I suggested that she simply reduce the animal products, and to make room for a goodly amount of fruits and vegetables. She did so and rapidly improved.

The South Beach Diet

The South Beach Diet was developed by Arthur Agatston M.D. and Marie Almon R.D. Dr. Agatston, a cardiologist, found some patients did not do well with the low-fat diets recommended for heart patients.

This diet allows more carbohydrates than the other low-carb diets because one of its goals is to moderately reduce the overall fat in the diet. The diet uses lean meats, poultry, fish, nuts and seeds, as the major sources of protein and fat.

The calories lost from the reduction of total fat are replaced by whole-food sources of carbohydrates, such as fruits, vegetables, beans and whole grains.

Caloric Ratio: Carbs 35-65% Fats 20-35%, Protein 15-25%.

Strong Points

- The diet eliminates refined carbohydrates and features whole foods.
- As with the Paleo Diet, this one restricts trans-fats, saturated fats and omega-6 fats, replacing them with foods that are rich in omega-3 fats.
- This diet is flexible and allows for individuals who may prefer more or less animal based foods. Dr. Agatston even provides for a vegetarian version of the South Beach Diet. [23]

Weak Points and Criticism

- This diet relies heavily on the glycemic index, which, according to many nutrition authorities, has only limited value in predicting the effect of a food on overall blood sugar.
- Though the diet permits a substantial amount of plant-based foods, the initial phase of the diet excludes carbohydrate foods entirely, which results in rapid loss of water-weight and loss of minerals.

Personal Note

Though this diet has been described as a low-carb diet, Dr. Agatston does not particularly care for that label. He points out that his diet is so flexible it would be inaccurate to call it "low-carb." He may have a point there. In one sense, this diet is like a bridge between the low-carb diets, described above, and the low-fat diets, described below.

Low-Fat Diets

The low-fat diets are also high in carbohydrates. Most of them rely on starchy plant foods, such as grains, potatoes and squash for the bulk of daily calories. A few of them reduce the starchy foods and replace them with more fruits and low-starch vegetables.

Caloric Ratio: Carbs 55-80%   Fats 10-20%   Protein 10-15%.

Strong Points

- Low-fat diets do away with the over-consumption of factory-farmed animal products.
- These diets, when done properly, have proven to be effective in reversing cardiovascular disease.

Weak Points and Criticisms

- This dietary approach can result in the over-consumption of grains and refined sugar, leading to weight gain, blood sugar issues and arthrtitis.[23]
- Low-fat diets tend to be mostly or completely vegetarian and therefore have been associated with deficiencies in vitamin B12, vitamin D and long-chain omega-3 oils, such as EPA and DHA, all of which can create neurological problems, as well as the same cardiovascular issues attributed to excessive protein and fat. For example, low levels of B_{12} can result in irreversible brain damage, as well as triggering high blood levels of homocysteine, which is associated with irritation of the inner lining of blood vessels, thus triggering vascular disease.

Three well-known examples of low-fat diets are the Macrobiotic, Pritiken and Ornish Diets.

The Macrobiotic Diet

Macrobiotics, developed by Mishio Kushi of Japan, utilizes the principles of Traditional Chinese Medicine as part of a comprehensive system for healthy living and nutrition. The percentage of carbohydrates, fats and proteins tends to be fairly close to the NIH guidelines, though the numbers can vary moderately.

Macrobiotics is basically an application of the traditional Japanese diet, using an abundance of cooked grains (typically rice) to provide the bulk of the calories, as well as cooked vegetables, legumes, sea vegetation and a moderate amount of fish and fermented products, such as miso. The diet has very little fruit. Onions and garlic are excluded because they are said to stimulate the appetite too much and promote overeating. Nightshades are also excluded.

Strong Points

- It uses mostly whole foods.
- It avoids refined and highly processed wheat and sugar.
- It eliminates the over-consumption of animal products.
- It reportedly has been used to help with degenerative conditions such as cancer, heart disease and arthritis.
- It can be done as a strictly plant-based diet or can include fish.
- In addition to the professed health benefits, the Macrobiotic Diet is economical, because grains and beans are both relatively inexpensive. It is probably the least expensive diet described in this book.

Weak Points and Criticisms

- It is high in sodium, grains and soy-based condiments.
- It has been criticized for not having enough fresh fruit.
- The above issues can be obviously mitigated by reducing the salt and grains and increasing the fresh veggies and fruit. However, the high-sodium soy-based condiments tend to be addictive, making it difficult to restrict intake.

The Pritiken Diet

The Pritiken Diet was the first of the modern low-fat diets. It was created by Nathan Pritiken, and modified by his son, Robert Pritiken, M.D. It is based on grains, legumes, vegetables and fruits. In this diet, fat and protein are each limited to 10%. Animal products are allowed in small amounts. As with the Atkin's Diet, this one shows great short term results, specifically in reversing cardiovascular disease, but eventually can have some long term problems, such as arthritis.

The Ornish Diet

Created by Dean Ornish, M.D., this diet, like the Pritiken Diet, is based on grains, legumes, vegetables and fruits. Fat is restricted to 10% or lower. A small amount of animal products are permitted.

Dr. Ornish developed this diet as part of a comprehensive system includeing exercise, yoga, meditation and support groups for patients that were diagnosed with cardiovascular disease. The results were impressive. The reversal of vascular disease was enough to lower the average patient's medical expenses by $30,000 per year. Not surprisingly, Dr. Ornish's program is now covered by many insurance companies.

Vegetarian Diets

The term "vegetarian" is often loosely applied to describe anyone who does not consume animal flesh, but might still eat dairy and eggs. **The Vegan Diet** is a version of vegetarianism that excludes all foods derived from animals. The term "ethical vegan" is applied to individuals motivated by humane, spiritual or environmental reasons. Such individuals exclude clothing or any other personal items using animal products or animal testing.

Strong Points

- Plant foods have fiber which is essential for a clean and healthy digestive tract.
- Plant foods tend to be higher in most minerals and vitamins, as well as containing a wealth of important phytonutrients and antioxidants not found in animal products.
- Growing plant foods is less taxing on the land than producing livestock.
- Plant-based foods tend to leave less toxic residue than animal products.
- A plant-based diet is associated with longevity. Here is an excerpt from an article written by Joel Fuhrman, M.D., author of *Eat To Live*:

> "Innuit Greenlanders, who historically have had limited access to fruits and vegetables, have the worst longevity statistics in North America. Research from both the past and present, show that they die on an average of about 10 years younger, and have a higher rate of cancer, than the overall Canadian population. Similar statistics are available for the high meat-consuming Maasai in Kenya. They eat a diet high in wild hunted meats, and have the worst life expectancy in the modern world. Life expectancy is 45 years for women and 42 years for men. African researchers report that historically, Maasai rarely lives beyond age 60."[25]

Weak Points and Criticisms

- Modern vegetarians and vegans often over-consume grains and highly processed soy products, both of which tend to produce allergic reactions.
- Although the traditional cultures that have been reported to enjoy above-average health and longevity do eat a predominantly plant-based diet, they also include small to moderate amounts of animal-based foods (1-10% of calories).[46] How important is that small amount of animal-based food? With our current level of knowledge, it would be premature to dismiss it as unimportant. Even when we account for B_{12} and omega-3 oils, there is still a

real possibility that other critically important factors are provided by those small amounts of animal products.
- Though the vegetarian diets, typically, are supposed to be low-fat, this is often not the case. In actual practice, it is tempting and easy to add substantial amounts of fatty foods on top of the already carbohydrate-rich meals, leading to the over-consumption of total calories. It is easy to slather on enough butter or margarine, pour on enough oil and munch on enough walnuts to turn the supposedly low-fat diet into a high-fat diet. Some vegetarians unknowingly get 30-40% calories from fat, while also consuming substantial amounts of carbohydrates, and then wonder why they gain weight on their "low fat" diet.
- The combination of fat and carbohydrates slows the digestion of carbohydrates, leading to bloating, gas and intestinal candida. Furthermore, when those high levels of dietary fats get into the blood, the fat tends to slow down the passage of blood sugar into the cells, leading to blood sugar issues and systemic candida.

Not surprisingly, vegetarian diets that have been used effectively for weight loss and cardiovascular health are careful to keep the fat portion of the diet down in the range of 10-20% of daily calories. Dr Joel Fuhrman's diet (see below) goes one step further by advising the individual to limit foods that have the highest concentrations of carbohydrates, favoring, instead, foods that pack more vitamins, minerals and phytonutrients.

Dr. Fuhrman's "Eat to Live" Diet

This is, essentially, a vegan diet that encourages you to eat all the fresh fruits and vegetables you want. It is low in fat, though not as low as the other vegan diets. There is less emphasis on keeping the fat very low, and more emphasis on the quality of the food.

The individual is advised to eat about one pound of raw vegetables, one pound of cooked vegetables and at least four servings of fruit per day. The greater abundance of fruits and vegetables reflects a proportionate reduction in cooked starchy foods, such as potatoes and whole grains. Starchy vegetables are favored over grains, but both are limited to one or two cups per day, on the average.

Nuts, seeds, avocados and tofu are limited to a few ounces per day. Animal products, fruit juice and dried fruit are generally avoided. However, Dr. Furman does provide options for individuals who want to use small amounts of animal products.

Raw Food Diets

Changing to a diet consisting exclusively of raw (usually vegan) foods is, for most individuals, a radical move that should be approached with care and thoughtfulness. Therefore, let us begin by looking at the advantages and disadvantages of cooking.

Advantages of Cooking

- Sterilizes food.
- Neutralizes some potentially toxic substances and antinutrients.
- Releases some of the nutrients (especially minerals) locked up in the plant fiber.
- Warms and softens food for easier digestion.
- Allows us to utilize food-sources, such as dry beans and grains, which are otherwise unavailable.
- Sterilizing food allows us to safely consume animal products.
- Allowed our ancestors to survive the last ice age and, later, develop civilization.

Disadvantages of Cooking

- It destroys some vitamins and phytonutrients and all enzymes.
- Cooking carbohydrates produces carcinogenic substances called acrylomides.
- Cooking oxidizes fats making them toxic (rancid).
- Cooking proteins at high temperatures produces protein-carbohydrate complexes called AGEs, (advanced glycation end-products) which promote low-grade inflammation, degeneration and aging of tissues.[26]
- Cooking might render part of the protein unavailable. The heat either denatures the protein (making it less digestible) or destroys amino acids. For example, cooking releases the sulfur from some amino acids (cysteine and methionine). As a result, the amino acids become non-functional and the sulfur becomes toxic.

Advantages of Raw Food Diets

- Raw food diets have been used to facilitate the elimination of serious pathologies resistant to other forms of treatment.
- The absence of cooked food means the body does not have to expend energy and resources to make the extra enzymes needed for the digestion and clean-up.

- Diets rich in raw fruits and vegetables have been shown to protect against cancer. For example, some of the nutrients in raw vegetables have been shown to facilitate removal of carcinogens and promote DNA repair. [85]
- In addition to the known nutrients that are destroyed or altered by heat, there might be other subtle factors. For example, there is an emerging body of evidence suggesting foods have electromagnetic qualities which seem to be strongest in freshly picked fruits and vegetables, especially those that receive the most sunlight, such as tropic fruit. These same qualities appear to diminish after the food is picked and are rapidly destroyed by cooking and processing.[102]

Disadvantages of the Raw Food Diet

- Even if a 100% raw diet is do-able from a logistical standpoint, it may still not be beneficial for a given individual due to the need for nutrients in concentrations that are unavailable or difficult to get in a totally raw vegan diet.
- Unless you're eating a lot of fruit, 40-70% of your daily calories will typically come from fat, in the form of extracted oils, avocados, olives, nuts and seeds.

Mostly Raw Diets

There are raw dietary systems that allow for a small amount of selected cooked food. The inclusion of cooked food allows the individual to get an ample amount of calories and protein without relying too heavily on high-fat raw foods. For example:

- The **Hallelujah Diet,** used by Hallelujah Acres, allows for 15% cooked food.
- The **Hippocrates Diet,** used by the Hippocrates Institute, advocates raw on most days, with an occasional meal that includes certain cooked foods, such as grains or squash.
- The **Gerson Diet,** used by the Gerson Institute, was developed Dr. Max Gerson to help individuals with cancer and other degenerative diseases. This diet uses raw fruits and vegetables and an abundance of freshly squeezed vegetable juice. Since Dr. Gerson's research suggested that most overtly fatty foods promoted tumor growth (except for flax oil), he excluded such foods. With fat restricted, the caloric needs are met by allowing a small amount of cooked plant-food in the evening meal.

The High-Fruit Diets

This type of diet is mostly or totally raw, and provides most or all of daily calories from fresh fruits, with the rest (perhaps) coming from a generous helping of vegetables and small amounts of high-fat foods, such as nuts, seeds and avocados. This sort of diet is usually, though not necessarily, very low in fat. Cooked or non-vegan foods are excluded or used in very small amounts, typically in the form of raw goats milk, raw (or soft boiled) egg-yolks, or small amounts of cooked or raw flesh foods.

Strong Points

- Individuals on this diet often report lots of steady energy, with no fluctuation or fatigue.
- Most of the nutrients in fruit are predigested, requiring minimum effort by the body.
- This diet is cleansing for the body because fruit has a high water content, lots of fiber, and the least amount of toxic residue of all food groups. Individuals on this diet report a virtual elimination of body odor, and they also claim that their feces "do not stink."
- Proponents of this diet assert when the body has been allowed to cleanse and balance itself, fresh fruits generally do not cause blood sugar problems and yeast overgrowth. The major cause of blood sugar problems and candida is said to be high levels of fat and other stressors which interfere with the body's ability to absorb and utilize sugars.[28]

Weak Points and Criticisms

- Critics say that such a diet can produce deficiencies in protein and fat-soluble nutrients, especially EPA and DHA, thus compromising brain function and perhaps the immune system.
- Some mineral deficiencies, such as zinc or selenium, may also occur.
- If this diet is practiced in a strictly vegan manner, it could produce a deficiency of vitamin B_{12}.
- The high amount of sugar in fruit is said to possibly raise blood triglycerides.

The 80/10/10 Diet

The 80/10/10 Diet is one version of the low-fat and high-fruit approach. It was developed by Dr. Douglas Graham, a chiropractor and natural hygienist[104.] Here are the key points:

- At least 80% of the daily calories come from carbohydrates. No more than 10% of calories come from protein. No more than 10% of calories come from fat. By the numbers, it is basically a raw version of the low-fat diets developed by Pritikin and Ornish. The main different is the source of calories — mostly by fresh fruit, instead of grains and starchy vegetables.[62]
- Essentially, the individual is guided to eat an abundance of fresh fruit and 1-2 pounds of tender vegetables per day.
- Dry fruit may be used sparingly. Fruit juice is typically not recommended, except for freshly squeezed orange juice.
- A small amount of high-fat whole foods may be added, such as 1-2 ounces of nuts or seeds, or an avocado. 100% raw is recommended, but not required.

The 100% Fruit Diet

The term "fruitarian" has been used loosely to describe anyone who gets the bulk of their daily calories (at least 75%) from fruit. However, some individuals claim to thrive on a diet consisting *entirely* of fruit, including non-sweet botanical fruits, such as tomatoes, cucumbers, peppers and avocadoes.

The 100% Fruit Diet is not recommended by most nutritional authorities, due to the low levels of protein, fats and minerals. Granted, the fat and protein can be increased through careful selection of fruit. However, the typical low-fat version of the fruitarian diet can have a caloric ratio that looks like this: Carbohydrates 90% / Fats 5% / Protein 5%

5% for fat and protein are very low compared to most other diets. Though protein is the nutrient that usually gets the most attention, the very low fat content might be a more serious issue. This is of special concern for young children, because their fat requirements are higher than adults. Specifically, there have been reports of mental and emotional instability and even deaths on such a diet.[101]

Some strict fruitarians resolve the fat issue by simply including a generous amount of fatty fruits, such as avocados, which can easily raise the fat content from 5% to 30%. Another strategy is to include more berries, since they tend to have twice the fat and protein as other fruits. Other fruitarians claim to thrive for many years on the low-fat version.

A Closer Look at Fruit

Fruit consumption is currently enjoying a rise in popularity, and more fruitarian books are emerging. One such book is called *Fruitarianism, The Path to*

Paradise, by Anne Osborne, who also happens to be a massage therapist.[61] In her book, she describes her experience of 17 years (almost 20 years, at the time of this writing) of excellent health and fitness on a 100% fruit diet. However, she does not claim to have all the answers on fruitarianism. Neither does she assert that everyone can succeed on this diet. She states, "I believe that fruit is a perfect food for humans, and whether it makes up all your diet or just a part of it, I hope that fruit will bring you many blessings." Osborne's article in the appendix of this book gives a more detailed description of her fruitarian diet and how it has affected her work as a massage therapist.

In her article and her book, Osborne also explains the two major reasons why many individuals are unable to sustain a long-term strict Fruitarian Diet:

- **Lack of Preparation.** The body needs time to cleanse and rebalance itself so it is capable of extracting sufficient nutrients from fruit alone. Like other fruitarian authors, Osborne suggests that once the body has had sufficient time to reset itself, it needs less food, because the individual absorbs and utilizes nutrients more efficiently. To highlight this point, she tells her own story: "When I started on the raw path, I could eat four good-sized avocados a day without gaining weight. Now, after seventeen years on fruit…I actually gain weight if I eat avocados."

- **Poor Fruit quality.** Conventionally grown fruit usually lacks the balance of nutrients necessary to sustain optimum health because of poor soil quality and the common practice of picking fruit before it is ripe. For example, by picking the fruit prematurely, the mineral content will be lower — as the fruit ripens, the higher sugar levels draw in minerals from the soil. Normally, the sweeter the fruit, the higher the mineral content.

Even if the two explanations given above prove to have merit, they should not be taken as a green light to jump into a 100% fruit diet, or even a mostly-fruit diet. On the contrary, the two challenges described by Osborne remind us that such a diet should be approached with caution, especially for individuals living in a temperate or cool climate, where fresh tree-ripened fruit are more difficult to get.

Even if these two issues are somehow addressed, some individuals might still have problems on the high-fruit diet, because of other, perhaps unknown, constitutional issues. Furthermore, as you may recall, fruit is rich in simple sugars (mostly glucose and fructose) that are readily absorbed into the blood. These sugars are, indeed, "high-grade fuel" for our cells. An abundance of such fuel might be entirely appropriate and perhaps ideal for a high performance athlete. But the average person who has been sedentary for a number of years, while consuming a large amount of cooked and fatty food, should be cautious about eating large amounts of this high-grade fuel.

Though the high-fruit diets may not be practical for a given individual, the overall nutritional profile, ease of digestion and efficient cleansing provided by fresh fruit present us with an option that has been mostly overlooked (or actively dismissed) by most dietary systems: the use of fruit as a staple food.

Fruit as Staple Food

Using fruit as staple food means it is not merely used as a snack or dessert or as a sweetener for the occasional vegetable smoothie. It is, instead, consumed in quantities that provide a significant percentage of daily calories.

Looking at the numbers, if, on the average, we consume enough fresh fruit to provide about 1/5 (20%) of daily calories, we could legitimately say that fruit is being used as a staple food. Based on the standard 2000-calorie diet, 20% is 400 calories. This translates into about 2 pounds of fresh fruit — more or less, depending on the caloric density of the fruit. For example, 400 calories can be provided by any of the following: 1 pound of bananas, 1.3 pounds of grapes, 1.8 pounds of oranges, or 2.8 pounds of strawberries.

However, you do not have to track the calories, unless you have a specific reason to do so. Generally, the calorically denser fruits will satiate faster, therefore you will tend to eat less without even trying. In other words, you can just eat the amount of fruit that feels right to you, and just leave it at that. Yes, it is that simple.

Balance of Feeding and Cleansing

The possibility of promoting fruit to the status of a staple food addresses an important issue that is often overlooked in the search for ones ideal diet: the need to balance feeding and cleansing. In the preceding survey of the various diets, the emphasis is on the nutrients. Little attention is given to the toxic residue of the foods in question.

For a diet to be sustainable, it must provide all the needed nutrients, while allowing the body to properly cleanse itself. A diet that is nutrient-rich, but causes a gradual increase in toxicity, eventually needs to be modified. Furthermore, the issues arising from the low-grade toxic build-up may develop so gradually as to be virtually undetectable to the individual, until serious pathologies arise.

In general, diets with the highest levels of grains and animal products tend to leave the highest toxic residue. These diets tend to be high in complex carbohydrates (starch), fats and protein, while being relatively low in vitamins, minerals, phytonutrients, plant fiber and water. In other words, whether we replace animal products with massive amounts of grains, or vice versa, the end result is less than ideal. We simply replace one form of toxicity and deficiency with another. This does not mean such diets are inherently bad. They simply need to take a lesson from the fruit-based diets and make room for enough fresh fruit and raw vegetables to allow the body to adequately cleanse itself and stock up on the vitamins, minerals and phytonutrients.

Even if a given diet is fairly clean and does not cause a significant build up of toxicity over time, the body seems to appreciate a rhythm consisting of a maintenance diet that provides all the needed nutrients, punctuated with an occasional period of cleansing. This is probably what our pre-agricultural ancestors did for many thousands of years. Once they moved away from the tropics and became more affected by the seasons, they had to observe periods of "cleansing" whether they wanted to or not. In other words, they had to fast or reduce their caloric intake during the colder months.

Yes, fasting is still the simplest and quickest way to cleanse. However, the quickest way may not be the most healthy or practical way. A more gentle method is to just increase raw plant fiber and clean water while perhaps decreasing total calories for a while, especially the calories derived from heavily processed or fatty foods. The simplest and safest way to do this is to eat mostly or totally raw fruits and vegetables for a while. You can do this regardless of the diet you favor.

Chapter 9
Eating and Emotions

This chapter focuses directly on a subject we have previously danced around. The connection between food and emotions is obvious to anyone who takes the time to ponder the matter. That connection is important for the student of nutrition, especially when the various sources of information are often contradictory and sometimes combative. It is just too easy to take sides. To the extent that we do, our ability to be objective declines.

Beyond the academic study of nutrition, the connection between food and emotions must be considered in order for any diet to succeed. Whether we are aware of it or not, the emotional element is a major factor in the everyday act of choosing our food and preparing our meals (next chapter).

There are a number of ways to logically explain why eating tends to be so emotional. The explanation that is most relevant to this chapter has to do with instincts.

The Eating Instinct

Animals in the wild eat by instinct. Such instinct is no less important for us civilized humans. No matter how much we educate ourselves on foods and nutrients, the body is likely to become malnourished and toxic if the eating instincts have been dulled or otherwise neglected. No matter how thoroughly we study nutrition, and no matter how meticulously we try to watch what we eat, the body will suffer if our food instincts have been disrupted.

A big part of the eating instinct is the sense of taste. Most nutritional authors would agree that the ideal relationship between the individual and his/her food is one in which the foods that taste good also promote optimum health. It obviously works for animals in the wild, but eating has become more complicated for civilized humans. Here are the two reasons:

- **Altered Foods:** Animals in the wild eat foods that are typically fresh, raw and eaten one at a time. On the other hand, the food eaten by civilized humans is usually not fresh and raw. Even raw food is shipped to us days or weeks after it is picked or slaughtered. We then store it, mix it with other foods and non-foods, and usually cook it. The result is that we "trick" our sense of taste. Our nervous system has a harder time "reading" the nutrients because the molecular language has been altered.

- **Altered Humans:** To complicate matters, our instinctual food-radar is intimately connected to our ever-present emotions. While the educated intelligence is at its best when it is logical and precise, the innate intelligence is soft, fluid, touchy-feely and very much influenced by emotions. The emotional connection in and of itself is not a problem. Instincts and emotions are supposed to be connected. Our instincts often "speak" through our emotions. Our instincts cause us to be emotionally drawn to things that are good for us and to be repulsed by things that can harm us. However, when our other emotional needs are neglected, we often compensate by using food as a means for experiencing pleasure or numbing pain. The result is that we eat to fulfill our emotional needs, sacrificing the body's needs.

The two situations described above probably did not exist until humans created artificial environments, including the cooking and mixing of foods. I am not suggesting here that our ancestors should not have left their Garden of Eden tropical paradise of raw fruits and vegetables. I am simply pointing out that our creation of artificial environments and artificial foods has had consequences. One such consequence is that the deeply intimate and mutually supportive relationship between our nutritional needs and emotional needs got torn asunder.

Therefore, for us modern humans, food selection is, at best, a harmonious dance between our innate intelligence (specifically, our food instincts) and educated intelligence (rational thinking). When that dance is harmonious, we find it fairly easy to select foods which taste good and promote health.

In real life, however, the dance between our innate and educated intelligence is often less than harmonious. The two partners seem to bump into each other and step on each other's toes. Ultimately, the educated intelligence is the one that is being the klutz. It makes decisions which essentially dis-empower the innate intelligence and scramble our food instincts.

Learning to Dance

This book, like other nutrition books, is about providing information for the educated intelligence. However, one of my goals is to provide the information in a way which recognizes the immense importance of the innate intelligence so the two can function in a mutually supportive manner.

In other words, healthy eating is not just about gathering information, and has little to do with developing "will power." It is, at best, an awakening of our instincts. Realistically, awakening our eating instincts means that we must do two things:

- Recognize and gently address our conditioned cravings for heavily processed foods.
- Untangle our nutritional needs from our emotional needs so both may be properly fulfilled.

Each of these two issues, acting alone, is like a monkey wrench that has been thrown into the neurological gears of the brain. The simultaneous presence of *both* issues constitutes a double whammy. This is when our "will power" crumbles like a house of cards in an earthquake.

How do we remove those two monkey wrenches? The first one (in and of itself) is pretty easy. You simply walk past the processed foods in the supermarket and proceed to the produce section. What makes it difficult is the second issue: the tangling of emotional and nutritional needs. Let us, therefore, give some thoughtful consideration to that second monkey wrench which is often called "emotional eating."

Emotional Eating

Firstly, the term "emotional eating" is a little deceptive because it seems to imply our emotions have no place at the dinner table. On the contrary, as suggested above, eating is inherently emotional. The act of eating, by design, is supposed to be pleasurable — a celebration. The anticipation of eating a tasty meal is generally experienced as a joyful expectancy.

The deep connection between emotions and eating must be recognized and respected if we hope to free ourselves of the curious and mysterious civilized habit called "emotional eating"— made even more mysterious by the fact that it has been misnamed.

Whatever the name, we simply need to see it for what it is: the deeply ingrained (no pun intended) habit of relying *too* heavily on food for emotional pleasure and comfort. That habit typically results in the sacrifice of physical health for the sake of emotional gratification.

However, this untangling process must be done with thoughtfulness and care. Our efforts to eat healthy are likely to backfire if we approach the food-emotion connection with an attitude of somehow surgically separating the two. If, in our ignorance, we try to "separate them," or, in our arrogance, think that we can willfully exclude our emotions and desires from the dinner table, the result is that both become more dysfunctional.

Our present exploration of emotional eating is not intended to separate eating from emotions, but rather to simply recognize where they become tangled. The rest is an inside job: each individual has to listen deeply and walk gently on his/her personal journey of gradually allowing emotional needs and nutritional needs to loosen the stranglehold they have on each other, thus re-establishing their mutually supportive relationship, wherein the two naturally bless each other.

In my opinion, restoring that relationship is of prime importance. Most of the dietary challenges that I have observed in my patients and myself have been directly related to the presence of emotional needs which often get projected on food.

Along with the obvious emotional need for loving touch and warm relationship with the people around us, I also include the more subtle spiritual needs, for the two are on the same continuum of consciousness. Emotions, expressed cleanly and freely, evolve into spiritual awareness. Likewise, spiritual awareness shows up in everyday life as a rebirth of emotional innocence and the capacity to take joy in the activities of daily living — such as eating!

To the extent we neglect our emotional and spiritual needs, we are likely to project them elsewhere, and food just happens to be a convenient place to do so. This is quite understandable when we remember the close connection between food and emotional comfort in the world of the infant. After mother's touch, food is the first form of comfort we experience outside the womb.

Food and Stress Reduction

As we develop from childhood to adulthood, if emotional needs are not fulfilled through loving relationship with the life around us, as well as the cultivation of a spiritual life, we often compensate by using food to give us pleasure or ease the pain. This is entirely appropriate for the new-born infant who uses mother's milk to mitigate the stress of life outside the womb. However, to the extent that we, as adults, become overly dependent on this infantile mode of stress reduction, the body is likely to suffer.

In one sense, we have to grow up! Specifically, we have to evolve and mature in the manner that we nourish ourselves. We have to eat in a way that nourishes the body, relate to each other in a way that nourishes our emotions, and commune with Life in a way that nourishes the soul. All three are inherently pleasurable; all three are, by design, mutually supportive.

However, even though we would intellectually agree that sacrificing physical health for the sake of emotional pleasure is less than ideal, I wish to emphasize that we must be careful about challenging those firmly ingrained patterns. As previously mentioned, a direct and "willful" frontal assault on our hidden emotional world is generally not successful, and typically does more harm than good.

To enter the inner domain of one's eating habits is to enter a deep and sensitive place. It is an extremely raw and fragile place that starts to quiver fearfully if we approach it with less than unconditional love. To judge our desires harshly or neglect our preferences, in favor of external teachings and dietary ideologies, is likely to provoke inner conflict. Such conflict detracts from the potential benefits of a given dietary system.

Kindness is the Key

A change in diet is more likely to be successful if it also includes a change in attitude toward our food choices: an attitude of patience, kindness and respect. Such a change is surprisingly easy and natural when our knowledge of nutrition is nested within a larger vision that says, "For every thing there is a season, and a time for every purpose under Heaven." Such an attitude helps to bring harmony between our inner world and the outer teaching, gently dissolving the conflict between what we want to eat and what we think we should eat. Yes, it is that simple.

As usual, kindness and patience will succeed where arrogance and urgency fail. The journey of true dietary transformation is a journey of self-discovery. Such an inner journey is usually not linear and direct, but rather is full of curves and loop-de-loops. It is like a meandering river that follows the contour of the land, sometimes flowing quickly, sometimes flowing slowly, sometimes swirling around in a whirlpool and seemingly going nowhere. As we float along that river on the (often flimsy) raft of conscious awareness, not having seen what lies downstream, the only reliable prediction we can make about the journey is that it is not very predictable. Sometimes, the most useful thing the rational mind can do is to remind itself the river knows where it is going.

Such mindfulness becomes even more important when we take on the role of teachers and health counselors. A given food may seem less than ideal if we use only our educated intelligence to judge the worth of the foods or diet in question. However, when we include our intuition and our capacity to empathize, we tend to see a bigger picture — one which reflects the whole person. That bigger picture includes biochemical, emotional and spiritual factors that might be unseen by the rational mind. In other words, there might be hidden wisdom behind the seemingly "bad" food choice or "cravings." Therefore, once you have chosen your food, bless it, give thanks, and enjoy.

The Bigger Picture

How do we invite such an expansion of our inner-vision? The simple answer is that our vision naturally expands when we are mindful of what we do not know. The good scientist would do no less. The same rational approach that gives us the scientific understanding of nutrition also demands that we frame our body of knowledge against a background of the unknown.

In other words, we must not assume that we know everything there is to know about food and nutrition. The rational mind is limited. It functions best when it recognizes its own limits. No matter how much we know about human nutrition, we do not know everything! This might seem plainly obvious, but, for some reason, we tend to forget. This is when we speak with unjustified certainly, often becoming arrogant and impatient, and fail to see the potential value of opinions other than our own.

When we do recognize the limits of our sight, our vision expands. That expansion quietly shows up as mental clarity and emotional serenity tempered with a generosity that is neither forced nor strained. We can sit down and "break bread" with those who see things differently. In other words, when we are intellectually honest enough to recognize the gaps in our knowledge, we tend to have sharper discernment, as well as invite the emergence of our natural gentleness and graciousness.

With regard to this book, I am simply suggesting that as you consider the information, you also allow your emerging nutritional knowledge to be nested within a larger container of spiritual wisdom; which, in practical terms, looks like kindness and respect. No matter how important the game may seem, the whole thing becomes meaningless if we forget the dignity and humanity of the players.

Such an attitude, at the very least, helps you to interpret the various dietary systems more objectively so you can make the best nutritional choices for yourself, as well as provide useful information for your clients. You will not be so confused by the many differing opinions. You will not become yet another pawn in the nutrition wars which seem to have erupted. Regardless of how "sold" you are on a particular dietary system, you will maintain the intellectual honesty that allows you to question the concepts you hold as true while being willing to recognize the value of other dietary systems.

Such an attitude will help you to remember that your primary responsibility is to your body which means your primary loyalty is to truth. More specifically, your primary loyalty is to the truth of what *your* body needs nutritionally. That truth is likely to change over time, simply because the body changes over time. It is entirely possible the nutritional teaching you reject or ridicule today might have some value for you tomorrow.

Body Food and Soul Food

The attitude of kindness and respect towards our own emotions and desires brings a measure of grace to our personal inner journey, including the part that involves our relationship to food. This is how the mind can quiet down enough to hear the truth about food as it relates to us personally. For example, the mind can finally understand that, no matter how delicious Mother Nature's unprocessed food happens to be, it is not designed to replace other forms of pleasure and comfort. Fresh fruit, regardless of how good it tastes, makes a very poor drug. It cannot numb the pain or provide the serenity and joy we were meant to experience through honest and loving relationships, joyful creative work and spiritual connection.

To the extent we deprive ourselves of our natural soul-food, we will, more than likely, deprive the body of its natural food. Therefore, if we choose to "clean up our diet," it necessitates the willingness to nourish ourselves on those other levels where we had perhaps been starving ourselves. We must tend to the deeper emotional issues and neglected spiritual hunger that, if unfulfilled, cause us to seek out "comfort foods." When that detail is handled, the little tricks for promoting healthy eating, described below, can actually work.

Techniques for Awakening the Eating Instinct

- Include foods in your diet which are appealing to you with no preparation or processing what-so-ever. Do not even cut it with knife. Be on the look-out for foods which taste good exactly as Mother Nature presents them.

- Visit the farmer's market, and re-discover the produce-section of the supermarket. Slow down and spend some time there. When you find some fruit that really appeals to you, and makes your mouth water, make a meal of it! You do not have to be a full-time fruitarian or raw-foodist to do this. You can just do it occasionally, whenever you happen to feel like it! If this is right for you, you will probably feel like it more and more often. In other words, the only discipline you need is the discipline of paying attention to your desires as you intentionally look for Mother Nature's unprocessed food that is simultaneously appealing to your senses and easy on the body. As you explore the produce section, expand your fruit-seeking vision beyond apples and oranges. Check out the kiwi, cactus pears, fresh figs, fresh dates, blackberries, papaya, persimmons, pomegranates, pineapples, mangos, muscadines, mamey sapotes, blood oranges, dragon fruit, longons and guavas.

- If you have a garden, rediscover the joy of just picking and eating. If your garden is big enough, you can make an entire meal of picking and eating. Along those lines, when you get a chance, go to a pick-your-own farm, and allow your nervous system to do what it was made to — eat right from the tree or vine in a beautiful natural setting. Most individuals would not think of making a meal entirely of raw and unprocessed tomatoes, broccoli, lettuce or okra, but if you pick them yourself straight from the garden, you might change your mind. Food is more satisfying when you pick it and eat it, while it is still brimming with life. This is one way you can gently reawaken your capacity to eat instinctively, as well as helping to restore the natural harmony between your nutritional needs and emotional needs. It is easier to eat naturally in a natural setting. Our instincts for healthy eating work best when we eat straight from the garden — because this how we were designed to eat!

Personal Experience

I have found that when my diet consists mostly (in terms of calories) of raw fruits and vegetables, overeating is actually difficult. If the foods I eat on any given day consists *entirely* of raw fruits and vegetables (or just fruit!), the only way that I can over-consume calories is to actually force myself to do so. No matter how delicious the fruit, no matter how fresh and tender the vegetables, I eventually reach a point where eating is no longer pleasurable. That point of satiation coincides with my stomach feeling nicely full.

In fact, in my early days of a high-fruit diet, on my total fruit-and-veggie days, the most challenging part of eating was that I sometimes consumed fewer calories than usual — without trying to do so. Obviously, if I did this on a regular basis, I would have lost weight. This is not a problem for someone who wants to lose weight, but if you choose to avoid such weight loss, you can intentionally select a certain amount calorically dense fruit, such as persimmons, Kiwi, bananas and dates. However, over the years, I have found that I generally feel better when I simply allow my body to determine how many calories it wants to ingest on a given day regardless of what the book says.

I have also found if I require anything besides raw fruits and vegetables, my body lets me know. For example, if I eat just fruits for a few days, I will eventually want some vegetables. If I eat just fruits and vegetables long enough, I may eventually start to crave some nuts and seeds, or an avocado. So, I eat some nuts, seeds or an avocado, or blend them up with some lemon juice and use them as salad dressing. The only catch is that I may have to practice moderation because the natural barriers to over-consumption are gone: I do not have to work to remove the nuts and seeds from the shells, and there are no blenders and food processors in Nature.

The same applies for any foods that have been mixed, cooked or otherwise processed. The more the foods are altered from their natural form, the more challenging they are for the nervous system to monitor. Some of these foods may be entirely appropriate, and provide real health benefits, but our instincts may need a little help from our educated common sense to determine when to stop. Eating slowly seems to help. Taking care of our other emotional and spiritual needs definitely helps!

Rediscover Mono-Fruit Eating

Mono-eating is what we commonly observe in Nature. Mono-fruit eating is what we see in anthropoid apes, which scientists say, are our closest animal relatives. In fact, the vast majority of non-human primates (apes, monkeys and related animals) eat this way.

Likewise, mono-fruit eating was probably a common practice among our earliest human and pre-human ancestors, as indicated by the microscopic ware-pattern in fossil teeth. Even though the author of the Paleolithic Diet does not specifically mention mono-fruit eating, we can imagine how our paleolithic ancestors may have done just that. Like some modern hunter/gatherers, they might have started their day by filling up on one type of fresh fruit (when available), which would then give them the energy to go out and hunt, without being weighted down and sedated by a heavy fatty meal.

The digestive physiology of modern humans, as far as we can tell, is fundamentally the same as that of our paleolithic ancestors, and quite similar to that of other primates.[93] In my opinion, once the body has had sufficient time to cleanse and rebalance itself, most modern humans can easily eat one or more mono-fruit meals during the day, as desired.

Eating one fruit until we are full is a natural thing to do. The only reason we don't do it is because we have been conditioned not to. Re-awaking that instinct is as simple as paying attention to it. You can also do the same with any vegetable if it is tender and juicy enough. For those who are looking for an easy and effective "cleansing program," this is it!

In Conclusion

Making friends with your food means that you make peace with your emotions. This is especially important if you want to eat mono-fruit meals on a somewhat regular basis. Raw fruits and vegetables are designed to fulfill our nutritional needs, not our emotional needs. Granted, as the "palate becomes cleaner," eating fresh fruit becomes increasingly more pleasurable. Furthermore, some of the nutrients found in fresh fruit, such as certain flavonoids, have been shown to help regulate the hormones and neurotransmitters associated with positive mental and emotional states. Bananas, for examples, reportedly have a soothing and uplifting effect on the emotions. However, no matter how good fruits taste, and no matter how loaded they are with brain-benefitting phytonutrients, they are not very effective at buffering us from our own emotional issues. Fruit does not have the titillating, adrenal-irritating and brain-zapping effects of heavily spiced, cooked foods, laden with stimulants and opiates. Furthermore, many of these commercially prepared foods have apparently been specifically formulated to maximize consumption, and keep us coming back for more.[12]

As a nutritional explorer, you do not necessarily have to totally avoid processed foods. However, since many of them are designed for over-consumption, you might find it difficult to refrain from doing so. This is where you get to exercise patience.

Some individuals are able to "eat just one" and some find it impossible to do so. Whatever choices you make, remember that you choose only for yourself. When you free yourself of the need to keep up with your neighbor (as well as the need to make your neighbor keep up with you) you are free, indeed. As my friend (a neuromuscular therapist who once walked all 2100 miles of the Appalachian Trail) once said, "Hike your own hike." Some individuals can benefit from practicing abstinence; others just need to indulge for a while. Which approach is best for you? Only your innate intelligence knows for sure.

What makes the dietary journey easier is a steady supply of clean, nutritious and delicious foods — supported by other forms of emotional fulfillment and spiritual connection that are harmonious with your nature. Eventually, eating fresh and raw fruits and vegetables in their unprocessed form will seem quite natural — because it is. You are simply reclaiming your natural eating instinct. That same instinct will also direct you to any other foods that are needed for optimum health. The awakened eating instinct is the key to effectively choosing your diet and planning your meals — which brings us to the next chapter.

Chapter 10

Time to Choose

For most individuals who are used to eating the standard civilized diet but are looking to "eat healthier," (like many massage clients), the Macrobiotic Diet, Pritiken Diet, Westin A. Price Diet and Paleolithic Diet are probably the easiest and most practical beginning. At the very least, any of these diets can be the first step, if not the only step.

For those who favor the low-fat strategy, the Macrobiotic or Pritiken approach might fit the bill. Just be careful you do not overdo it on the grains, salt and soy-based condiments. For the individual who is more motivated, Dr. Fuhrman's diet, with its greater abundance of raw fruits and vegetables, would probably produce more dramatic results in weight loss, greater vitality and possible reversal of degenerative diseases.

For those who favor the low-carb strategy, the Westin A. Price Diet is doable for the average person because it allows all the food groups people are used to. They will simply favor high-quality organically produced foods. You just have to be mindful about not over-consuming high-fat flesh foods and dairy, or creating deficiencies of the vitamins, minerals and phytonutrients found in plant foods. As an alternative, the Paleolithic Diet would fit the bill for those who choose to go easier on the fat, especially saturated fat, and eliminate dairy and grains, while allowing for more fruits and vegetables.

As you consider any of the various diets for yourself or your clients, be aware that even the well-established dietary systems are sometimes modified in response to new findings and challenges that were not anticipated by the founders. For example:

- The Adkins Diet was eventually modified to include more vegetables and even allows some fruit.
- The Pritiken Diet has eased up on the consumption of grains, and no longer restricts the consumption of fruit.

- The Paleolithic Diet has evolved into a system which now allows occasional meals that include starchy foods.
- Some of the raw food diets were modified to allow a modest amount of cooked food and even non-vegan foods.
- Some vegetarian authors have acknowledged that they occasionally eat fish or take supplemental fish-oil.[29]

There is nothing wrong with this. It is certainly not a sign of weakness to change your mind in the face of new information. On the contrary, it is sign of integrity, especially when it is done candidly. For the student of nutrition, the lesson in this is to simply question authority! Your educated intelligence is at its best when it maintains an open mind, tempered by healthy skepticism.

The information offered by the presenters of various diets might be useful and may have some scientific evidence to support it, but the high degree of certainty they express is often unjustified. The nutritional information, no matter how convincing it sounds, could have hidden flaws, or might be problematical for a given individual. Any dietary system is useful only to the extent that we remember that the ultimate decision maker is the innate intelligence of the individual.

And Now, Choose Your Diet

Below is a list of the major dietary systems that we surveyed in chapter 8. Let your eyes casually scan list.

Name	Type	%Carbs	% Fat	%Protein
Atkins	Low Carb	5-20	60-75	20-30
Westin A Price	Low Carb	10-35	45-60	20-30
Paleo	Low Carb	22-40	28-47	20-35
Zone	Low Carb	40	30	30
Blood Type	Mixed	35-65	15-45	15-25
South Beach	Mixed	30-55	20-35	15-25
Macrobiotic	Low Fat	55-65	15-20	10-15
Pritiken and Ornish	Low Fat	80	10	10
Raw (high fruit)	Low Fat	70-90	5-20	5-15
Raw (low fruit)	Usually Low Carb	20-45	40-70	10-15

Some of these diets are radically different from one another in terms of the caloric ratios and types of foods. To keep it simple for yourself, do not try to figure out which one "is right" in the absolute sense, but rather listen to your inner signal as to which of these diets, if any, is right for *you*.

Ideally, food choices are based entirely on instinct, but this is usually not practical, because the inner signal may not be as clear as we would like. One way to make it easier is to choose from a list, rather than having to pull the information out of the "ethers." Your innate intelligence is not loyal to any external doctrine. Neither is it contrary to any doctrine. Its usual mode of operation is simple: It guides your educated intelligence in applying any information that is right for you in the present moment. In other words, as we encounter choices in the external world, our innate intelligence responds with a silent (or not so silent) "yes" or "no."

The point is this: Whether your decision seems to be based on logic, a gut-feeling or some combination of the two, you and no one else must choose. This important job, in my opinion, should not be delegated to any external authority because no one knows you better than you. Furthermore, when you choose, you choose for yourself and no one else (unless you are the parent of a young child, of course).

Once you feel you have a sense of direction about how you want to eat, creating your meal is fairly simple. The meal options given below include choices which can accommodate all of the major dietary systems discussed in chapter 8. You will notice that in virtually all the meal options described below, the bulk of the calories are provided by fat or carbohydrates. Typically, if one is high, the other is low. This feature is particularly useful for individuals who are trying to lose weight or want to avoid gaining weight.

What's for Breakfast?

Fasting cleanses the body. Eating nourishes the body. Morning is a transition time for the body. It is when we "break the fast." The longer you refrain from eating concentrated food, the longer the body remains in the cleansing mode. Ideally, your body tells you when to start eating. However, if the signals have become a bit weak or hyperactive, here is a rule of thumb: Individuals with any sort of blood sugar issue generally do well with a breakfast that has a goodly amount of protein or slow-burning unrefined complex carbohydrates. Other individuals may have no appetite at all, until later in the morning or noon. Still others may go through cycles: they might go through a period of feeling the need to eat a hearty breakfast upon rising, and then they might go through a cleansing phase, wherein they might feel the need to do just vegetable juices, fruit or water alone in the early morning.

As a point of caution, keep in mind that, regardless of the condition of your body, skipping breakfast means you have to tap into your reserves of vitamins, minerals and glucose. This is not a problem, if your tanks are full and get refilled daily. However, if the body is already depleted (which is fairly typical in the general population), skipping breakfast entirely will deplete the body even more. This is when the adrenal glands secrete stress hormones to "get you going." Later in the day, the blood sugar is likely to fluctuate, triggering tiredness, irritability and mood swings. Therefore, the individual might crave sweets or over eat.

Three General Breakfast Strategies

- Many individuals seem to do well with a hearty breakfast containing a goodly amount of protein (eggs, breakfast steak) and foods rich in unrefined complex carbohydrates (toast, oat meal). As a general guiding principle, you can either use the high fat/protein foods or the high carbohydrate foods as the dominant source of calories.
- Once the blood sugar is sufficiently stable and the body has ample reserves of nutrients, some individuals feel better with a light breakfast of freshly squeezed vegetable juices or fresh fruit. This provides the body with easily absorbed vitamins, minerals and a moderate amount of easily digestible or predigested carbohydrates, fatty acids and amino acids, so you will not experience blood sugar fluctuation or have the need to tap into the body's nutrient reserves. Also, the absence of concentrated foods allows the body to remain in the cleansing phase longer.
- Just drink water until lunch. There are some rare individuals who do well with this. In other words, they abstain from food until noon (more or less), and then do not overeat and feel good throughout the day without energy fluctuations. Even if you do not do this every day, you might feel inclined to do this occasionally, perhaps on weekends, as a way of doing a "mini-fast," giving your digestive system a little extra time to rest and cleanse.

Specific Options for Breakfast

1. 1-2 eggs. You can prepare them anyway you like, but in general, sort of breaking and frying will introduce more oxidation to the lipid component of the egg. Soft boiled eggs are the cleanest and most nutritionally intact. Next are hard boiled eggs. With your eggs, you can have breakfast meat or one or two slices of whole grain toast with dairy butter or nut butter. Instead of the toast, you can have a small portion of organic grits, millet or oat meal.

2. Any whole grain hot cereal, with or without a small amount of eggs or breakfast meat.

3. Any whole grain cold cereal with organic milk, nut/seed milk.

4. Start with freshly squeezed orange juice, followed by whole grain toast with raw nut butter (tahini, almond/walnut/pumpkin seed/sunflower seed butter).

5. Start with freshly squeezed orange juice, followed by a bowl of raw organic nuts/seeds and some fresh or dry fruit. The nuts and seeds can be walnuts, almonds, pecans, macadamias, pumpkin seeds, sunflower seeds, etc. The fruit can be sliced or diced apple, raisins, dates, dried apricots, dried figs, etc. It is best to soak the nuts, seeds and dry fruit for easier digestion.

6. Yogurt, by itself or with fruit, granola, or raw nuts and seeds.

7. A bowl of fresh organic fruit, either mixed fruit, or better yet, a fruit mono-meal, consisting entirely of one type of fresh fruit.

8. A tall glass of freshly squeezed vegetable juice, including green leafy vegetables.

9. A quick green drink consisting of water and barley grass powder or other powdered greens.

10. Those who go to work or school can have freshly squeezed orange or vegetable juice in the early morning and easy to mix green drink or fresh fruit as a mid morning snack. For those following a low-carb diet, some fresh berries (blueberries, raspberries, strawberries, and blackberries) or other in-season fruit, would make an ideal mid morning snack.

What's for Lunch?

Some of the lunches described below can easily be prepared in the morning and taken to work. If preparing lunch in the morning does not work for you, the good news is that healthy eating is becoming more popular, and many restaurants offer soups, salads and sandwiches as healthy "fast foods."

1. Baked fish, chicken, turkey or beef with assorted steamed or sautéed vegetables, such as broccoli, cauliflower carrots, string beans or other

veggies. If you want to limit the consumption of meat, you can also include a small amount of brown rice or a small piece of whole grain bread

2. A large vegetable salad with or without a light toping of animal products (see dinner below) and baked potato.

3. Rice and black beans with steamed or sautéed broccoli. You can replace the black beans with other legumes, such as lentils or black-eyed peas.

4. One or two whole grain sandwiches. Fill them with one of the following: tofu, tempeh, natto, organic cheese, nut butter peanut butter, or hummus. (Hummus is a paste made from garbanzo beans, lemon juice and garlic). The meal can also include raw veggies such as romaine lettuce, tomato, alfalfa sprouts. For extra flavor and moisture, you can swipe on some butter, mayo or mustard.

5. Same as #3, but use whole grain pita (pocket) bread instead of sliced bread.

6. One sandwich (regular or pita), plus vegetable soup or small salad.

7. Medium sized salad and a side dish of hummus and crackers or whole grain bread.

8. Raw mono-meal, consisting of the fruit of choice. Eat slowly. Eat until you are full, or use it as the first course, to be followed by a second course consisting of any of the above options.

What's for Dinner?

1. Baked or grilled fish, chicken, turkey or grass-fed beef, with an abundance of steamed or sautéed broccoli, carrots, green beans or other veggies. If desired, you can include a small amount of brown rice or sourdough roll dipped in melted herb butter or olive oil.

2. Whole grain pasta and a side dish of beans and steamed or sautéed vegetables. For the pasta, some wheat alternatives include spelt, buckwheat and rice noodles.

3. Rice and beans with steamed or sautéed broccoli or other vegetables, seasoned with tamari. Instead of beans, you can use tofu or tempeh,

which you can steam or sauté with the veggies. Or you can simply add the tempeh without steaming to preserve the nutrients that were produced through fermentation.

4. Same as above, but replace the soy products with fish or chicken, which are cooked separately or cut up and added to the stir fry. You can also include a small side dish of rice.

5. A large salad made with any combination of the following: Shredded romaine lettuce, finely grated carrot, beet and celery. You can also add larger pieces of softer things, such as sliced tomato, cucumber, zucchini, yellow squash and green onions. You can also sprinkle on any of the following toppings: Chunks of fish, chicken, raw organic goat cheese, hard-boiled egg, avocado, nuts, seeds, tempeh or olives. The dressing can be as simple as olive oil and lemon juice. Or you can also add a bit of dill, garlic powder and salt, thickened with ground up flax seeds. Instead of flax seeds, you can use other ground up nuts or seeds such as hemp seeds, almonds, sunflower seeds, pumpkin seeds, walnuts or macadamia nuts. If you get the dressing right, you can make an entire meal of the salad, using all raw ingredients, if you wish. For variety, you can reduce the size of the salad and add a side dish of hummus and crackers or bread. Again, the hummus and crackers can be raw, if you wish. In addition, or instead of the crackers, you can use carrot sticks or any cut vegetable to dip into the hummus.

6. Quick and Semi-raw: Left-over cooked rice and sprouted beans (lentils, mung beans, adzuki beans, etc) seasoned with tamari and a dash of organic olive oil. You might be surprised at how tasty it is. You can also include a quick side dish of grated carrots and shredded zucchini topped with miso dressing.

7. A first course consisting of fruit (ideally, acidic or enzyme-rich fruit, such as oranges, kiwi, pineapple or papaya). Let that settle for 15-20 minutes and follow it with lean meat and steamed or sautéed vegetables.

8. A first course consisting of the acidic or enzyme-rich fruit, as above, followed by a large salad with a dressing of blended nuts and seeds with lemon juice. You can also throw in some bits of baked chicken or hardboiled egg.

Advising Your Client on Diet

- Keep it simple. Give the client enough data to make sense of things, but do not go overboard.
- Do your homework and know the science well enough to be able to translate the information into laymen's language.
- Whether or not you give your clients any technical information, listen to them. Guide them to the dietary system that seems best suited for them, based on their stated needs and preferences.
- Ideally, just provide them with information. Let them make the decisions. Remember, your client's innate intelligence is smarter than your educated intelligence. Engage them in such a way that they tell *you* how they will eat, rather than you telling them. This becomes easier, as you become more knowledgeable on the subject.
- Naturally, if they have a medical condition, advise them to consult with their physician before making a big change in diet.

Part II
Clinical Application

Nutrition and the Massage Practice

Stress

Fibromyalgia

Bones and Joints

Cardiovascular Health

Blood Sugar and Yeast Overgrowth

Advising Your Clients on Weight Loss

Depression and Addictions

Hippocrates said, "Above all else, do no harm." The secret of doing no harm is balance between knowledge and wisdom. Knowledge gives us power—the power to make changes. Wisdom gives us serenity—the serenity to let things be. When we take steps to increase outer knowledge, it necessitates a deepening of inner wisdom.

Chapter 11

Nutrition & the Massage Practice

The domain of massage therapy includes three broad areas:

- Pain relief
- Healing and rehabilitation from injury
- Stress reduction

A skillful massage therapist, even one who chooses to specialize, should have some knowledge of all three areas. In addition, regardless of your area of specialty, your clients can benefit from nutritional support that complements your treatment. Quite often, your therapeutic effect is marginal if you do not enroll the client in making nutritional adjustments. Even if you already get good results, your work is likely to get even better results with the right kind of nutritional support.

Below are some specific conditions that often motivate individuals to seek massage therapy:

- Muscle and joint pain
- Muscle spasms
- Insomnia
- Fibromyalgia
- Arthritis
- Depression
- Constipation
- PMS

These conditions tend to respond favorably to nutritional support or massage. Combining the two is likely to produce even better results. From a business perspective, the best form of advertisement is the good results you get with your existing clients.

Dietary Stressors and Sore Muscles

- Caffeine – Stimulant
- Alcohol – Creates acidity in the body, irritates nervous system, depletes the body of vitamins, mineral and enzymes.
- Sodium – Contributes to hypertonicity, irritability and insomnia.
- Acid Forming Food – increase muscle soreness and hypertonicity
- Colas – Contain caffeine, phosphoric acid, sodium and sugar. All of these contribute to hypertonic muscles and irritability.
- Grains – In large amounts, grains can contribute to muscle and joint pain.
- Protein – In large amounts, dietary protein, especially grain-fed meat can contribute to muscle and joint pain.
- MSG – Excites the nervous system, contributing to chronically sore muscles.

Sore Muscles and Aching Joints — The Big Four Causes Your Client on MSG

In his book, *Health and Nutrition Secrets That Can Save Your Life*, Dr. Russell Blaylock, a neurosurgeon, states that removal of monosodium glutamate from the diet can eliminate or greatly reduce pain from fibromyalgia. He also suggests that elimination of MSG might be of great benefit for individuals with chronic pain in general.[41]

Your Client on Sodium

Sodium (Na) is needed for the normal conduction of nerve impulses. Sodium has a general excitatory effect on nerves. Excess sodium results in the following:

- Irritability
- Hypertonicity
- Insomnia
- Muscle fatigue
- Greater tendency toward edema and inflammation
- Joint deposits
- Dry skin
- Excessive stimulation of heart

Your Client on Acid-Forming Foods

Hypertonicity, muscle soreness and insomnia may have brought your clients to your services; therefore, they might be interested in knowing that such conditions may be caused or aggravated by an acid forming diet. They may or may not be motivated enough to alkalize, but they will probably be more likely to take action if they know that the same sort of acid forming diet has been associated with a number of more serious conditions, such as:

- Arthritis
- Kidney stones
- Asthma
- Stroke
- Osteoporosis

Your Client on Grains

Since sore muscles and aching joints are common in massage clients, the therapist should know that both have been associated with the high consumption of grains, especially gluten-containing grains (wheat, rye, barley and oats). Other symptoms of gluten sensitivity include fatigue, abdominal pain, depression and compromised immune function.

Gluten sensitivity, when severe enough to show up on a blood test, is given the medical diagnosis of celiac disease. However, mild (subclinical) intolerance of grains can also contribute to the client's health issues. Since gluten sensitivity is technically an autoimmune problem, it becomes just one more factor which contributes to general adaptation syndrome.

Relaxing Minerals

Potassium (K) works with sodium for the proper conduction of nerve impulses. Both are regulated by carrier molecules in the cell membrane, known as sodium/potassium pumps. Potassium tends to have a relaxing effect on muscles and nerves. Since sodium and potassium are physiologically connected, excess sodium causes the body to excrete potassium. Likewise, one way to support the body in flushing out excess sodium is to take extra potassium.

Magnesium (Mg) has a wide variety of functions such as tissue regeneration. For the massage therapist, it is important to note that magnesium is essential for proper relaxation of muscles.

Calcium (Ca), among its many functions, has a general relaxing and calming effect. An excellent source of calcium is dark green, leafy vegetables and oranges. If it is taken as a supplement, we should keep in mind that calcium and magnesium are physiologically connected, just like sodium and potassium. We need magnesium for the proper metabolism of calcium.

Better Results Through Better Nutrition

The best way to promote your practice is to get great results. One of the best ways to create great results with your clients is to encourage them to mineralize.

The typical diet is rich in sodium and deficient in potassium, magnesium, and perhaps calcium. Most clients who suffer from chronic pain and tension can greatly benefit from increasing potassium, calcium and magnesium, and decreasing sodium. Most fruits and vegetables, especially the latter, are good sources of potassium, calcium and magnesium. These minerals can also be taken as supplements, but minerals are better absorbed (and cheaper) when received in whole foods.

Your Client on Fruits and Vegetables

In addition to providing alkalizing minerals that promote detoxification, muscle relaxation and emotional calmness, fruits and vegetables are also rich in flavonoids, some of which promote mental clarity, emotional serenity, cheerfulness and muscular relaxation, mostly by promoting higher levels of certain neurotransmitters (such as serotonin) and hormones (such as melatonin).

Flavonoids are especially abundant in fruits high in vitamin C such as citrus, strawberries, kiwi, pineapple, papaya and mangos. Brain benefitting flavonoids are also available in a number of herbs and teas such as ginkgo biloba, chamomile, St. John's wart and passion flower. These herbs, which are readily available in health food stores, have been traditionally used to promote positive mental and emotion states.

Home Remedies for Your Clients

Most massage therapists do not have the training to do extensive nutritional work with their clients. That is why it is good to develop a working relationship with a skilled nutritionist, unless you become sufficiently inspired to continue your nutritional exploration to the point where you can become a nutritional councilor, in earnest. However, even if you do not travel that far, the basic principles described in this book will allow you to share information with your clients that will support them in greater health. Here are some specific suggestions you can make to your clients to support the work they receive from you. These suggestions will promote pain relief and allow your clients to rest better at night without having to resort to drugs.

Epsom Salt Bath

Dissolve half of a four-pound box of Epsom salt into 2-3 inches of warm water in the bathtub. Get into tub and rub the remaining salt on your body, paying attention to sore areas. Then, fill the tub and soak for 20 minutes. The Epsom salt soak is a good initial self-care modality following the first massage treatment, because the client might have soreness.

Effects:

- Mg – soothing
- Sulfur – cleansing
- Provides relief from arthritis
- Reduces stiffness and soreness of joints
- Relieves muscle aches and pain from overexertion
- Soothes painful bruises and sprains

Contraindication: Not to be used with diabetics or pregnant women.

Vegetable Broth

This is an excellent way to get your clients to get more of those relaxing minerals without necessarily taking supplements. The broth is rich in alkalizing minerals, especially potassium. It is a gentle way to cleanse and alkalize. It is especially recommended for the client suffering from an acid condition in urgent need of relief from neuromuscular pain, tension, anxiety, constipation, depression, restlessness and fatigue. Here is the recipe:

- 1 cup of carrots, shredded or sliced
- 1 cup celery, chopped, shredded – include leaves
- 2 cups any combination of these: beet greens, broccoli, turnip or collard greens, Swiss chard, kale, spinach

The broth can be flavored with garlic, onions, kelp, dolse, or any spice high in potassium. Place vegetables in a stainless steel pot and add 1.5 quarts of water. Simmer for 30 min. Strain and serve warm. You can recommend the broth after treatment along with Epsom salt soak. The combination of the two will reduce the soreness following massage and improve the client's response to treatment.

As an added service, you can call the client one day after the initial treatment and ask them how they feel and if they followed up on your suggestions to soak in Epsom salt and/or drink the broth to reduce toxicity and soreness.

This might seem like a lot of homework for your client, so you might suggest this only if the client seems committed. Generally, individuals who are in pain are more likely follow these recommendations.

The Slippery Elm Tonic

Throw a heaping tablespoon of slippery elm powder in a blender with about 12 oz of warm water. This remedy is excellent for soothing and healing an irritated gastrointestinal tract. Its high silica content helps calm nerves and repair irritated tissues. It is excellent for stressed out clients or anyone with an ulcer, irritated GI tract or sore throat.

Quick Aids for Fibromyalgia

The major remedy for fibromyalgia is rest. Get to bed early and get regular massage treatments. Malic acid and magnesium are helpful. Malic acid is found in a number of fruits like apples. Magnesium is found vegetables. Chapter 13 addresses this condition in more detail. Also, feel free to give your fibromyalgia client the hand-out in the appendix entitled, *A Cure for Fibromyalgia*.

Enemas and Colonic Irrigations

Colon cleansing might be a helpful adjunct to massage therapy. When the large intestine is sluggish, toxins are absorbed into the blood and lymph, and can influence the rest of the body (autointoxication). This can produce a wide variety of ailments, including a compromised immune system. For this reason, enemas and high colonics can be of benefit to the entire body.

Case study

An older male client came to the office of a neuromuscular therapist. His eyes were glazed and he showed signs of adrenal exhaustion. The abdomen was bloated and he had body odor. His legs were often numb and his hands were clammy. He ached all over. In addition to providing neuromuscular therapy, the therapist suggested a series of high colonics. When he returned, his eyes were clear, he had lost some weight and the feeling had returned to his two legs. The results were augmented by the fact that the colon therapist had given the individual a cleansing diet.

Palpation and Nutrition

In addition to getting information about your client through their description of life style and diet, you can also get a general idea about their nutritional status through palpation. There are two basic ways of getting information through palpation: the client's *subjective* response and your *objective* appraisal. The major subjective response is pain under palpatory pressure. The major objective finding is hypertonicity. The other objective finding is how the skin feels under your touch. Specifically, does the skin feel unusually dry or scaly? Muscle tightness and soreness can be caused by high sodium, caffeine, acid forming foods and some drugs. Dry or scaly skin indicates dehydration or excess sodium, both of which are very common.

Case Study

A massage therapist had a client who complained of neck pain and tension. The muscles were tender under palpation (subjective finding). The therapist also noted hypertonicity (objective finding). The therapist had been in practice several years; long enough to realize that the level of tenderness and hypertonicity were unusual. In fact, the hypertonicity had a quality that she had not felt before. She reported that the client's muscles felt like "beef jerky." Since the client's condition did not respond as well as expected, the therapist asked her about her diet and life style. This was when the client realized that the unusual tension began after she started taking a certain diuretic drug. In addition, she realized that she had been feeling emotionally "uptight" since she started the drug treatment. Naturally, the therapist did not advise the client to get off the drug, as that would have been "practicing medicine." Nonetheless, the client elected to discontinue the drug without any encouragement from the therapist. When the client returned for her next visit, she reported that the tension was significantly better when she got off the drug. Palpation revealed a noticeable reduction in tenderness. The therapist also noticed that the muscles no longer felt like beef jerky.

Chapter 12

Stress

Even though many individuals come to massage therapists to de-stress, they are usually not aware of the powerful effects of massage in stress reduction. Neither do they know that the effects of stress go beyond the tight muscles, headaches and insomnia that motivated them to seek treatment from a massage therapist.

The physiological changes associated with stress have been linked to serious degenerative diseases and aging of the body.[31, 49] For example, when the body is chronically stressed, the blood becomes thicker and more prone to clotting, which accelerates the formation of plaque on the inner walls of arteries.

The massage therapist who is knowledgeable on the physiology of stress will be more effective in helping the client de-stress, as well as in educating clients on ways to de-stress on their own. When such knowledge includes an understanding of the nutritional aspects of stress, your treatment can become that much more effective.

What is Stress?

Stress is a stimulus (a change in the internal or external environment) that challenges our ability to adapt and maintain internal equilibrium. A certain amount of stress is normal and healthy. However, when the level of stress chronically exceeds our ability to adapt, the body experiences a gradual physiological decline. The normal condition of homeostasis gives way to a series of disturbances, which, until recently, have received very little medical attention, despite of being associated with the major degenerative diseases responsible for the most fatalities in industrialized nations, and accounting for most of the money spent on health care. The subtle changes associated with stress are collectively known as General Adaptation Syndrome (GAS).

The Physiology of Stress

General Adaptation Syndrome is also known as Adrenal Stress Syndrome, because the adrenal glands are the primary organs which allow us to adapt to stress. The concept was first developed by a Hans Selye M.D.[48] As a medical student in 1926, he found that whether stress was due to infection, chemical toxicity or psychological disturbances, the body shows the same basic reaction, which he described in three phases:

Phase 1: Alarm Phase. The body reacts to stress by an outpouring of adrenal hormones (adrenalin and cortisol), which mobilize the body's energy to adapt to the stress. Most individuals associate the adrenal glands with heavy exercise, physical injury or emotional upset, all of which can produce the "adrenalin rush." Less obvious, but equally significant, the same adrenal alarm can be activated by low-grade infections, environmental toxins, drugs and food. If the stressful event is brief, the body quickly recovers. If the stress continues, the body goes through a brief period during which the overall secretion of adrenal hormones decreases, and individual might feel fatigue, but eventually, the body moves into phase two.

Phase 2: Resistance Phase. The body tries to adapt to the ongoing stress. Tissues are broken down to mobilize amino acids and fatty acids, and bone may be broken down to mobilize minerals. In this phase, the individual might feel fine and may actually feel great because the stress hormones are inhibiting pain and inflammation, while giving the individual a "lift." Furthermore, the immune system is on high alert and successfully keeps infections away (for the most part), and the brain is supplied with the needed nutrients and oxygen.

Even when people do not feel totally well in phase 2, they still feel like they are "coping okay," perhaps with the help of stimulants and tranquilizers, such as caffeine and alcohol, which become part of their daily routine. Therefore, they have little motivation to correct the situation. They might eventually become prone to little inconveniences such as a stuffy nose, constipation, headaches, difficulty waking up in the morning, dry mouth, urinary incontinence and menstrual difficulties, most of which might be considered normal, because so many other individuals seem to have similar issues. The upper respiratory infection in the winter is blamed on a virus, the allergies in the spring are blamed on the pollen, and heavy perspiration in the summer is blamed on the heat.

The situation for the individual in phase 2 is not unlike a consumer living on credit cards. If the person starts out with "good credit" (healthy body with a robust bank-account of nutrient reserves), phase 2 can go on for a long time, during which the body gradually becomes depleted of nutrient reserves and becomes progressively weaker, until eventually, the body moves into phase 3.

Phase 3: Exhaustion Phase. The gradual depletion and breakdown can no longer be easily ignored. The immune system is unable to cope, and obvious pathological conditions emerge. The five-day flu gives way to a two-week lower respiratory infection, which could easily progress to life-threatening pneumonia, if not for antibiotics. Years of fluctuating blood sugar gives way to diabetes mellitus. The accelerated killing of brain cells due to the chronically high cortisol levels, eventually shows up as senile dementia. The stress-induced thickening of blood and high blood pressure, which had been silently causing arterial plaquing over a period of years, eventually show up as cardiac arrest.

The actual disease processes that show up can vary from person to person, but regardless of the specifics, the tissues, essentially, dry up and the vital organs and glands shrink away. The entire body is on a course of accelerated aging.

The Vicious Cycle

When the body goes deeply enough into GAS, the condition is likely to become self-perpetuating — stress begets more stress. For example, too much stress during the day prevents the body from resting and regenerating at night. The blood-levels of cortisol remain high, even after the individual goes to bed, and interfere with sleep. The next day, the individual may have low energy, and therefore takes a stimulant such as coffee, which will stress the adrenal glands even more and throws the body deeper into GAS.

The fact that coffee and other stimulants are so widely used is testimony to the fact that a large percentage of individuals living in industrialized areas have GAS. The morning coffee (without which many individuals would find it difficult to start the day) is followed by a "coffee break" a few hours later, and probably a few more cups later on, along with the extra caffeine from the soft drinks and chocolate candy.

Coffee pots and coffee machines seem to be as indispensible as fax machines and telephones in the place of business.

In other words, GAS leaves us feeling weak, which drives us to use stimulants. The stimulants drive us deeper into GAS, we feel weaker, and so we reach for stronger stimulants, and so on.

In one sense, when the body goes deeply enough into GAS, it "forgets" how to restore itself. For example, in addition to general sleeplessness, the individual has a harder time reaching the deep dreamless (delta) sleep, during which the pituitary gland sends out a surge of growth hormone (GH) that promotes regeneration. The individual, literally, cannot relax and is trapped in a feedback loop, a vicious cycle, in which the body breaks itself down at an ever-increasing rate.

The actual basic mechanism of that vicious cycle and its relevance to massage can be understood first reviewing the autonomic nervous system.

Review of the Autonomic Nervous System

The autonomic nervous system controls our visceral functions. More specifically, it consists of motor neurons that supply smooth muscle, cardiac muscle and glands. Smooth muscle is found on the walls of the digestive system, air passages and blood vessels. Cardiac muscle forms the heart. Glands include the exocrine glands (such as sweat glands, oil glands and salivary glands) and endocrine glands (which secrete hormones). To understand how stress impacts the autonomic system, we need to look at its two parts, called the sympathetic and parasympathetic divisions.

The **parasympathetic division** allows the body to rest and regenerate. It promotes activities which result in the conservation and generation of energy. For example, it slows the heart, slows down breathing, constricts air passages and promotes digestion.

The **sympathetic division** promotes activities that expend energy. For example, sympathetic stimulation tends to increase heart rate, increase the rate and depth of respiration, dilates air passages and inhibits digestion. Not surprisingly, one of the effects of the sympathetic division is to stimulate the adrenal glands, which, in turn, intensifies, prolongs and broadens the effects of the sympathetic division.

In other words, the parasympathetic system allows us to relax, heal and regenerate, while the sympathetic system brings us to attention and maintains a state of alertness. From an energetic standpoint, the parasympathetic system generates and stores energy, while the sympathetic system spends energy. Massive dominance of the sympathetic division is called the fight or flight response.

General Adaptation Syndrome is, essentially, a low-grade on-going flight or flight response. It is chronic sympathetic dominance.[49] The body cannot relax and gather its energy because it perceives it is under attack, but is unable to successfully "fight back" because the attack is coming from within.

Thus, the body remains in a perpetual state of hyper-vigilance which disrupts the normal restorative functions, resulting in a gradual depletion of resources and aging of the body. The sense of futility and helplessness makes things worse, as the individual goes from one desperate measure to another — trying to put out fires by doings things that actually start new fires! The body is fighting for its life but does not realize that the only way to win this particular battle is to just stop fighting.

Eliminating GAS

Here are four powerful ways of helping the body reverse GAS.

- **Rest.** There is no getting around this one. The body needs to rest in order to regenerate. Even if the individual does all the other beneficial things, the body does not properly regenerate if it cannot rest.

- **Exercise.** There is no getting around this one, either. One of the reasons that the body becomes increasingly stressed out is that it gets too much of the wrong kind of stress and not enough of the right kind of stress, in the form of physical activity that challenges the muscles and promotes good circulation. In fact, lack of proper physical exercise may be considered a "passive" form of stress.
- **Nutrition.** Stress (physical, mental or emotional) causes the body to use up nutrients more rapidly. Those who live under constant financial worries, stressful family life, broken homes, etc., have to use larger amounts of their nutritional reserves every day. To effectively manage and eventually reverse GAS, the body needs the raw materials necessary to strengthen itself, especially B vitamins, vitamin C, minerals and omega-3 oils. These nutrients are best obtained from whole foods, but if the higher levels of required nutrients are not available from whole foods, supplementation may be used to help the individual navigate through a prolonged stressful period, without leaving a legacy of GAS.
- **Massage.** This is one of the best therapeutic modalities for reversing GAS. Why? One simple explanation is that massage helps to balance the sympathetic and parasympathetic divisions. As chiropractors and osteopaths are well aware, the body depends on sensory input to keep itself running properly. Such input is essential because it helps the nervous system to adjust the many reflexes that keep us alive and healthy. The motor (efferent) side of these vital reflexes collectively make up the autonomic nervous system. When body workers mobilize joints, massage muscles and stretch the deep fascia, the nervous system receives the sensory input and uses it to reset reflexes. A feature of massage therapy that makes it particularly powerful is the fact that it is applied, typically, for an hour, during which the client is, for the most part, lying still and being quiet, while soothing music is playing in the background. Thus, the body is allowed to gradually reach levels of relaxation that would not be possible with modalities that are done in much less time and with less attention to the environment.

The Healing Power of Touch

As you are well aware, simple hands-on techniques, such as effleurage, petrissage and kneading are effective for relaxing muscles and promoting a general sense of well-being. However, what many massage therapists do not realize is that the same massage techniques also provide the sensory input that helps to "reset" the reflexes that keep our internal organs and glands working properly.

In other words, an effective way to help the body to remember how to heal itself is to simply give it enough touch, as in a series of full body, Swedish massages. Your technique does not have to get more complicated than that.

When massage is combined with the right nutritional support, and the client is guided to get proper rest and exercise, years of GAS can be reversed. Your client's physiology undergoes a subtle but powerful shift that allows him or her to feel better in the present, and slow down or stop the degenerative changes associated with GAS. You are doing nothing less than improving the quality of life, as well as promoting longevity.

Chapter 13
Fibromyalgia

In the past, individuals exhibiting the signs and symptoms associated with fibromyalgia were often dismissed as neurotic or hypochondriacs. However, with increased awareness of the effects of stress on the body, we now know that fibromyalgia syndrome is yet another pathological condition that can develop after years of General Adaptation Syndrome.[66]

Here are the major symptoms:

- Widespread musculoskeletal pain
- Stiffness, especially in the morning
- Persistent fatigue and/or anxiety
- Depression
- Hypersensitivity to smells, sounds, lights and vibrations
- Digestive disturbances
- Dizziness and palpitations
- Non-refreshing sleep

The individual with fibromyalgia syndrome tends to be very driven or very compliant. Symptoms may appear gradually or suddenly after a stressful episode, such as illness or trauma. Assessment is made by the presence of tenderness at eleven of eighteen specific points for a period of over three months, as shown in figure 15.

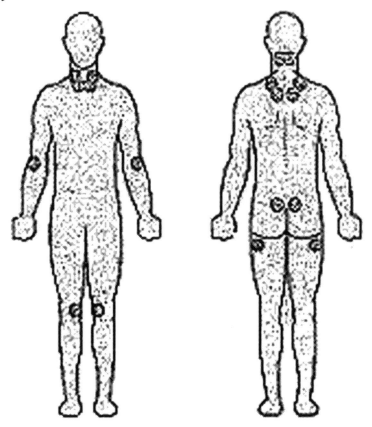

Figure 15: Tender Point in Fibromyalgia

Some of the symptoms of fibromyalgia may be attributed to underproduction of growth hormone (GH), produced by the pituitary gland.[67] GH stimulates the production of protein. The most abundant protein in the body is collagen — a major component of ligaments, tendons, joints and muscles.

Individuals with fibromyalgia frequently have disturbed sleep in which they do not get adequate amounts of deep, dreamless (delta) sleep during which the pituitary gland secretes a large amount of GH. Instead, the individual spends more time in the lighter phase of sleep which is characterized by dreams – often unpleasant.

The heaviest secretion of GH generally occurs between the hours of about 10 p.m. and 2 a.m. According to some researchers, when healthy test subjects were deprived of delta sleep for three weeks, they developed all the symptoms of fibromyalgia.

The presence of widespread pain makes it even more difficult to get adequate delta sleep. Furthermore, the common medication that is given for fibromyalgia — antidepressants — also disrupts delta sleep.

Incidentally, growth hormone is also secreted during exercise. Not surprisingly, individuals who exercise regularly tend to drop down into delta sleep more easily and stay there longer. On the other hand, individuals with fibromyalgia are less likely to exercise, due to the pain and fatigue, thus exacerbating the condition.

Treatment

Individuals with fibromyalgia are probably experiencing the end result of stage 3 GAS. Therefore, they are likely to benefit from a similar treatment strategy:

- **Good nutrition** is important. If the diet seems less than ideal, you might suggest a high potency vitamin and mineral supplement, and of course, you can also suggest they eat more fresh fruits and vegetables.
- **Relaxing herbs**, such as valerian, hops, passion flower, or skull cap can be beneficial for promoting deep restful sleep.
- **Malic acid and Magnesium.** Both of these support the cells of the body generate ATP. Individuals with fibromyalgia who take Mg and malic acid show a significant reduction in pain and fatigue. Malic acid is found in common fruits, especially tart apples. Magnesium is found abundantly in fruits and vegetables. Malic acid and Mg supplements (formulated together for fibromyalgia) are available.
- **Omega-3 oils** can be beneficial in reducing pain, inflammation and depression.
- **Hydrolyzed collagen** supplements, reportedly, promote growth hormone secretion, while providing the specific amino acids that are used to make collagen. Over the years, I have seen a number of individuals experience relief from fibromyalgia with the use of these products. Some of these products have the added benefit of promoting a deep restful sleep, which is essential for regeneration. Such products may be purchased in most health food stores or on line.
- **Eliminate MSG.** Dr. Russell Blaylock, a neurosurgeon, states that removal of monosodium glutamate from the diet can greatly reduce pain from fibromyalgia. MSG overexcites neurons, inhibits the secretion of growth hormone from the pituitary gland and stimulates secretion of cortisol from the adrenal glands. All three can contribute to fibromyalgia. Dr. Blaylock sites clinical studies in which some patients diagnosed with fibromyalgia were simply guided to eliminate MSG from their diet and experienced significant reduction in pain.

- **Massage.** Massage has been shown to be beneficial for individuals with fibromyalgia.[69] The massage does not have to be painfully deep. The main therapeutic effect is the touching itself. During that one hour of stillness, quiet and bodywork, the sympathetic system tones down, the parasympathetic system wakes up, and the many reflexes which govern the internal organs and glands can reset themselves.

To motivate your client to follow through on your recommendations, you can give them a copy of the article on fibromyalgia in the appendix of this book. It is specifically written for the massage client with fibromyalgia.

Chronic Fatigue Syndrome

Chronic fatigue syndrome and fibromyalgia syndrome may be looked upon as two versions of the same condition. Both can be brought on by long-term GAS. With both conditions, the individual suffers from chronic pain, stiffness, fatigue, depression, anxiety and disturbed sleep. The main difference is that, in fibromyalgia, the major symptom is pain, whereas in chronic fatigue syndrome, the major symptom is fatigue. Treatment and recommendations for chronic fatigue syndrome are virtually the same as Fibromyalgia.

Chapter 14
Healthy Bones and Joints

The key to healthy bones and joints is regular exercise combined with an abundance of fruits and vegetables, especially the latter. It really is that simple. To understand why this is so, let us consider the two major pathological conditions which afflict the human skeleton: osteoporosis and arthritis.

Osteoporosis

Osteoporosis refers to a loss of bone density. Eventually, the bones can become so brittle, they can fracture. Since the same dietary and life-style factors that cause chronic muscle tension and pain can produce osteoporosis, the massage therapist is likely to encounter clients with this condition. Some of them will have already been medically diagnosed with osteoporosis and perhaps had been advised to take a drug or calcium for the condition. Both might be helpful, but neither address the actual cause. To understand how you can help such individuals, let us first review the basic tissue structure of bone.

Bone tissue is a form of connective tissue which means it consists of a loose scattering of cells embedded in a non-living matrix. In the case of bone tissue, the matrix is rigid and consists of two components: **collagen fibers** and **calcium salts**. The most abundant of these salts is calcium phosphate. Another is calcium carbonate.

Calcium salts give the bone rigidity. Collagen fibers give the bones tensile strength. Both are necessary for making strong bones. With collagen fibers alone, the bone would not be bone, it would be ligamentous tissue. With calcium salts alone, the bone would be rigid, but it would be brittle, like chalk.

In osteoporosis, both the collagen fibers and the mineral content diminish. Therefore, the bone is weaker and more susceptible to fractures, especially compression fractures. For example, hip fractures usually occur in older individuals, typically females, after years of progressive bone loss. The hip fracture typically consists of a compression fracture of the neck, of the femur, or a breaking of the acetabulum due to pressure from the femur head.

Causes

- Lack of exercise.
- Acid-forming diet (typically too much meat, dairy and grains).
- Vitamin C deficiency.
- Mineral deficiency.
- Malabsorption of calcium, possibly due to lack of vitamin D.
- Decrease in estrogen production, especially in post-menopausal women.
- Anti-inflammatory drugs, especially cortisone, can accelerate osteoporosis.[32]

The Cure: Exercise and Nutrition

Bones must be exercised in order for them to maintain their density. Osteoporosis can be reversed, even in elderly individuals, by exercising regularly. The results are even better when the exercise is combined with proper nutrition. On the nutritional side, the three major factors that are essential for preventing and reversing osteoporosis are vitamin D, vitamin C and alkalizing minerals.

The importance of these three nutritional factors becomes clear when we remember that the matrix of bone is made not just of calcium salts but also collagen fibers. Abundance of vitamin C is necessary for optimum production of collagen, while vitamin D is important to assure that the calcium is properly absorbed from food and deposited upon the collagen fibers of our bones. Likewise, a diet rich in alkalizing minerals is essential to assure that calcium remains on the bones. If the diet becomes too acid-forming, the body will pull calcium from the bones to maintain the alkalinity of the blood.

Animal products and most grains, nuts and beans tend to be acid forming because they are high in acid forming minerals. This does not mean these foods need to be eliminated, but rather consumed at a level which leaves room for sufficient qualities of foods that are rich in alkalizing minerals and vitamin C. Such foods are fruits and vegetables. The vitamin D is best obtained through adequate exposure to sunlight (preferably while the individual is exercising outdoors).

What about taking calcium supplements or drinking milk? Contrary to popular belief, extra calcium, by itself, has not been found to be effective in preventing and reversing osteoporosis, if the three key factors, described above, are not addressed. Of course, adequate calcium intake is essential. However, calcium is easily provided by consuming the same fruits and vegetables that contain the other alkalizing minerals and vitamin C.

In other words, *lack of calcium is typically NOT the major causative factor in osteoporosis.* Therefore, giving the individual extra calcium, by taking supplements or drinking milk, is unlikely to be of much benefit. In fact, multiple studies throughout the world have shown that individuals who consume the most dairy products also show the highest incidence of osteoporosis and hip fractures.[33]

Arthritis

The term, arthritis, refers to any inflammatory or degenerative condition of a joint. To understand arthritis and how it can be corrected, let us review the basic anatomy of joints.

There are three types of joints in the body: Fibrous joints, cartilaginous joints and synovial joints.

- Fibrous joints are held together by fibrous connective tissue, as in the sutures of the skull.
- Cartilaginous joints are held together by slabs of cartilage, as in the intervertebral disc that holds together adjacent vertebral bodies.
- Synovial joints have a fluid filled space between the articulating bones. These joints are the most freely movable and the most abundant in the body. Since all forms of arthritis involve synovial joints, we will take a closer look at them.

Synovial Joints

The free movement of synovial joints necessitates the presence of many nerve endings to allow the nervous system to monitor the activity of the joints. Many of these nerve endings are pain receptors. Therefore, any disruption of synovial joints is likely to produce pain. In other words, synovial joints *tend to be painfully expressive*. Furthermore, since they are freely moveable, they are greatly influenced by the action of skeletal muscles which means that massage therapy can benefit painful conditions involving synovial joints.

Here are the four major features of synovial joints:

- The **joint cartilage** (articular cartilage) is a layer of hyaline cartilage which covers the articular surfaces of the bones.
- The **joint cavity** is the space between the articulating bones.
- The **synovial fluid** is the thick syrupy substance that fills the cavity. It has three functions: It is a lubricant (like motor oil), it nourishes the articular cartilage, and it contains scavenger cells that remove bacteria and debris.
- The **joint capsule** is the membrane that encloses the joint cavity. It consists of two layers. The outer layer is made of fibrous tissue which fuses with the periosteum of the bone. The inner layer is made of synovial membrane which secretes the synovial fluid.

Figure 16: The Typical Synovial Joint

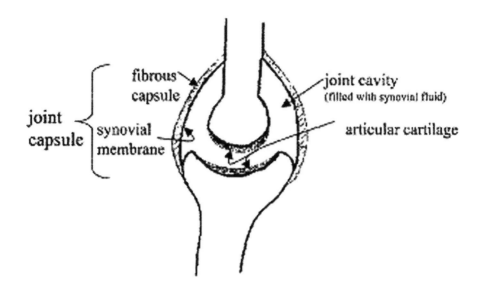

Three Main Types of Arthritis

There are three main types of arthritis that afflict synovial joints. They are osteoarthritis, rheumatoid arthritis and gout. In all three types, the soft tissue, cartilage and even bone tissue, described above, can be affected.

Osteoarthritis

Osteoarthritis is also known as degenerative joint disease (DJD). This condition is often called the wear-and-tear arthritis. It is generally associated with old age and involves an erosion of articular cartilage.

Eventually, the bone surfaces become sclerotic (more dense) and bone spurs may develop. Also, the fibrous tissue associated with the joint (articular capsule and ligaments) may become less flexible and perhaps infiltrated with calcium (hardened). Severe cases may result in fusion of the bones.

Causes

- Excessive use of the involved joint.
- Traumatic injury.
- Inadequate levels of synovial fluid.
- Inadequate circulation (lack of nutrition) to the articular cartilage due to sedentary lifestyle or from joint fixation (immobility).

- Subluxations (misalignments) of the bones, causing the articular surfaces to be in an unfavorable position.
- Dietary stress (lack of needed nutrients and the presence of toxic substances) can add to the irritation initiated by mechanical stress.

Treatment

- Passive range of motion
- Massage
- Alternating hot and cold applications.
- Glucosamine sulfate — a naturally occurring substance found in joints which can be given in supplement form. Glucosamine sulfate has been shown to decrease joint pain and stimulate regeneration.[44] Its principle action is to stimulate the regeneration of cartilage. It is a key building block for chondroitin sulfate, which forms the matrix of cartilage (along with collagen).
- Adequate vitamin C — important for supporting collagen production.
- A diet that provides alkalizing minerals (fruits and vegetables). Too much acidity irritates joints and promotes inflammation.
- Long-chain omega-3 oils (as found in fish oil) — has been shown to be beneficial in bringing relief to chronic joint pain.

Rheumatoid Arthritis

This condition involves substantial inflammation of a joint, due to an autoimmune attack on the joint tissues. The articular cartilage breaks down and scar tissue may bridge the articular surfaces of the bones. The scar tissue may become calcified, which means the joint is effectively fused.

Treatments

- Digestive enzymes, such as bromelain, to reduce inflammation.
- Dietary stressors include wheat, dairy, nightshade vegetables (tomatoes, potatoes and peppers) and excessive meat. Avoidance or restriction of these foods has produced positive results in this condition.
- Avoid high intake of foods high in omega-6 oils, such as corn, soy and safflower oil.
- An alkalizing diet, rich in anti-inflammatory foods and sources of omega-3 oils (fruits, vegetable, flax seeds, fish oils) can be very beneficial.

- Black cherry juice and noni juice, reportedly, can bring relief. I have found noni juice to be helpful with inflamed and painful joints.

Gouty Arthritis

Gout is an inflammatory condition resulting from irritating uric acid crystals that accumulate in the joint. Uric acid is a byproduct of protein metabolism. Though this condition has a different causation than rheumatoid arthritis, both can be triggered by the same dietary stressors: excess meat, dairy, and nightshade vegetables. Certain foods, like beef and shellfish, especially irritate gout, because they tend to be high in uric acid. High levels of any protein in general will cause the body to make more uric acid, but animal protein tends to be more concentrated. Furthermore, as soon as the animal dies, the tissues start to decompose, resulting in the accumulation of uric acid and other waste products. In addition, problems with the liver and kidneys can contribute to high uric acid levels.

Treatments

- Cold packs and digestive enzymes to reduce inflammation.
- Avoidance or restriction of high-protein foods, tomatoes and peppers can make a big difference. In particular, excessive animal protein, especially liver, kidneys and shellfish is generally helpful.
- As with osteoarthritis and rheumatoid arthritis, an abundance of alkalizing anti-inflammatory foods can be very beneficial.
- As with rheumatoid arthritis, black cherry juice and noni juice, reportedly, can bring relief.

Chapter 15
Cardiovascular Health

The circulatory system is of special interest for the massage therapist, especially one who has an interest in nutrition. Here are the reasons:

- Massage greatly benefits the circulatory system. Swedish massage was specifically designed to promote good circulation.
- Cardiovascular disease is the biggest cause of death in industrialized nations.
- In studying the workings of the circulatory system, we can come to understand edema and inflammation, both of which are emphasized in massage education. In addition, chronic low-grade inflammation has been found to be the common thread in virtually all degenerative diseases.
- The circulatory system provides us with the foundation for comprehending the secrets of that mysterious and immensely important process called immunity. We can understand the auto-immune conditions such as rheumatoid arthritis, lupus, multiple sclerosis and even common allergies. Once we understand these autoimmune issues, we can also understand how food can have an immense effect on these conditions.
- The circulatory system, along with the digestive system, is the one that is obviously and profoundly influenced by diet. This is quite understandable when we remember that food must first pass through the digestive system, and, from there, into the blood.

Not surprisingly, both digestive and cardiovascular disturbances are very common in industrialized nations, where heavily processed and devitalized foods are more the rule than the exception. However, cardiovascular issues command public attention more than digestive issues. This is understandable, because poor digestion is not immediately life threatening. Granted, chronic problems with the digestive system can eventually contribute to other serious problems, but most individuals are concerned with indigestion because of the associated social problems, not because of the long-term health consequences. In contrast, cardiovascular issues can be immediately life threatening.

Unfortunately, cardiovascular problems (unlike digestive problems) may go completely unnoticed until the condition is very advanced and critical. The first actual sign that the individual has cardiovascular issues is sometimes a fatal heart attack. Until recently, medical science did not see the profound connection between diet and cardiovascular health. It is easy to connect bloating, gas and constipation with your last meal, but it has taken a lot longer to connect heart attacks with specific foods that were eaten in the preceding twenty years.

Now it is becoming clear that diet is one of many stressors that can compromise cardiovascular health. Apparently, stress in any form can compromise cardiovascular health. To do justice to this important subject, let us first review the basic anatomy and physiology of the circulatory system.

Review of the Circulatory System

Overall Anatomy

The circulatory system consists of the blood vascular system and lymph vascular system.

- The **blood vascular system,** also known as the cardiovascular system, consists of the heart, arteries, veins and blood capillaries. Arteries are blood vessels that channel blood away from the heart. Veins are blood vessels that channel blood to the heart. Capillaries are microscopic blood vessels that link arteries and veins.

- The **lymph vascular system** or lymphatic system consists of lymph vessels and lymphatic organs. Lymph vessels start as blind-ended lymph capillaries which converge into progressively larger vessels. Along the course of many lymph vessels, we find lymph nodes, which filter the lymph, while producing certain types of white blood cells (lymphocytes and monocytes). The other lymphatic organs are the tonsils, spleen and thymus.

Figure 17: The Circulatory System

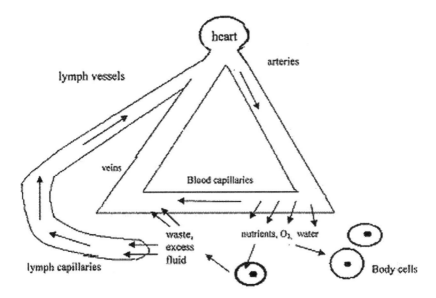

Overall Physiology

The circulatory system is all about body fluids. The three major body fluids are **blood**, **lymph** and **tissue fluid**. Tissue fluid, which is mostly water, bathes the cells of the body. Our cells absorb nutrients and oxygen from the tissue fluid, and they expel their waste products into that same fluid.

If tissue fluid is stationary, it quickly stagnates, becoming depleted of nutrients and polluted with cellular excrements. For this reason, we have the circulatory system. Figure 17 illustrates how the blood and lymph vascular systems interact.

As blood flows through capillaries, the sheer pressure of blood on the walls of the capillaries causes some of the blood components to filter out. This is how tissue fluid forms. Meanwhile, some of the water and waste products in the tissue fluid diffuse back into the blood capillaries. Any excess fluid that cannot be reabsorbed by the blood capillaries is absorbed by the lymph capillaries. Once the tissue fluid seeps into the lymph capillaries, it is no longer called tissue fluid, it is called lymph, which then flows through a series of progressively larger lymph vessels that eventually merge with two large veins (the subclavian veins) close to the heart.

Blood

Blood is a mixture composed of plasma and formed elements. The formed elements are the blood cells. The three types of blood cells are red blood cells, white blood cells and platelets, all three of which are produced in the red bone marrow.

- **Red blood cells** are filled with hemoglobin which carries oxygen.
- **White blood cells** defend the body from pathogens. There are five types of WBCs: neutrophils, eosinophils, basophils, monocytes and lymphocytes. The lymphocytes come in two varieties, B lymphocytes and T lymphocytes, otherwise known as B cells and T cells.
- **Platelets (Thrombocytes)** are cell fragments which contain most of the clotting factors. When a blood vessel is damaged, the platelets are ruptured by the rough edges and release the clotting factors, thus initiating the clotting reaction.

The plasma is a yellowish fluid composed of water and a number of dissolved chemicals. These chemicals include three types of plasma proteins: antibodies, fibrinogen, and albumins.

- **Antibodies** are protein molecules which bind to potentially harmful substances and render them harmless.
- **Fibrinogen** is one of our clotting factors. It is produced by the liver.
- **Albumins** are the most abundant of the plasma proteins. They are similar to the albumin that forms egg white. Their presence draws excess water from the tissue fluid, back into the blood capillaries. One of the symptoms of severe malnutrition is swelling of the tissues, especially in the abdominal region. The swelling is due to excess tissue fluid, which results from a depletion of albumins in the blood.

Edema and Inflammation

Edema is the build-up of excess tissue fluid in the tissues spaces. It may be caused by any one of a number of factors. For example, edema may be caused by sluggish lymphatic or venous drainage, both of which can be assisted by massage. This is how the developer of Swedish Massage, Pehr Henrik Ling, got the idea of doing effleurage toward the heart.

Inflammation is the tissue's response to injury or irritation. The four cardinal signs of inflammation are edema, redness, heat and pain. Inflammation may occur in response to traumatic injury, chemical irritants or infection. The damaged tissues release chemicals that initiate the inflammatory response. Such chemicals include histamines, which do two things:

- Cause dilation of local blood vessels, which results in redness.
- Make capillaries more porous which results in edema.

Food and Inflammation

Chronic low-grade inflammation has been found to be a major common thread that links many degenerative diseases. Chronic low-grade inflammation is greatly influenced by diet, which means that *virtually all degenerative diseases have a dietary connection, to some degree.* Regarding food and chronic inflammation, the bottom line is this: some foods are pro-inflammatory and some are anti-inflammatory.

Numerous studies suggest that a simple way to prevent and sometimes reverse degenerative conditions, such as cardiovascular disease, is to eat an abundance of anti-inflammatory foods and to limit the pro-inflammatory foods.

Pro-inflammatory Foods

- All foods containing high levels of omega-6 fatty acids, such as corn oil and soy bean oil.
- Most grains and grain-fed beef.
- Dairy

Anti-Inflammatory Foods

- Foods rich in omega-3 oils, such as fish and flax seeds.
- Fruits
- Vegetables

The Heart

The heart is a pump that drives blood through the blood vessels. The inner wall of the heart is lined with a thin membrane called the endocardium. The thick middle layer is composed of cardiac muscle tissue and is called the myocardium. The outer side is covered by another thin membrane called the pericardium. Inflammation of the inner and outer layers is called **endocarditis** and **pericarditis**, respectively.

The heart is two pumps in one. The right side of the heart receives oxygen-depleted blood from the body and pumps it to the lungs. The left side of the heart receives freshly oxygenated blood from the lungs and propels it through the body.

The Arteries

The walls of arteries are thick and elastic (rubbery). The large arteries have the most elasticity because they have to accommodate the surge of the high pressure blood from the heart. When the heart contracts, arteries expand in response to the increased pressure. When the heart relaxes, the arteries shrink back to their original size, thus giving the blood a little extra push.

If the arteries were not elastic (hardening of the arteries), the surge of high pressure blood during cardiac contraction could cause the pressure in the arteries to become dangerously high, resulting in damage of the tiny blood vessels and perhaps a rupturing of weakened arteries.

Blood pressure is the force that blood exerts on the walls of blood vessels. Blood pressure is greatest as it leaves the heart and surges through the large arteries. It drops steadily as it flows through the smaller arteries, capillaries, small veins, and large veins. It is lowest in the largest veins, just before merging with the heart.

Arterial blood pressure is an important diagnostic tool because if the pressure is too high, the arteries may be damaged, and if it is too low, nutrients will not filter out of the capillaries fast enough to feed the body cells.

When we measure arterial pressure, we record two numbers: the systolic pressure, which reflects the pressure during cardiac contraction, and diastolic pressure which reflects pressure during cardiac relaxation. For diagnostic purposes, blood pressure is measured in the brachial artery (just above the elbow). At this point the normal systolic pressure is 120 mm Hg (millimeters of mercury), and the diastolic pressure is 80 mm Hg. We indicate this as 120/80.

Veins

Veins have thinner walls than arteries because the blood traveling through veins is under much less pressure compared to arteries. In fact, the pressure in veins is so low that blood might actually flow backwards were it not for the valves found in many veins. Veins are also more numerous than arteries. Some veins are deep and follow a parallel course to arteries. Others are superficial and have no arterial counterparts. The blood vessels we can see on the surface of the body are the superficial veins.

Vascular Problems

The major pathological conditions associated with arteries are as follows:

¤ **Arteriosclerosis**, also known as hardening of the arteries, is a condition in which collagen stiffens and calcium becomes deposited on the walls of arteries. As a result, the large arteries cannot expand sufficiently which can contribute to high blood pressure.

- **Atherosclerosis** is a condition in which fatty and fibrous material becomes deposited on the walls of arteries, thus narrowing the passageway for blood. If these obstructions occur in the small coronary arteries that supply the heart muscle, the restriction in blood flow can cause pain on the left side of the chest and upper extremity (angina pectoris) and cardiac arrest. The actual sequence of events that leads to acute coronary insufficiency is more subtle than previously thought. It is usually not as simple as cholesterol and other material gradually accumulating in the inner lining of arteries, but rather has to do with the rupturing of the plague, sort of like a pimple spontaneously popping, which, in turn, initiates a clotting reaction that ultimately clogs the artery and deprives the heart muscle of blood.[56]
- An **aneurism** is a ballooning out of the arterial wall. The ballooned area tends to be weaker than the surrounding areas on the arterial wall, and is thus more vulnerable to rupturing, especially if the blood pressure is too high. Massage therapists are advised to be aware of older clients who might have an abdominal aortic aneurism. On such individuals, it is prudent to ease up on the abdomen, or totally avoid it.
- **High Blood Pressure** is a serious condition for reasons other than endangering arteries that are already weakened by aneurisms. High blood pressure increases the wear and tear on otherwise normal arteries, as well as increasing the likelihood that clots will form within blood vessels. The common factors that tend to increase blood pressure are lack of exercise and obesity, kidney issues, excessive dietary sodium, oral contraceptives, stimulants, diet pills and cold and allergy medicine.

Abnormalities with veins tend to be less devastating than that of arteries. The two major problems encountered with veins are varicose veins and phlebitis.

- **Varicose veins** (varicosities) are abnormally distended veins, due to sluggish circulation and perhaps vitamin C deficiency. Varicosities are most common in the superficial veins of the lower extremities.
- **Phlebitis** is inflammation of a vein. It is accompanied by redness of the overlying skin and throbbing pain. It is usually caused by bacterial infection or local trauma. Phlebitis may progress to thrombophlebitis, a condition in which a blood clot develops in the affected vein. The thrombus may become dislodged and form an embolus, which later becomes lodged in a small artery and obstructs blood flow to a vital organ. An embolus that gets lodged in a small artery in the brain may result in a stroke. An embolus that gets lodged in the heart or lungs may be fatal. Therefore, massage therapists are advised to steer clear of areas that show signs of phlebitis.

Causes of Arterial Plaquing

Arterial plaquing starts with irritation of the delicate inner lining of the artery, known as the endothelium.[56] If such irritation exceeds the body's ability to prevent or heal it, chronic low-grade inflammation sets in. Once the inflammation is established, it tends to perpetuate itself, leading to further degenerative changes that include the growth of arterial plaques, consisting of fibrotic material and fat, such as cholesterol. As the plaques grow, they progressively obstruct the flow of blood. As mentioned above, the most dangerous place for this to happen is in the coronary arteries that supply the heart muscle.

Non-Dietary Factors

- Lack of exercise has been positively connected with arterial problems. Lack of exercise can also contribute to varicose veins, but of course, this gets much less attention than arterial issues. Like muscles and bones, the heart and blood vessels must be used in order for them to maintain their integrity. The human body is simply not designed to be sedentary. Nutrition gets most of the attention, but physical exercise is of equal importance. To have optimum health, we must be physically fit.
- General Adaptation Syndrome can contribute to the progression of cardiovascular disease. Chronic stress tends to thicken the blood and elevate blood pressure, both of which can compromise the health of the heart and blood vessels.

Dietary Factors

There was a time when any health care provider who suggested that vascular disease could be related to diet was considered a quack. Now the evidence has become irrefutable that vascular diseases can be caused by diet, as well as be prevented and reversed by diet.[74] Here are the main dietary factors that influence cardiovascular health:

- Lack of vitamin C and C complex (such as flavonoids). Both are important for collagen production, which is critically important for maintaining the integrity of the arterial endothelium.[75]
- Lack of omega-3 oils. These important oils keep inflammation in check and help maintain the smoothness and elasticity of the inner lining of blood vessels.[76]
- Lack of dietary antioxidants. Much of the damage that leads to arterial plaquing is caused or accelerated by free-radical damage.[77]

- Lack of vitamin B_{12} and folate can lead to high levels of homocysteine (which is a form of the amino acid, cysteine), that irritates the inner lining of blood vessels.
- Too many pro-inflammatory foods and not enough anti-inflammatory foods. In other words, too much dairy, grains, refined vegetable oils high in omega-6 (safflower and corn oil), grain-fed beef, and not enough fruits and vegetables.
- Any foods that contain substances which irritate the inner lining of blood vessels, such as oxidized oils and partially hydrogenated vegetable oils, can trigger the formation of arterial plaque.
- Saturated fats in the diet tend to raise blood cholesterol (specifically LDL cholesterol), which speeds up the process of plaque formation.
- Oxidized cholesterol is especially damaging. Animal studies suggest that a relatively small amount of oxidized cholesterol (0.3% of ingested cholesterol) can cause damage to the walls of arteries. Cholesterol is oxidized by cooking, especially at high temperatures, as in broiling, deep-frying and industrial canning. Also, high levels of heme iron (found in red meat) can trigger oxidation of cholesterol in the body. [58]

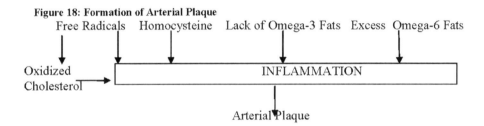

Figure 18: Formation of Arterial Plaque

Nutritional Support

- A diet that is **low in sodium** and **rich in magnesium, potassium and calcium** can be very effective in lowering blood pressure. This is easily provided by an abundance of fruits and vegetables, which have the additional benefit of alkalizing the body, providing **antioxidants,** keeping inflammation in check and maintaining the integrity of blood vessels.
- **Pomegranate** juice contains a powerful blend of antioxidants that promote vascular health. It also helps to thin blood and reduce blood pressure. Human and animal studies suggest that pomegranate juice can help to reverse atherosclerosis.[65]
- **Garlic** has been shown to thin the blood, lower blood pressure and reverse atherosclerosis.

- **Hawthorne** has been used to treat angina, arrhythmia, high blood pressure and high cholesterol. It has been shown to strengthen cardiac contraction.
- **Ginkgo Biloba** promotes microcirculation to all internal organs, thins the blood just as well as aspirin (without the harmful side effects), helps reduce arrhythmias, and contains powerful antioxidants that prevent oxidation of LDL cholesterol.
- **Natto** (a form of fermented soy) contains nattokinase, which has been shown to thin blood and reduce blood pressure.
- **Omega-3** oils, found abundantly in flax, fish and egg yoke.
- **Adequate vitamin B_{12} and folate.** B_{12} is found abundantly in animal products. Folate is found abundantly in green leafy vegetables. If the individual on a vegan diet has good absorption and gets an abundance of organic raw fruits and vegetables, especially mushrooms, B_{12} supplementation might not be necessary. However, most nutritionists advise vegans to supplement with B_{12} or, at least, check it periodically.
- **Vitamin E and coenzyme Q_{10}** are both powerful antioxidants as well as supporting the utilization of oxygen by heart cells. Since both are fat soluble, they also act as important antioxidants that help prevent oxidation of LDL cholesterol.
- **Vitamin C and associated flavonoids.** In addition to being important in the production of collagen (which forms the walls of blood vessels), these nutrients have strong antioxidant activity. As an antioxidant, vitamin C indirectly helps to prevent oxidation of LDL cholesterol by restoring the antioxidant power of vitamin E. Though the right kind of vitamin C supplement can be of benefit, studies suggest that vitamin C is more effective when obtained from whole foods.[73] For optimum health, around 1000 mg of vitamin C per day has been suggested. I am inclined to agree, because it reflects the level of vitamin C we would get if we consumed a fairly large amount of raw fruits and vegetables. Here are some options for getting about 1000 mg of vitamin C from whole foods: One to two pounds of high-vitamin C fruits (such as citrus, kiwi, pineapple, papaya, mango and strawberries), and then two pounds of green vegetables (such as kale, spinach, romaine lettuce, broccoli and chard).

Chapter 16

The Immune System

The previous chapter described how dietary stress (as well as other forms of stress) precipitate cardiovascular problems. One aspect of the circulatory system is its central role in the so-called immune system, which is responsible for keeping the body free of pathogens. Not surprisingly, the same stressors that trigger degenerative changes in the circulatory system also compromise the body's defenses. To understand how stress affects the immune system, let us consider its basic operation.

Review of the Immune System

Our Two Lines of Defense

Defense of the body occurs in two phases. They are called the innate defense and adaptive defense.

Innate defense, as the name suggests, is our inborn defense. It responds to all pathogens in pretty much the same way, therefore, it can also be called the non-specific defense. The innate defense includes the following:

- Physical barriers, such as the skin and mucus membranes.
- Phagocytosis (the process by which defensive cells engulf pathogens.).
- Natural Killer Cells: Lymphocytes that attack and destroy tumor cells and virus-infected cells.

Adaptive defense consists of the body's ability to target specific pathogens. Adaptive defense is carried out by the T lymphocytes and B lymphocytes that have been specifically "programmed" to attack certain pathogen.

- T lymphocytes directly attack and destroy specific pathogens.
- B lymphocytes produce antibodies in response to specific pathogens.

Antigens, Antibodies and Immunity

An antigen is any substance that stimulates the proliferation of T and B lymphocytes. Antigens may be molecules that are ingested, inhaled or absorbed through the skin, or molecules produced by microorganisms invading the body. Once the specific T lymphocytes and antibodies are produced, they will be drawn to the antigens and render them harmless in various ways.

After the pathogens have been eliminated, the specially programmed T and B lymphocytes remain. Therefore, if the same pathogen returns, it is quickly eliminated with little or no symptoms. In this manner, the adaptive defense gives us immunity against pathogens encountered in the past.

Immunity Gone Bad

In an **autoimmune** response, the body's defenses respond in such a way as to irritate or destroy the body's own tissues. Autoimmune diseases include type I diabetes, lupus, MS and rheumatoid arthritis.

Many autoimmune diseases are triggered by improperly digested protein, which can occur by simply eating more protein than the body can comfortably digest. In addition, some types of protein, such as dairy and soy, can be problematic even in moderate amounts. For example, when improperly digested milk protein (casein) gets into the blood, the immune system recognizes it as a foreign invader and makes antibodies against it. Unfortunately, when the immune system is not as well-tuned as it needs to be, it may be unable to distinguish between foreign proteins from the body's own proteins, especially when the foreign protein closely resembles our own. In the case of dairy, the antibodies often do not distinguish between dairy protein and the proteins found on the pancreatic cells that make the hormone, insulin. As a result, the immune system destroys the insulin-producing cells. This is a major cause of type I diabetes in young children. In susceptible individuals, the condition can be prevented by simply taking the child off cow's milk.[34]

Common allergies are due to a poorly functioning immune system. The most common symptoms associated with allergies are fatigue, headaches, nasal congestion, dark shadows under the eyes (allergic shiners), abdominal pain, muscle and joint pain, bladder symptoms, nervousness, irritability, or feeling "spaced out."

Allergens that cause gastro-intestinal irritation can prevent the proper digestion and absorption of nutrients. The subsequent undigested food molecules can then produce more allergic reactions. All that irritation rings the adrenal alarm, which brings us back to General Adaptation Syndrome.

General Adaptation Syndrome Revisited

Upon initial exposure to an allergen, the body is "shocked," causing an increase in adrenal hormones, thus producing the alarm stage of GAS. If the individual continues to take in the allergen, the body goes into the adaptation stage. Continual consumption of the allergen will cause the body to reach the exhaustion stage, with accompanying illness.

Quite often, the person may actually feel better after eating the allergen because there is an adrenalin rush. Eventually, however, there will be a worsening of GAS.

Many health food store remedies or "energizers" may just be producing very mild allergy alarm reactions. For example, many people have slight pollen allergies that they may be unaware of. While a small, infrequent exposure to bee pollen may energize them in the short-term, it will eventually contribute to fatigue.

Allergies and Addictions

A food craving may signal the presence of allergens. The most common source of food allergens include wheat, corn, coffee, milk, peanuts, chocolate, eggs, tobacco and beef. It takes about five days to eliminate the effects of an allergen from the system. If the individual eats wheat bread on Monday, it would take until Friday for it to clear from the body. Therefore, it is best to give up all allergens at the same time. The individual may initially experience withdrawal symptoms, but will eventually feel better. For example, alcoholism typically involves addiction to the food derivatives in the beverage – such as wheat, rye, grapes, yeast or hops. Alcoholics often have candida overgrowth and hypoglycemia. Bipolar disorder (manic depression) might also involve an allergic reaction.

Dietary Factors That Stress the Immune System

- Saturated fats and partially hydrogenated vegetable oils. The cell membranes are composed primarily of fats (phospholipids) with a light scattering of protein. The integrity of the membrane is greatly influenced by the quality of the fats making the membrane. When the right fats are not provided through the foods we eat, the body uses whatever is available. Since saturated fats and partially hydrogenated oils are "stiffer" compared to the omego-3 oils, the result is a reduction in the cell's ability to "sense" what is happening in its external environment. This can have a number of devastating effects, such as the inability to cope with a virus or other pathogens.
- White flour and white sugar. Both deplete the body of vitamins and minerals.
- Stimulants - caffeine, nicotine, constant bad news, violent movies.
- Environmental poisons - tap water, mercury, fluoride, pesticides.
- Antibiotics (see below).
- Vaccines (see below).

Antibiotics

Antibiotics are chemicals that disrupt the metabolism of bacteria. Used judiciously, they are a great blessing, because they can save the person's life. However, there are two main issues with the long term use of antibiotics:

- Antibiotics tend to breed bacterial strains that are more virulent. For example, five years after penicillin was discovered, it showed signs of becoming less effective. What happened? In a word, the bacteria "evolved." When a species is challenged in such a way that most of its members are wiped out, the few that are genetically suited to survive will do so and reproduce after their own kind. This is known as *natural selection*.

- Antibiotics tend to weaken the body's natural defenses. For example, antibiotics destroy beneficial bacteria, which are actually an important part of our immune system. The body is weakened, thus paving the way for yet another infection and another round of antibiotics. In other words, the use of antibiotics is, by its very nature, self-perpetuating. The repeated use of antibiotics creates the need for more antibiotics. It creates a closed loop of dependency. First seeming to defeat an infection, while in the reality, the antibiotic leaves the host more susceptible for the next bout.

Vaccinations

Whereas antibiotics are used to knock out existing bacterial infections, vaccinations are used to render the individual immune to a given virus or bacteria. A vaccine consists of a killed or weakened microorganism that is associated with a given disease. The theory behind vaccinations is that the killed or weakened organism will not cause the disease but will trigger the body's immune system to mobilize its defenses against that disease.

Vaccinations are even more controversial than antibiotics. One reason is that many vaccinations have been made mandatory. Children are not admitted into schools unless they have been vaccinated against certain diseases. Some vaccinations are even being given at birth.

Aside from infringing on the individual's freedom of choice, there is a growing body of evidence suggesting that many of the vaccinations that were once considered safe and effective actually are not. Rather than mobilizing the immune system against one specific disease, many vaccinations weaken the immune system, as well as having other severe and sometimes fatal side effects.

Over the years, articles and books have been published by medical doctors and scientists (as well as parents who claimed that vaccinations were responsible for their children becoming severely ill or even dying) describing the problems with our past and current vaccination policies.

The studies that followed mandatory vaccinations for polio, measles, diphtheria, rubella, mumps, tetanus, pertussis and others, have revealed some recurring patterns:

- Mass vaccinations for a given disease did not lower the incidence of that disease.[83]
- Mass vaccinations against a given disease were sometimes followed by an *increase* in the incidents of the disease.[83]
- The highest incidents of the disease often occurred in individuals who were considered fully immunized.[84]
- The documented harmful side effects often outweigh any potential benefit.[83]

Ways of Boosting the Immune System

- **Good Nutrition.** Limit saturated fat, and avoid products made with refined carbohydrates (sugar and flour) and partially hydrogenated vegetable oils.
- **Chiropractic.** A properly functioning nervous system is essential for a smooth running immune system.
- **Massage.** A full body massage boosts the white blood cell count. Furthermore, as described in chapter 12, massage helps to de-stress the body, promoting balance between the sympathetic and parasympathetic divisions of the autonomic nervous system.
- **Exercise.** Exercise boosts circulation, allowing the cells to be more efficiently cleansed and nourished.
- **Vitamin C and Vitamin D3.** Both are vital for the immune system. Vitamin C is best obtained from fresh fruits and vegetables, anything else is second best. However, when whole-food sources of vitamin C are limited, supplementation can be beneficial. Vitamin D is best obtained from natural sun light, but here again, supplementation can be very helpful during stressful times, or when access to sunlight is limited.
- **Probiotics.** A big chunk of our immune system is actually rooted in the gastrointestinal tract, with the beneficial microbes playing a major role. The right kind of probiotic supplements can assist the body's defenses, especially after having taken antibiotics, which typically devastate our intestinal microbes.

Chapter 17
Blood Sugar

In my anatomy and physiology and nutrition classes, I would sometimes ask, "How many of you know someone who has diabetes?" Most of the students usually raise their hands. The incidents of blood sugar disorders have skyrocketed in recent years. If you have been in practice for a while, you have probably already treated a number of clients with substantial blood sugar issues. Many of them do not know that it is related to stress or that it is very treatable with diet and exercise.

How Does the Body Regulate Blood Sugar?

Our blood sugar is glucose. It is the primary fuel for our body cells. Fat provides an important secondary source, except for brain cells and red blood cells, which normally burn only glucose.

Since glucose is a simple sugar, the molecules are easily absorbed by the body cells. There are a number of hormones that influence the levels of glucose in the blood. The two primary hormones are insulin and glucagon, both produced by the pancreas.

As you may recall, the bulk of the pancreas is involved in the secretion of digestive enzymes, but also contains clumps of tissue called the Islets of Langerhans, which produce the two hormones. Glucagon, which is produced by the alpha cells, increases blood glucose, by stimulating the breakdown of glycogen in the liver. Insulin, which is produced by the beta cells, decreases blood glucose.

When large amounts of glucose enter the blood from the gut, the pancreas releases extra insulin, which causes our cells to absorb the glucose. Some of the glucose is burned for energy, and the rest is handled in one of two ways:

- It is converted into *glycogen* within the cells of the liver and muscles.
- It is converted into *fat* and stored in the fat-storage cells, located in the superficial fascia (under the skin) and around the internal organs.

Overworking the Pancreas

The ability of the pancreas to regulate blood glucose can be overtaxed by a number of factors. However, the bottom line is this: the amount of glucose that enters the blood (from the GI tract), exceeds the body's ability to move the sugar into the body cells. Logically, this log-jam of glucose in the blood can occur for one of two reasons (or both):

1. The amount of glucose moving from the gut into the blood is excessive. In other words, the individual is simply eating too many carbohydrates, or the wrong kind of carbohydrates.

2. The cells' ability to absorb the blood glucose has been compromised.

Most of the attention in addressing blood sugar problems has been on #1. However, #2 is equally important. Either way, glucose levels in the blood become too high. Either way, the pancreas has to produce extra insulin. If the insulin levels are too high, it "overshoots the mark." In other words, it pulls too much glucose out of the blood, resulting in blood glucose levels dropping too low. This is when the individual might feel the urge to eat more of the concentrated sugary foods that triggered the extra insulin release, in the first place. If this is done habitually, the individual develops **hypoglycemia,** a condition of chronically low blood sugar. The symptoms are fatigue, irritability, depression, moodiness and craving of sweets. Hypoglycemia is often associated with General Adaptation Syndrome. After a number of years, the hypoglycymia can progress to diabetes mellitus.

Diabetes Mellitus

Diabetes mellitus is a condition characterized by chronically high levels of glucose in the blood. The high levels are due to a decrease in the body's ability to move the glucose from the blood and into the body cells. The lack of proper nutrition of cells can lead to blindness, slow wound healing and ulcers, especially on the feet. In addition, the body responds to the lack of glucose availability to the cells by putting more fat into the blood, which increases the likelihood of atherosclerosis.

Excess blood glucose causes it to pass out through the urine, which in turn causes water to follow by osmosis. In other words, there is increased in urine production. Not surprisingly, a person with diabetes is thirsty a lot.

To understand how to treat diabetes mellitus, we must first understand its two forms: type I and type II:

- **Type I diabetes** is a condition in which the pancreas does not produce adequate amounts of insulin. This condition was formerly called juvenile diabetes, because it typically occurred in children. For many years, this condition was assumed to be entirely genetic. However, the genetic predisposition seems to require a trigger – diet. Apparently, certain foods can induce an autoimmune destruction of the insulin producing cells in the pancreas. This typically happens in response to chronic ingestion of allergens, most notably, dairy.[34]

- **Type II diabetes** is characterized by insulin resistance, wherein the body cells become "numb" to the presence of insulin, resulting in a gradual elevation of blood glucose. Insulin resistance forces the pancreas to secrete more insulin. Eventually, the pancreas becomes exhausted, insulin levels drop and blood sugar levels skyrocket. Since type II diabetes accounts for 90% of diabetic individuals, let us take a closer look at insulin resistance.

Insulin Resistance

Here are the major dietary and life-style factors that greatly influence the insulin sensitivity of our body cells:

- **Physical Activity.** The level of physical activity has a profound effect on insulin sensitivity. The more we exercise, the greater the insulin sensitivity, and vice versa.

- **Dehydration.** Insulin resistance and dehydration can form a positive feedback loop, wherein each contributes to the progression of the other. Specifically, dehydration makes the cells more resistance to insulin, which eventually causes an increase in blood sugar.[78] When blood glucose is high enough, it escapes through the urine. The presence of glucose in the urine results in greater water loss from the body, thus contributing to more dehydration, and therefore more insulin resistance, and so on. In other words, a simple way that an individual can promote proper blood sugar levels is to exercise regularly and make sure the body is well hydrated.

- **Stimulants.** Overstimulation of the adrenal glands results in high cortisol levels, which lead to insulin resistance. Caffeine is the main dietary stimulant that is used to arouse the already tired adrenal glands. Another one that is often consumed in large amount, usually without the person knowing it, is MSG, which is now used widely in restaurants and processed foods. Beyond the dietary stimulants, anything that over-stimulates the adrenal glands, including emotional stress and lack of sleep, can contribute to insulin resistance and blood sugar issues. Likewise, *anything that promotes stress reduction is likely to improve insulin sensitivity* (hint, hint).

- **Dietary Carbohydrates.** In addition to exhausting the pancreas, as described above, the chronic overconsumption or carbohydrates, especially refined sugars and refined grain products, leads to insulin resistance.
- **Dietary Fat.** Too much fat in the diet can trigger insulin resistance, as described below.

The Fat Factor

The role of refined or simply excessive amounts of refined carbohydrates in diabetes is widely recognized. However, a well-established, but often ignored, factor that contributes to insulin resistance is dietary fat in excessive amounts.[36] High levels of fat in the blood inhibit the absorption of other nutrients, such as glucose, into the body cells. The pancreas responds by secreting more insulin.

More specifically, fat can destabilize blood glucose in two ways: Extra bodyfat makes the pancreas work harder because the high fat content in the fat-storage cells makes them more insulin resistant. In addition, the fats circulating in the blood interfere with glucose uptake by *all* body cells. In one study, college students were given an abundance of fatty foods, such as eggs, cream, and butter. Within two days, their blood sugar elevated to diabetic levels.[57]

According to one study, a burger's worth of beef or three slices of cheddar cheese boost insulin levels more than two cups of cooked pasta. Baked goods, along with high protein foods, were found to trigger high secretion of insulin.[79] The fat, per se', may not cause the immediate insulin elevation (like carbohydrates and protein), but the long term effect of a high fat diet is an increase in insulin resistance, which means the body will be forced to secret more insulin. Likewise, low fat (high-carbohydrate) diets, done properly, seem to be effective in managing (or reversing) diabetes.[95, 96]

As previously mentioned, in the natural world, concentrated carbohydrates and fats do not occur together in the same food. However, this combination is quite popular with civilized humans: cookies, cakes, sweet bread, ice-cream, pizza, baked potatoes with sour cream or butter, potato chips, French fries, etc. The combination of concentrated carbohydrates and concentrated fats results in digestive disturbance and insulin resistance. It is a safe bet that the typical individual with type II diabetes got that way by chronically over-consuming foods that have unnaturally high levels of carbohydrates and fats.

Saturated fats, omega-6 fats (most vegetables oils) and trans-fats are especially problematical. Studies show that high levels of saturated fats in cell membranes are linked to increase in insulin resistance.[36] On the other hand, omega-3 fats (in the proper amounts) have been shown to promote insulin sensitivity and decrease blood sugar levels in diabetics.

Effect of High Insulin Levels

Besides causing blood sugar issues, insulin resistance has other serious long-term consequences. Since the cells are numbed to the presence of insulin, the pancreas is forced to produce higher levels of this hormone, which harms the body in a number of ways:

- Inhibits the secretion of growth hormone and thereby accelerates tissue degeneration.
- Stimulates arterial plaquing.
- Interferes with the removal of cholesterol from the blood.
- Damages the kidneys.
- Damages the retina of the eyes.

The Glycemic Index

The glycemic index is a measure of how readily a given food sends glucose into the blood. There are two ways of measuring the glycemic index. One system uses white flour as the reference to evaluate other foods. Another system uses pure glucose as the reference. In the latter system, the index ranges from 0 to 100. Pure glucose has the maximum value of 100. Using this system, the glycemic index of a given food is evaluated as follows:

Classification	range	Examples
Low GI	55 or less	Most fruits and vegetables, grainy breads, legumes, milk, pulses, fish, eggs, meat, some cheeses, nuts, cooking oil, brown rice.
Medium GI	56 - 69	Whole wheat products, basmati rice, sweet potatoes.
High GI	70 and above	Corn flakes, baked potato, watermelon, croissants, white bread, some breakfast cereals (e.g. rice krispies), straight glucose.

Glycemic Index Ratings

cherries (23)	corn (59)
grapefruit (26)	bananas (62)
lentils (29)	raisins (64)
milk (34)	soft drinks (68)
yogurt (36)	water melon (70)
chickpeas (36)	potatoes (70)
apples (39)	whole wheat bread (71)
spaghetti (42)	white rice (72)
grapes (45)	white bread (73)
oranges (46)	refined cereals (80)
oatmeal (54)	honey (87)
sweet potatoes (48)	cooked carrots (92)

The usefulness of the glycemic index in managing blood sugar levels is debated. Some nutritional authorities are cautious about placing too much weight on the glycemic index to evaluate a given food, because other factors, such as the fat and protein content and the presence of soluble fiber, vitamins and minerals may be more important than the glycemic index, regarding how the food will influence blood sugar. In general, however, individuals with blood sugar issues are well-advised to favor the lower glycemic foods.

In the above list, notice that the higher glycemic foods are cooked starchy foods and products made with refined sugar. These are the same foods that are often combined with fats, resulting in blood sugar chaos.

The Bigger Picture

Some authors advise caution or moderation on fruit consumption for individuals with blood sugar issues. As a general principle, this is a good idea; however, we must look at bigger picture:

- Most fruits are middle or low glycemic.
- The usual alternatives to fruit (as a way of getting calories) are cooked starchy vegetables and grains, which tend to have a higher glycemeic index than most raw fruits.
- The other alternative sources of calories are fatty foods, which can cause insulin resistance.
- Fresh fruits offer other benefits that often outweigh the glycemic index, such as the high level of soluble fiber, which helps to stabilize blood sugar (see below). In addition, some of the other nutrients in fruits

may have similar benefits. For example, pomegranate juice has a glycemic index of 67, but it also contains phytonutrients that help regulate blood glucose.

Soluble Fiber and Blood Sugar

Plant fiber, in general, slows down the passage of simple sugars into the blood. As you may recall, plant fiber is an indigestible complex carbohydrate. The soft fiber in fruit is called pectin, a form of soluble fiber which tends to be soft and absorbent. Soluble fiber is especially effective in stabilizing blood sugar. Though fruit pectin is the most readily available and abundant source of soluble fiber, it is also found in some vegetables, grains, legumes and seeds. Flax seeds are very rich in soluble fiber and have been shown to lower blood sugar.

Treating Diabetes and Maintaining Proper Blood Sugar

- Regular exercise is as important as proper nutrition for supporting the body in maintaining healthy blood sugar levels.
- Stay well hydrated.
- Eat whole foods, especially fresh fruits and vegetables, that are rich in soluble fiber, vitamins and minerals.
- Use moderation with foods that are high in fat or very concentrated carbohydrates. This includes oils, fatty animal products, dried fruit and fruit juice. Trans fats, refined sugars and white flour products should be avoided.
- Foods and supplements that have been used effectively in diabetes mellitus, include the following:
  - **Alpha-lipoic Acid**: Powerful antioxidant, encourages the absorption of glucose by the body cells, and relieves diabetic neuropathy (numbness of the extremities).
  - **N-Acetyl Cysteine**: Encourages the absorption of glucose by body cells.
  - **CoQ_{10}**: Powerful antioxidant, lowers blood sugar, and promotes proper utilization of glucose and oxygen.
  - **Omega-3 oils**: promote insulin sensitivity.

- **Chromium:** Promotes insulin sensitivity.
- **Zinc:** Promotes production and utilization of insulin.
- **Cinnamon:** Promotes insulin sensitivity and works synergistically with insulin to lower blood glucose.
- **Other Foods that lower blood sugar:** bitter melon, ginseng, cumin, cucumber, garlic, and any food that is rich in soluble fiber.

Yeast Overgrowth

High levels of glucose in the blood are often associated with yeast overgrowth. Yeast is a single-celled fungus. The one that grows in the body is called candida albicans. This is not the same as the yeast used in baking bread and brewing beer, which is called saccharomyces.

A certain amount of candida in the gastrointestinal tract is normal. Certain stressors create an environment that permits the yeast to overgrow. Such stressors include refined and highly concentrated carbohydrates, especially simple sugars, a high fat diet, hormonal problems, antibiotics, birth control pills, steroids, emotional stress, mercury fillings and alcohol. All of these weaken the immune system and promote the overgrowth of yeast.

Health problems associated with yeast overgrowth are fatigue, PMS, urinary tract infections, vaginitis, gas, bloating, depression, "brain fog," skin rashes, psoriasis, hives, headaches, feeling bad all over, athlete's foot and jock itch.

The Yeast-Free Diet

A yeast-free diet is designed to deprive the yeast of food. Different authors have varying views on how to eliminate candida over growth. There is general agreement that the following should be avoided:

- Refined carbohydrates, especially sweets
- Alcohol
- Condiments (vinegar and spices can be moldy)
- Processed and smoked meats
- Dried fruits
- Fruit juices (1/2 cup fresh squeezed is OK)
- Leftovers
- Coffee & tea
- Cheese

Beneficial Foods

- All vegetables.
- Chicken, fish, eggs, turkey, beef (2x week).
- Almonds, sunflower seeds.
- Whole Grains – brown rice, whole wheat, etc.
- A few pieces of fruit per day. Some authors will allow substantially more fruit, provided that the fat in the diet is restricted. Those who advocate a high fruit diet claim that we can eat a large amount of fruit while cleansing candida, provided that the fruit is fresh and the fat intake is low.[38]
- Anti-fungal agents: Pau'd Arco, caprylic acid, oregano oil, citrus extract.

After two to four weeks of following the above program, probiotics may be added to replace the beneficial intestinal bacteria. You might feel worse as the yeast in your system starts to die and give off toxins. You can experience cravings for foods that will feed the yeast, such as sweets.

Chapter 18

Counseling Your Client on Weight Loss

Virtually all the dietary systems that have emerged in recent years are marketed, at least partially, for their ability to facilitate weight loss. This is quite understandable since obesity has reached epidemic proportions in industrialized nations, with the United States leading the pack. There are two primary reasons for this:

- Decrease in physical activity.
- Increase in the consumption of foods that are simultaneously rich in macronutrients (calories) and deficient in micronutrients (vitamins, minerals and phytonutrients).

These two factors translate into the body ingesting more calories than it can burn on any given day, with the excess stored as body fat. Likewise, effective and safe weight loss is a matter of increasing physical activity and decreasing the consumption of high-calorie/low-nutrient foods. Yes, it is that simple. However, "simple" is not the same as "easy." Below is a more detailed summary of what we know about safe and effective weight loss. Once we grasp these basic principles, simple can also become easy.

The Stop Signal

The same instinct that tells us what to eat, also tells us when to stop. The stop signal (satiation) is activated in response to three primary factors:

- **The presence of bulk in the stomach.** As the stomach becomes fuller, we feel less inclined to eat. It is not so much the weight of the food, but the volume.
- **The presence of sufficient calories.** The more calories that are present in a given food, the more quickly we feel satiated.
- **The presence of sufficient micronutrients in the foods.**

More than likely, there are other nutritional factors that tell the brain when it is time to stop eating. In addition, the emotional factors that are also ever present must be respectfully recognized, if any diet is going to work.

The good news is that, once they have been recognized, the three core factors described above are fairly easy and straightforward to work with. Ideally, all three factors should be present in just the right amounts to give us the feeling of satiation, while meeting our nutritional needs. This is what we generally encounter in unprocessed whole foods. The more we consume foods that are reasonably close to the way Nature presents them, the more clearly our innate intelligence can guide us in consuming the right amount of food. On the other hand, as foods become more processed, the three satiation factors become progressively unbalanced. The typical result is the over-consumption of calories, which are stored in the body as fat.

Nature Has the Answer

If we look to the natural world, with an eye that has been sensitized to our current weight issues, we cannot help but notice a conspicuous absence of obesity in wild animals. Neither do we see obesity in pre-industrialized societies that live on whole un-processed foods. Likewise, our ancestors living in the wild were unlikely to become obese, because they simply did not have the luxury of being able of over-consuming protein, fats and carbohydrates. On the contrary, their main challenge was to get sufficient amounts of these macronutrients. In other words, their top priority was to get enough calories to keep from starving. In contrast, the situation is reversed for most humans living in industrialized nations. Specifically, there are three main features in modern diets that produce obesity:

- Unlike our ancestors, we have an abundance of high-calorie foods, in the form of grains, starchy vegetables and animal products, which sets the stage for obesity and the other health issues associated with it. The body we inherited from our ancestors is simply not designed to deal with extra calories for an extended period of time.
- These same high-calorie foods are relatively low in bulk (fiber) and micronutrients, resulting in a delay of satiation. This is especially true for the highly refined products, such as white flour, sugar and vegetable oils, which have had most of their fiber (bulk) and micronutrients removed. To complicate matters, most processed foods have been specifically blended and spiced to maximize consumption. Therefore, by the time the stomach is full enough to give us a good clear stop signal, we have over consumed calories.
- Eating too many calories is especially easy when the diet has both an abundance of carbohydrates *and* fats. This confuses the brain and stresses

the body, because the combination of high carbohydrates and high fat typically does not occur in whole foods provided by Nature. Either one, when consumed in excess, gets stored as body fat, but if the extra calories consist of carbohydrates *and* fats in the same meal, we have a double whammy for rapid weight gain: The body will preferentially burn the ingested carbohydrates for the immediate energy needs, while storing most of the ingested fat. This is because the body is designed to be as efficient as possible with energy. Carbohydrates are easier and "cheaper" to burn, while fat is easier to store. Fat is the ideal way for animals to store surplus fuel, because it packs the maximum calories in the minimum amount of space and the least amount of weight. It also does not require any major alterations; it literally goes from your GI tract to your hips. In contrast, the body must expend substantial energy to convert extra carbohydrates into body fat. Therefore, the body will do so only if it has more carbohydrates than it can burn or store as glycogen.

Four Principles for Safe and Effective Weight Loss

Once we understand the issues that produce obesity, we can easily grasp these four principles for safe and effective weight loss

- **In addition to facilitating weight loss, the diet should promote overall health.** In other words, the diet that allows you to lose weight should also support a healthy heart, blood vessels, kidneys, immune system, blood sugar, bones and joints.
- **The amount of calories that are burned must exceed the calories that are ingested.** This is generally accomplished by exercising more and eating fewer calories. Any weight loss system that claims to circumvent this principle is in denial of the laws of physics, or is simply forcing the body to make metabolic changes that are, ultimately, unhealthy.
- **Replace some of those refined high-calorie foods, with unprocessed fruits and low-starch vegetables.** Fruits and vegetables are relatively low in calories, while providing large amounts of fiber and micronutrients that give us a feeling of satiation. This can be accomplished by using either the low-carb or low-fat approach, described in Chapter 8.
- **The diet can feature substantial amounts of carbohydrates or fats, *but not both*.** The individual must restrict one or the other, because high levels of both encourage the over-consumption of calories, and sets up the physiological conditions that trigger blood sugar issues and fat storage.

The low-carb diets tend to produce a more rapid weight loss, compared to the low-fat diets. One of the reasons that weight loss tends to occur more rapidly with low-carb diets is that the digestion and metabolism of protein and fat takes longer and requires the body to expend more energy. In other words, the body must work harder (burn more calories) when it has to process larger amounts of fats and protein. This is especially true for protein, which requires the greatest energy expenditure by the body, of the three macronutrients. This may not seem like a problem, and might actually seem like a good thing, since expending more energy translates into faster weight loss. However, faster is not necessarily better. As described in chapter 8, the individual must be mindful of not ingesting too much fat and protein, because they can produce toxicity, especially the latter.

Given the potential toxic effects of too much dietary fat and protein, individuals who choose the low-carb approach for weight loss are advised to make sure that the diet has enough carbohydrate foods to prevent the overconsumption of protein and fats, as well as providing the critically important micronutrients. For example, the Paleolithic Diet recommends that 50% of daily calories come from plant foods, most of which is in the form of fruits and vegetables, with modest amounts of nuts and seeds.

For individuals who do not tolerate substantial amounts of fat and protein, or simply are concerned about the long-term effects of a high-protein and fat diet, the low-fat approach can be just as effective in weight loss, though it might take longer. The individual must simply reduce the high-calorie grains and starchy vegetables, while increasing fruits and low-starch vegetables. An example of such a diet is the one recommended by Dr. Joel Fuhrman, in his book, *Eat to Live*. With such a diet, even though total calories are moderately reduced, the individual can still feel satiated, because the other two signals of satiation (fiber and micronutrients) are abundantly present. For the same reason, this sort of diet has been associated with cardiovascular health, strong bones, limber joints, cancer prevention and reversal of diabetes.

Raw vegetables are especially effective for weight loss, because they are rich in fiber and micronutrients, while having the least amount of calories of all the food groups. In fact, most raw vegetables actually cause the body to burn more calories than the food provides! In other words, *the more vegetables you eat, the more rapidly you lose weight* – healthfully.

What to Tell Your Clients

Here are the key points to explain to your clients who are interested in weight loss:

- **Burn more calories than you consume.** In clear and simple terms, explain to them that the amount of calories they burn must exceed the calories they ingest, which means they need to increase exercise and reduce the consumption of high-calorie foods.
- **Eat for Health.** Tell your clients that the easiest and healthiest strategy for weight-loss is to replace some of the processed high-calorie foods with fresh fruits and low-starch vegetables. Explain to them how this will reduce their overall calories, while still providing the body with the fiber, vitamins and minerals that are essential for health.
- **Eat a moderate amount of high-calorie foods.** These foods are consumed in portions that are small enough to allow for healthy weight loss, while large enough to provide sufficient fuel and building material to maintain the body in a healthy state. The moderate amount of high-calorie foods should include relatively clean sources of protein, fats and carbohydrates, such as grass-fed beef, free range poultry, wild caught fish, occasional eggs, beans, whole grains and starchy vegetables (like potatoes and squash).
- **Favor either low-fat or low-carb meals.** By avoiding eating foods in the same meal that are simultaneously high in carbohydrates and fat, the individual will be less likely to overeat. Virtually all successful weight loss programs do this. For example, if the meal has a substantial amount of meat or cheese, the person would avoid high-starch foods or use them sparingly. If the meal has a substantial amount of high starch foods, such as potatoes, bread or rice, the person would avoid animal products or use them sparingly. This means that all foods that are rich in both carbohydrates and fats (cookies, cakes, candies, pizza and many other processed foods) are reduced, though not necessarily eliminated. The more these foods are restricted, the more rapid the weight-loss.
- **Listen to your Body.** Tell your clients, "No one knows your body better than you. Consult with the experts, but remember that you are in charge." All else being equal, the low-carb approach seems to work faster. However, either strategy works. It is a matter of what is most appropriate and doable for the individual. You do not have to figure out which approach is better for your clients. They will tell you!
- **Be Firm and Flexible.** Since the body changes over time, so do our nutritional needs. Remind your client that it is okay to make course corrections. Stay with the program that works, and be willing to make changes when the body requires it.

You can supplement your nutritional guidance by giving your clients the article on weight loss, in the appendix of this book. Naturally, if a client has major health issues, other than extra body-weight, you should advise him or her to consult with a primary health care provider, before making major dietary changes.

Chapter 19
Depression and Addiction

Can massage help individuals with these conditions? The answer is yes. Even before there was much scientific validation for it, there was apparently an understanding among psychology professionals that touching the body is good for the mind.

Massage therapists often team up with psychotherapists. In fact, in the many years that I have been involved in massage education, I have noticed that individuals troubled by depression or addictions are sometimes guided (often by other institutions or their psychotherapists) to enroll in massage school.

Both depression and addiction are apparently associated with stress[68,70]. Therefore, both are likely to benefit from nutritional support and massage, as discussed in chapter 12. Massage provides the neurological input that allows the nervous system to "reset" itself, while nutritional support provides the brain with the needed nutrients. Working on both fronts at the same time is likely to produce better results than either one working alone.

Depression and addiction are prevalent in industrialized nations. However, unlike the other "civilized diseases," like diabetes and heart disease, depression and addiction are less socially acceptable, more difficult to talk about and easier to conceal — until they are too problematic to keep hidden. When the individual finally does address the issue, the connection to stress can be made, and healing can begin.

Stress and Depression

As the body goes deeper into GAS, the mind is more likely to experience depression. In fact, some individuals go to a massage therapist (perhaps unconsciously) as a way of addressing their chronic depression. When such individuals tell you, "I'm stressed out," they might actually be saying, "I'm depressed."

Massage can help with depression in several subtle ways. For example, physical touch has been shown to trigger the release of serotonin, a neurotransmitter in the brain which tends to be low in individuals who have depression. However, the level of stress might be deep enough as to limit the benefits of massage. Depressed clients might give up on massage and, in their urgency for relief, resort to legal and illegal drugs, which often have harmful side effects. For such individuals, any guidance you can offer in nutrition and life-style can make a significant difference and complement the therapeutic effect of your work.

Here are some specific ways of helping to lift depression, while reducing GAS:

- **Physical Activity.** Regular exercise has been shown to be quite beneficial in lifting **depression. Exercise, like loving touch, increases production of serotonin.**
- **Sun Light**. In the winter, lack of sunlight can contribute to depression by disrupting the production of hormones and neurotransmitters. Getting extra sunlight or spending time under a sun lamp can be beneficial.
- **Vitamin D.** Lack of sunlight in the winter can result in low levels of vitamin D, which has been associated with depression. Such individuals often experience a lifting of depression when they take a vitamin D supplement.[72]
- **Adequate cholesterol levels**. Too much cholesterol in the blood is not good for cardiovascular health, but low cholesterol levels can contribute to depression.[63] This is important to know, for vegans and individuals on cholesterol lowering drugs.
- **Adequate protein.** Not enough protein can lead to depression.[50] Lack of protein can deprive the brain of the amino acids needed to make adequate amounts of certain neurotransmitters. For example, serotonin is made from the amino acid, tryptophan. However, low dietary protein is just one of many factors that may contribute to depression. Since excessive protein results in toxicity (and might also *contribute* to depression), one should not blindly load up on protein as a shot gun approach for treating the depression, but rather to get adequate protein. Unfortunately, there is disagreement as to the appropriate amount of protein. This, in my opinion, reflects the variations in dietary needs among humans. As a rule of thumb, the proper amount of protein to feed the brain is the same amount that allows for proper nourishing and cleansing of the body as a whole.
- **Omega-3 oils.** These oils, especially DHA and EPA, have been shown to improve depression.[39, 40]

DHA and the Brain

In addition to being linked to depression, lack of DHA has been associated with impulsiveness, aggression, reduced intelligence, sleep problems, temper tantrums, alcoholism, schizophrenia, and manic depression.[86,87] One study showed that when women supplemented with DHA during pregnancy and lactation, children's IQ at 4 years of age was higher, compared to control groups.[88]

Stress and Addiction

Addiction has been linked to environmental stress.[71] One of the single greatest stressors, which perpetuates suffering in the present and paves the way for disease in the future, is your client's relationship to food. Not surprisingly, that relationship is often addictive.

One reason some foods are addictive is that they stimulate the adrenal glands. We can become addicted to any substance that gives us that subtle adrenal rush Furthermore, some foods have opiate-like substances or produce opiates in the body, during digestion. Here are some common foods that could have addictive qualities:

- **Grains** and some other seeds – contain opiates. For example, wheat contains about fifteen opiates.
- **Dairy protein** – produces opiate-like substances when broken down in the body.
- **Cooked food** in general might produce a subtle stimulation the adrenal glands, as well as alert the immune system.[99, 100]
- **Caffeine** – stimulates the adrenal glands.
- **Red meat** – contains high levels of uric acid, which stimulate the adrenal glands, similar to caffeine.
- **MSG** (monosodium glutamate) found in many processed foods, and used widely in restaurants, especially fast-foods, over-stimulate neurons in the brain.
- **Many allergens,** such as peanuts, are addictive by virtue of the fact that they stimulate the adrenal glands.
- **Alcoholic beverages**– have a numbing effect on neurons, resulting in a reduction of physical pain and anxiety. In addition, such products are made from fermented plant foods which often contain allergens that produce a low-grade stimulation of the adrenal glands.

As with many other addictions, food addictions are usually not recognized as such, but are concealed behind a vale of denial or rationalizations. Even if the addiction is recognized, it tends to assert itself anyway, overpowering the will and putting to shame our best intentions. When will-power tries to overcome our feelings (in this case, cravings), the latter generally wins. In this regard, food addiction is especially powerful and subtle, because, unlike a drug or an obviously abusive relationship, we cannot just "leave it." One way or another, you have got to eat!

As with other addictions, food addictions are perpetuated by physical or emotional stress. Individuals who intentionally change their diets, often go back to the familiar foods during stressful situations. When we are stressed out, we reach for the comfort-foods to sedate us, and then, we reach for the stimulants to get us going again. In other words, GAS opens the door to addictions, which then deepens GAS, which, in turn, deepens the addictions, etc.

If the above description gives you the impression that addiction is like a monster that is too powerful to defeat, take heart. There is a way out.

Overcoming Addiction

Logically, if stress perpetuates addiction, stress-reduction techniques can be (and have been) used to help free the individual from addiction. This is an obvious lead-in to massage, however, before we even get to that, we should remember that most of the stress experienced by the average individual (like your stressed-out clients) is self-inflicted. It commonly shows up as harsh judgment. To be continuously badgered is stressful, and it is no less stressful when the badgering is self-inflicted.

Like other addictions, food addiction thrives on harsh judgment. There are two reasons for this:

- When we habitually condemn ourselves, we will eventually seek comfort. The typical response is to use the coping mechanism with which we are most familiar.
- Every time we condemn ourselves or others, we stimulate the adrenal glands, thus adding to the existing GAS, which feeds the addictions. In fact, it would not be unreasonable to suggest that we become addicted to harsh judgment for the same reason that we become addicted to caffeine — it stimulates the adrenal glands!

In particular, addiction is perpetuated by the self-recrimination that often follows the repeated fall from the proverbial wagon. This can become yet another vicious cycle that drives us more deeply into GAS. However, this also provides us with a simple key to unlock the door of the addiction prison.

As surely as harsh judgment tightens the knot of addiction, kindness loosens it. Perhaps it does not do the job as quickly as we would like, but kindness does the job, in its own time and season. Yes, it is that simple. We just have to remember that simple is not necessarily synonymous with "easy" or "fast."

Kindness Gets Clinical

Kindness can be extended to anyone, whether they are in pain or not. We give and receive kindness simply because that is one of the ways we nurture each other. The giving and receiving of kindness reduces stress. The happy feelings associated with kindness have been linked to the release of the feel-good neurotransmitters in the brain.

When kindness is applied to one who is facing physical, mental or emotional challenges, we call it compassion. If kindness is food for the soul, compassion is the medicine.

Just as kindness nourishes both the giver and receiver, compassion brings healing to both the giver and receiver. Our human sensibilities are designed to thrive on the regular giving and receiving of this "energy," whether it is the food called kindness or the medicine called compassion. Without this regular exchange, we become quietly desperate and unconsciously grasp for anything that can ease the emotional pain.

As with the kindness that we (hopefully) give and receive throughout the day, the giving of compassion is also normal and natural. It is natural to desire to help someone who has fallen. To empathize with someone who is suffering or struggling, and to wish to lend a hand, is as natural as smiling when we are happy or crying when we are sad.

What is often difficult is to keep the compassion flowing in a clinical setting where we are being paid to extend healing service. It might be especially difficult to extend compassion when the individual's troubles seem to be self-inflicted — which is often the case with individuals who are stressed out and addicted. However, that is generally NOT the real reason we withhold compassion. Clinical setting or not, the withholding of compassion has little to do the worthiness of the receiver. It has to do with the mind of the giver, as described below.

The Key to Compassion

The key that unlocks the door to compassion is the understanding that it cannot be given to one person if it is withheld from another. The compassion described above, which brings healing to both the giver and receiver, is not the superficial compassion that is given to a perceived victim and withheld from the perceived villain, for this is just self-indulgence in disguise. I am referring to the deep compassion that is born of the mother called truthfulness and the father called mindfulness. When we practice truthfulness and mindfulness, we naturally give birth to compassion, without forcing or straining. The daily practice of truthfulness deeply nourishes our capacity for compassion, while mindfulness supports, sustains, energizes and enlivens our truthfulness.

We cannot help but bring forth compassion when we are truthful, because when we express our truth, we relate. To relate is to emotionally connect. To connect is to recognize oneself in the other person. To recognize oneself in the struggling or suffering individual is to feel compassion.

Likewise, to withhold compassion from others requires that we deny or reject the part of one self that is connected to the other. Whether we know it or not, compassion withheld from others, is compassion withheld from self. The two are inseparable.

For health care providers, it means that if we withhold nurturing and kindness from self, we will withhold it from those we serve. This is usually done unconsciously. One simple way to know that we are withholding kindness from self is that we are harsh or critical of others, or coldly indifferent to their suffering. Under such circumstances, the most respectful thing we can do is to be mindful enough of our own internal condition to refrain from harming others.

Do No Harm

Hippocrates, the recognized father of Western medicine, realized that harmlessness is the necessary prerequisite for healing. The Buddha recognized the same principle on the larger social level. Hippocrates said, "Above all else, do no harm." Similarly, Buddhist philosophy says that if you cannot be kind and helpful to others, then, at the very least, do no harm. The same philosophy advises the individual to give compassion to self before extending it to others.

The possibility of doing harm to others is very real as long as we withhold kindness and compassion from ourselves. This is precisely why the words of Hippocrates and the Buddha still have value for us today, especially health professionals.

The simple guidance given to us by these two Masters from the ancient world provide powerful instruction, reminding us that self respect and service to others are inseparable. Thus, we free ourselves from the mistaken idea that it is possible to bring healing to others by first abusing ourselves, or that we can nourish others by starving ourselves. Such subtle indulgence in martyrdom might give us the consolation of noble suffering, but ultimately becomes yet another addiction.

The moment that we do become aware that kindness toward self and others are inseparable, we tend to relax and soften, and real compassion starts to spontaneously flow into all the hurting places, inside and outside. There is no thought of reserving it for the worthy and withholding it from the unworthy; the very idea is meaningless. There is no need to ration it, for the supply seems vast beyond measure. It must be given freely and unconditionally, or it cannot be given at all. When it is set free, it flows abundantly and with such ease and grace, that we cannot take credit for it — as if it were emanating from a source beyond the separate self.

Genuine compassion, when extended to others, is the voice that says, "That person could be me." Compassion toward others flows naturally when you see that the individual who seems angry, scared, self-destructive or otherwise acting "unconsciously," could be you, given the right set of circumstances. Such compassion does not require years of spiritual training, but rather, the capacity to just be honest with oneself. Such compassion is what carries you across the threshold, from the realm of the therapist to that of the healer.

Compassion, given or received, stops our inner warfare. This is how the vicious cycle of self-hatred and addiction is ended. This is how we slow down and stop the downward spiral of general adaptation syndrome, and replace it with an upward spiral of relaxation and healing.

Your Stressed-out Client's Food Addictions

On the more practical side of relating to your clients, if stress perpetuates addiction and depression, stress reduction techniques can certainly help to reverse them. Massage is the easy part. However, the benefits of the massage can be limited, because many individuals struggling with depression and addictions unknowingly perpetuate their condition with the foods and beverages they ingest every day.

Should you try to get them to change their diet or give up their coffee or alcohol? In general, the answer is no. Challenging them in that manner usually adds to the existing stress. If you feel yourself urgently wanting to "save them from themselves," or judging them harshly for not taking better care of themselves, that is the time to look into their eyes and remind yourself that their innate intelligence is smarter than your educated intelligence.

The demon we call addiction is, indeed, too subtle and powerful to defeat, as long as we perceive it as a demon that must be defeated. Instead, you, as the therapist, can simply encourage your client to rediscover the simple pleasure of eating delicious fresh fruit; whichever fruit appeals to them, as much as they want (provided they do not have a major blood sugar issue, in which case you can gently guide them to the lower glycemic fruits). Tell them once, and then do not even mention it again, unless they seem genuinely interested in receiving further support in this area. The more they eat fresh and raw fruits and vegetables (when doing so feels easy, natural and pleasurable), the more they reawaken their instinct for food selection. If your client seems receptive to this, you might also suggest some of the techniques for awakening the eating instinct in chapter 9.

In other words, the focus is not so much on abstaining from the habits that perpetuate their suffering, but rather on doing something that brings pleasure in the present moment, while helping to gently cleanse and nourish the body. This is about getting in touch with what it feels like to eat something you love — that also loves you back.

As your client begins to feel better physically, he or she will be even more motivated to eat foods that simultaneously taste good and promote health. The individual will tend to spontaneously decrease the consumption of the problematic food, until it reaches a level that is no longer problematic. As previously stated, when we eat enough raw fruits and vegetables, our own instincts will, more than likely, guide us to eat anything else that the body might need, whether it happens to be starchy foods, animal products or nuts and seeds.

One subtle way that fresh fruit can complement your work in stress reduction is by gently helping the brain maintain optimum brain chemistry. For example, many fruits contain nutrients, such as flavonoids, which can help raise serotonin levels in the brain.[63] Meanwhile, your massage work will also silently assist in raising the serotonin levels, as well as balancing the sympathetic and parasympathetic divisions of the autonomic nervous system, so the adrenal glands and the rest of the body can finally get some rest.

Your Brain on Fruits and Vegetables

Some flavonoids seem to have subtle but powerful effects on brain chemistry, such as promoting higher levels of neurotransmitters (serotonin) and hormones (melatonin) that are associated with positive mental and emotional states. Specifically, flavonoids seem to be anticonvulsive, anti-depressant and mood-elevating. They reduce anxiety, calm the mind, facilitate muscle relaxation, and might be beneficial in Parkinson's disease.[98]

Flavonoids are largely responsible for the mental and emotional benefits associated with certain herbs, such as ginkgo biloba, chamomile, St. John's wart and passion flower. However, the same brain-active flavonoids are found in commonly available fruits and vegetables. Studies done with flavonoid-rich fruits and isolated flavonoids indicate that these phytonutrients have the potential to protect neurons against injury, improve memory and cognition, and might help to prevent cerebrovascular problems (strokes).[98]

In other words, one of the hidden contributing factors for the high incidence of depression and addictions in industrialized nations might be the lack of flavonoids and other phytonutrients that are normally provided by an abundance of fruits and vegetables.

Long ago, our ancestors had to change from a diet of fruits and vegetables to one that was calorically dominated by grains, meat and dairy. They were obviously able to survive, but apparently, optimum brain function still requires that our brain cells be continuously bathed in a rich chemical soup that is supposed to include an abundance of plant-derived flavonoids.

The Body Awakens

When the body is allowed to physiologically rest, its innate capacity for self-healing awakens. It slowly and quietly undergoes a biochemical transformation, reversing the various manifestations of GAS. As stress hormones go down, so does insulin resistance. Therefore, the brain's favorite fuel, glucose, can reach the cells more easily. Since less insulin is needed, the insulin-producing cells in the pancreas can take a breather, too. Furthermore, since the tissues of the body are finally being adequately nourished and cleansed, the adrenal alarm is switched off, and the sympathetic system is toned down, allowing the body to conserve energy and build up its reserves.

Meanwhile, the levels of serotonin, melatonin and growth hormone go up, which allow for even deeper rest and regeneration. The individual is set free from that sense of quiet desperation that comes from being at war with self and feeling powerless to stop it. The mind and body are no longer at odds with each other; each gets what it needs. Thinking becomes clear and emotions flow more freely and happily. The tissues are no longer suffocated from lack of oxygen. Brain cells can finally rest and regenerate, because they are finally receiving a steady supply of nutrients, without having to be constantly slammed with insulin, cortisol and an endless barrage of stimulants and sedatives. Gradually, the individual can de-stress to the point where he or she may not be so dependent on food for sedation or stimulation.

Through time, the sense of taste becomes progressively liberated — restored to its original function of simply providing pleasure in the present moment, through the ingestion of foods that are both delicious and nutritious.

In other words, this process does not require a will of iron. You, as the therapist, do not have to tell your client to give up anything. That decision, if it is right, comes entirely from within the client.

This process is about inviting an inner sense of ease that makes draconian abstinence unnecessary, because the problematical substances are no longer desired or no longer problematical. Eventually, the repressed needs and desires that had been projected on food, such as the need for loving touch, emotional closeness, creative expression and spiritual communion, are gradually reclaimed – without you having to say a word.

A series of full body massages, supported by the simple act of eating delicious fresh fruit (when the person feels like it), might quietly and modestly awaken an ancient memory of the deep primordial connection between loving touch and good nutrition; a memory that dates back to the first time that the infant nursed on the mother's breast.

If all this seems a bit lofty, bear in mind that the process described above is not a magical and instantaneous transformation. Nor is it likely to occur on our pre-set time schedule. Neither does it always look as pretty as we would like. It is, rather, a gradual inner journey that is best completed when it is allowed to proceed in accordance with the person's unique cycles and seasons, which are barely known to the individual and totally unknown to the therapist. Therefore, the rule of thumb in supporting anyone with their depression, food issues or some form of substance abuse is to say as little as possible.

Just put the food on the table, and let them eat if and when they want to. Beyond making the suggestion to eat delicious fresh fruit when they feel like it, you, as the therapist, are just doing your massage as effectively and respectfully as you know how.

APPENDIX

Information for Your Clients

Study Guide for You

Information for Your Clients

This section consists of various articles on health and well-being. Each is designed to be suitable for the general public, with an emphasis on individuals that are likely to seek massage. Feel free to copy this information and give it to your clients.

Overcoming Stress

A Cure for Fibromyalgia

Nutrition in a Nut Shell

Selecting Your Food

Fasting

A Guide to Milk Alternatives

Losing Weight Safely and Effectively

How to Keep Your Brain Youthful

Facts on Mercury Dental Fillings

Is Your Cookware Safe?

The Gluten-Free Diet

The Seventh-Day Adventist Health Plan

Fruitarian and Massage Therapist

Living Foods

All articles were written by the author, unless otherwise indicated.

Overcoming Stress

What is Stress?

Stress is anything that challenges your body. Stress can be physical or psychological. A moderate amount of stress is appropriate and actually necessary to maintain health. However, when the stress is excessive, the body undergoes a number of unhealthy changes. The technical term for these changes is *General Adaptation Syndrome*. When your body goes into General Adaptation Syndrome, it becomes depleted of energy and is unable to repair and regenerate as well as it should. In essence, the body starts aging faster.

Short Term Effects of Stress
- Fatigue
- Mood swings
- Depression
- Unrestful sleep
- Craving sweet

Long Term Effects of Stress
- Depressed immune system
- Allergies
- Fibromyalgia
- Cardiovascular Disease
- Cancer
- Diabetes Mellitus
- Death of brain cells, especially those involved in memory and orientation.

How to Overcome Stress
- *Good Nutrition.* The body needs the raw material necessary to strengthen itself in the presence of stress, especially B vitamins, minerals and omega-3 oils.
- *Get some rest.* The body must have rest and quiet time in order to recover its energy and regenerate.

- *Exercise.* Exercise promotes regeneration in a number of ways, such as facilitating restful sleep.
- *Massage therapy.* When the body becomes stressed out enough, it tends to remain that way and "forgets" how to relax and regenerate. An effective way of helping the body to remember is through touch. Massage is one of the most potent therapeutic tools to get the body out of General Adaptation Syndrome. For this purpose, a series of massage treatments (10-12) is recommended.
- *Give Yourself 90 Days.* Any health-promoting activity that is done consistently and mindfully for about three months is likely to make a significant change in your health. In this case, taking the time to de-stress the body through exercise, rest, good nutrition and massage. These four health-promoting activities combined will help the body greatly reduce the short-term and long-term effects of stress listed above, as well as promote greater health and longevity.

A Cure for Fibromyalgia

Fibromyalgia is typically the result of chronic stress. Symptoms can also appear suddenly after a very stressful episode, such as illness or trauma. One of the physiological changes that accounts for the pain in fibromyalgia is lack of growth hormone, which is important for maintain healthy tissues. The underproduction of growth hormone seems to be due, at least partially, to disturbed sleep; in particular, the individual has trouble reaching the deep, dreamless sleep, during which growth hormone secretion greatly increases. When healthy test subjects are deprived of deep dreamless sleep for three weeks, they develop the symptoms of fibromyalgia.

Symptoms

- Widespread pain with tenderness
- Non-refreshing sleep, morning stiffness
- Fatigue, anxiety and depression
- Digestive disturbances
- Dizziness and palpitations

Treatment

- **Exercise** promotes a number of positive changes, such increased production of growth hormone.
- **Rest**, especially deep restful sleep, is essential for regeneration for a number of reasons — such as increased production of growth hormone.
- **Relaxing Herbs,** such as valerian, hops and passion flower can promote safe and restful sleep.
- **Good Nutrition.** The body needs the proper nutrients to strengthen itself in the presence of the stress. Specifically, it needs an abundance of B vitamins, Vitamin C and omega-3 oils, preferably from whole foods.
- **Remove monosodium glutamate (MSG) from diet.** Research indicates that removal of monosodium glutamate from the diet can eliminate or greatly reduce pain from fibromyalgia. MSG overexcites the nervous system,

inhibits the secretion of growth hormone, and stimulates the secretion of the stress hormones from the adrenal glands. MSG is found in many packaged foods. It is commonly used in Chinese restaurants and fast-food restaurants.

- **Malic acid and magnesium.** Taken together, they can reduce the pain and fatigue associated with fibromyalgia.
- **Massage therapy.** In fibromyalgia, the body has forgotten how to relax. It is stuck in a vicious cycle, where one stressor leads to another. An effective way of helping the body remember how to relax is through touch. A series of full body massages (10-12) helps to reduce pain, for short term relief, as well as helping to restore balance to the body, so it can gather its self-healing power to correct the fibromyalgia.

Nutrition in a Nut Shell

Healthy eating is not one-size-fits-all. One person may handle beans very well, while another may not. Furthermore, nutritional needs can change within the same person as time passes. However, there are some commonalities, which are described below.

The Basics

The three major nutrients that we extract from food are carbohydrates, fats and protein. In addition to these three main nutrients, we need smaller amounts of vitamins and minerals and phytonutrients.

- *Protein* is the brick and mortar of the body. Protein is the major building material for making our bones, muscles, skin, nerves, blood vessels and internal organs.
- *Carbohydrates* are the preferred fuel of the body. Carbohydrates are burned (broken down) to provide us with the energy we need to stay alive and healthy.
- *Fats* have several functions, such as providing us with an important second source of fuel, so the body is not totally dependent on carbohydrates. In addition to their fuel value, fats are used to build our tissues, especially the brain and nerves, as well as providing regulatory functions.
- *Vitamins, minerals and phytonutrients* are used mainly for their regulatory roles and, therefore, are needed in smaller amounts, compared to protein, carbohydrates and fats. Phytonutrients are thousands of different chemicals found in plants that we need to maintain a healthy body.

Opinions vary regarding the requirements for these nutrients. Furthermore, in recent years, other nutritional concerns have been voiced besides the presence of proteins, carbohydrates, fats, vitamins, minerals and phytonutrients. For example:

- **Fiber.** We need lots of plant fiber to maintain a healthy digestive system.
- **A Balance of Cleansing Foods and Building Foods.** Building foods are the ones that are rich in proteins, carbohydrates and fats. Cleansing foods

include most fruits and green leafy vegetables, especially in their raw state. Cleansing foods tend to be rich in fiber and water. Green leafy vegetables also have chlorophyll, which is the chemical that makes plants green. Chlorophyll is Mother Nature's own internal cleanser.

- **Raw and Unprocessed Foods.** Ideally, we should consume some food in its raw state because cooking destroys many nutrients and generates byproducts that may be toxic to the body.

- **80% alkaline-forming foods and 20% acid-forming foods.** In order for the body to be healthy, it must have the proper acid/alkaline balance. To achieve this, the diet should consist of 80% alkaline-forming foods and 20% acid-forming foods. Alkaline-forming foods leave an alkaline residue in the blood. Acid-forming foods leave an acidic residue in the blood. The main alkaline-forming foods are fruits and vegetables. Acid-forming foods include animal products and most grains, nuts and seeds. The typical diet in industrialized nations, consisting mostly of acid forming foods, increases the toxic burden on the body, promotes degenerative diseases and accelerates aging. Likewise, a favorable acid/alkaline balance encourages cleansing and regeneration, lessens painful conditions and promotes mental clarity and emotional calmness.

- **Moderation with Animal Products.** Animal products tend to be very acid-forming, can overburden the body with toxic residue and contribute to the onset of degenerative diseases, such as heart disease, hardening of the arteries, cancer and arthritis. Therefore, individuals who eat animal products should include a generous helping of cleansing foods, especially raw green leafy vegetables.

- **Moderation with Grains.** Grains, like animal products, tend to be acid-forming, are rich in calories, and relatively low in vitamins and minerals. In fact, grains contain phytic acid, which can pull minerals out of the body. Many grains also have gluten, a protein that triggers allergic reactions in many individuals. Therefore, as with animal products, do not fill up on grains, but leave room for the vitamin and mineral-rich fruits and vegetables.

The Key to Healthy Eating

The above information might seem complicated, but the good news is that all of the above-mentioned concerns tend to be automatically handled when we apply a simple rule of thumb: *Eat an abundance of high-water-content foods.* High-water-content foods are the foods that tend to produce a copious amount of watery juice when put through a juice extractor. These foods include most fruits and vegetables, as well as the young sprouts of grains and legumes. When we enrich the diet with high water content foods, we derive the following benefits:

- We tend to automatically eat the right amount of protein, carbohydrates and fats.
- We tend to get the vitamins and minerals we need.
- We get an abundance of plant fiber.
- We get a good balance of cleansing foods and building foods.
- We tend to eat the right balance of acid and alkaline forming foods.
- We reduce the amount of processed foods in the diet.

How do you know if you are consuming the right amount of high-water-content food for you? In general, if you consume enough high-water-content foods to have 1-3 bowel movements per day (that do not smell too bad), you are in the right ballpark.

Bless Your Food

There is more to good nutrition than biochemistry. Whether we are aware of it or not, food is, for most of us, a highly charged emotional issue. After mother's touch, food is the first form of comfort that we receive outside the womb. Even as adults, food is a major source of pleasure and comfort, as well as being a vehicle for social interaction. In addition, many cultures attach spiritual or religious significance to food.

Our emotional state has a great impact on how the body processes food. In particular, our attitude toward the food itself can influence the body's ability to handle it. The more we appreciate and enjoy the food, the more thoroughly we tend to digest it. So, the bottom line is this: After you have made your food choice, bless it, give thanks and enjoy.

Simple Guidelines for Healthy Eating

- *If you eat red meat:* look for grass-fed meats, and eat it in moderation.
- *If you eat poultry:* look for free-range poultry and eat it in moderation.
- *If you eat fish:* It is in moderation and gravitate toward the smaller short-lived fish (such as salmon and sardines), and go easy on the larger long-lived fish (such as tuna and swordfish), which tend to accumulate substantially more mercury.
- *If you eat grains:* gravitate toward whole grains, and eat them in moderation.
- *If you eat soy:* gravitate toward fermented soy, and eat it in moderation.
- *If you like tofu:* eat it like cheese — in relatively small amounts. Do not fill up on soy, but rather, make it part of a meal that includes a modest amount of whole grains and a generous helping of vegetables.
- *If you like fruit:* eat as much as you want.
- *If you don't particularly like vegetables:* Find ways to make them more appealing so you will want to eat more of them.
- *If you are on a low-carb diet:* Make sure that your diet includes some fruit and an abundance of vegetables.
- *If you are on a low-fat or vegan diet:* Favor vegetables, whole fruits and whole grains, and ease up on the white flour and refined sugary things. Make sure you are getting ample omega-3 oils and Vitamin B_{12}.
- *If you are on a high protein (low-fat and low-carb) diet:* Get off it as soon as possible!
- *If you do not have a bowel movement at least once a day:* increase your veggies and fruits.
- *If your log quickly sinks to the bottom of the bowl:* increase your veggies and fruits.
- *If you feel constipated or "toxic:"* increase your veggies and fruits.
- *If you have blood sugar issues:* Avoid all refined carbohydrates (white flour and sugar). Also, avoid over-consuming fats, especially saturated fats and partially hydrogenated oils, because they can inhibit the body's ability to regulate blood sugar.

- *If you are concerned about getting too much sun or other forms of radiation:* increase foods that are high in antioxidants.
- *If you want to maintain the youthfulness of your body:* Increase foods that are high in antioxidants.
- *If you just want to eat healthier in general:* Try to include at least one food from each of the following categories in your meals (not necessarily all in one meal):
  - *Dark green leafy veggies:* kale, spinach, collards, dandelion greens.
  - *Colorful veggies:* carrots, beets, sweet potatoes, yellow squash, red peppers, red Swiss chard.
  - *Lettuce:* romaine and leaf lettuce.
  - *Cruciferous vegetables:* broccoli, cauliflower, Brussels sprouts, cabbage.
  - *Fruit:* Whatever is in season and, preferably, grown locally: apples, pears, peaches, apricots, red and green grapes, blue berries, blackberries, cherries, watermelon.

Fasting

During a fast, the digestive organs can rest and the large amount of energy that is normally used to digest food can be directed toward helping the body cleanse and heal. If you have never fasted before, do it for one day, just to get the feel of it. Choose a day when you do not have to work, so you can rest and be quiet. After you are comfortable with a one day fast, you can try a two and then three day fast. After several days of fasting, hunger may vanish and energy levels may increase. However, different individuals respond differently. For example, if the fast continues for several days, the rapid removal of waste can result in a cleansing crisis, in which case, the individual feels "sick," experiencing flu like symptoms, headaches, lethargy, nausea and skin eruptions. If you would like to fast beyond seven days, it is best to do so under skilled supervision.

The Water Fast

Fasting on just water produces the most rapid results. According to the Natural Hygienists, the only kind of a fast is one in which the individual simply drinks water. However, Natural Hygiene also emphasizes that fasting should be done only under the right conditions, and preferably under skilled supervision. The reason for this is that the water fast produces vigorous cleansing of the body, releasing large amounts of toxins from the tissues that can overload the elimination organs. Furthermore, people with blood sugar issues can become weak and unable to carry on their normal routine while fasting on water alone.

The Juice Fast

Freshly prepared vegetable juices are loaded with vitamins, mineral, enzymes, phytonutrients and just enough calories to tone down the cleansing effects, making it more manageable for individuals who are not used to fasting. To tone it down even more, vegetable broth and herbal teas may be included.

How to Break a Fast

If the fast lasts for more than 3 days, it should be ended carefully.

- **Day One** Breakfast: 1-2 apples or the equivalent amount of any other fruit.

    Lunch: Same as breakfast, or small raw salad (with lemon juice dressing).
    Dinner: Freshly squeezed vegetable juice, or same as breakfast.

- **Day Two** Breakfast: Same as day one. Can add another piece of fruit, later in the morning, as a snack.

    Lunch: Same as breakfast, or a larger vegetable salad.
    Dinner: vegetable juice or soup (no added salt).

- **Day Three** Breakfast: same as Day Two.

    Lunch: Salad and with a few nuts, or cooked vegetables, including starchvegetables.
    Dinner: rice and beans or bread and beans, potatoes or sweet potatoes.

- **Day Four** Resume normal eating.

If you have fasted longer than 10 days, the break-in period should be extended one day for every three days of fasting. The cleansing, regenerative processes will continue if a good diet is followed afterward. It is good to do a three- to seven-day fast every fall and spring to assist the body in housecleaning and preparing the blood for different weather.

A Guide to Milk Alternatives

If you wish reduce or eliminate dairy products, but would like to continue to enjoy the experience of consuming something that resembles milk, here are some alternatives.

- *Soymilk* is readily available and relatively inexpensive. Since soy is a legume, the protein complements the whole grain cereal that you place it on. However, soy milk is not as nutritionally complete as dairy milk, and should not be viewed as a nutritional replacement for it. Like other unfermented soy products, soymilk is not that easy to digest and contains substances (such as phytoestrogens) that could be detrimental for some individuals, especially if consumed in large amounts. Therefore, as with dairy milk, do not depend on it as a staple food, and use it in moderation.

- *Rice milk* is hypoallergenic and easier to digest than soymilk. However, as with soymilk, it is still not as nutritionally complete as dairy milk. Therefore, do not rely on it as a staple, but use it when you feel like having some "milk" as a quick beverage or to put on you cereal.
- *Nut/seed milk* has a closer resemblance to dairy milk, compared to soy and rice milk. For example, it provides a significant amount of protein and is rich in beneficial fats. Many nuts and seeds provide omega-3 oils, unlike soy, which is high in omega-6. If the milk is made from raw (and organic, preferably) nuts and seeds, it is also rich in vitamins, minerals and other nutrients. The most readily available nut/seed milk on the market is almond milk. Nut/seed milk is also relatively easy to make at home. One recipe is given below.
- *Coconut milk.* The liquid part of the coconut, though pleasantly sweet, is generally too watery to serve as a milk substitute for most people. However, when the water from a young coconut is blended with some of the coconut meat, the two combine into a delicious and satisfying drink that, for many individuals, replaces the flavor, texture and satisfying quality of dairy milk.

As dairy alternatives, all four of the above milk-substitutes can vary greatly in quality. Read the label. Look for organic ingredients and a minimum amount (zero, preferably) of added sugar. Also, be aware that the store-bought milk alternatives that are not refrigerated come in cartons that are typically lined with aluminum.

What about Babies?

Babies and young children often have problems with cow's milk. Furthermore, there is evidence that giving children (especially babies before age two) cow's milk can trigger type I diabetes. None-the-less, the above four milk alternatives are not very suitable for infants. Soy milk is of special concern, for the reasons given above, as well as the high levels of glutamate, an amino acid that is known to over-stimulate and damage brain cells, when introduced in large concentrations. Mothers who are unable to breast feed their infants and would like to avoid formulas that are based on cow's milk, can explore these options:

- A wet nurse
- A milk bank
- Goat's milk. Compared to cow's milk, it is more nutritious, is less likely to produce allergic reactions, and is actually similar to human milk.

Nuts and Seeds Commonly used to Make Milk

- Nuts and seeds, in general, tend to be rich in beneficial fats and minerals.
- Almonds are tasty and tend to have a higher protein and lower fat content than other nuts and seeds.
- Flax seeds are an excellent source of omega-3 fats.
- Walnuts are loaded with nutrients that benefit the brain.
- Brazil nuts are extremely rich in selenium. One Brazil nut easily provides the daily recommended allowance of selenium.
- Pumpkin seeds are rich in zinc and have oils that help to eliminate intestinal parasites.

Recipe for Almond/Flax Milk:

Using a powerful blender, such as Vitamix:

- Blend one cup of almonds and 1-3 table spoons of flax seeds, with 25-32 ounces of water.
- You can vary the water to create the desired consistency. You can also remove pulp from the blended milk by using a sieve or cheese cloth.
- You can vary the proportion of almonds to flax seeds to change the flavor or nutritional profile.

Using a coffee grinder and regular blender:

- With the coffee grinder, grind up the almonds and flax seeds.
- Blend the powdered almonds and flax seeds with enough water to make a beverage of desired consistency.

Variations:

- Sweeten with honey, maple syrup or dates.
- Use other nuts and seeds, such as walnuts, sunflower seeds, Brazil nuts and pumpkin Seeds for variety of flavor and nutritional content.
- You can greatly reduce the water to make pudding, which can then be frozen into "ice-cream."

LOSING WEIGHT SAFELY AND EFFECTIVELY

Programs that are effective in weight-loss have one thing in common: they guide us in burning more calories than we consume. In practical terms, this means that we eat less and exercise more. In addition, *safe* and effective weight loss requires that we decrease high-calorie foods and increase foods that are higher in vitamins, minerals, fiber and water.

High-calorie foods are grains, starchy vegetables, vegetable oils, nuts and seeds, meat, dairy and eggs. The foods that are low in calories and high in vitamins and minerals are fruits and low-starch vegetables.

Two Basic strategies for weight loss:

- **The Low-Carb Strategy.** The low-carb diets provide the bulk of calories from protein and fat, while reducing the carbohydrates. One reason that weight loss occurs quickly with low-carb diets is that the digestion and metabolism of protein and fat takes longer and requires the body to expend more energy (burn more calories), compared to the digestion and metabolism of carbohydrates. In other words, the body must automatically burn more calories on a low-carb diet, even if the exercise level is the same. However, faster is not necessarily better. You must be mindful of not ingesting *too* much fat and protein, because they can produce toxicity and increase the risk of cancer, cardiovascular problems and osteoporosis.

- **The Low-Fat Strategy.** Low-fat diets, done properly can be equally effective in weight-loss, compared to low-carb diets. The difference is that low-fat diets may take longer (which might actually be a healthier strategy, depending on the individual).

Guidelines for Losing Weight Safely and Effectively

Whether the individual favors the low-carb or low-fat approach, losing weight safely and effectively requires that he/she observes the following simple guidelines:

- **Burn more calories than you consume.** The individual consumes enough calories to fuel the body and feel satisfied, while avoiding excess.

- **Eat lots of fruits and vegetables.** Even though calories are reduced, the diet should still provide an ample amount of vitamins, minerals and other nutrients. This is done by simply consuming enough fruits and low-starch vegetables. As an added benefit, the increase in fruits and vegetables provides enough bulk to create a sense of fullness and satisfaction, even though calories have been reduced.

- **Eat a moderate amount of high-calorie foods.** These foods are consumed in portions that are small enough to allow for healthy weight loss, while providing sufficient fuel (calories) and nutrients to run the body. The high-calorie foods can include relatively clean sources of protein, fats and carbohydrates, such as grass-fed beef, free-range poultry, wild caught fish, eggs, beans, whole grains and starchy vegetables (potatoes and squash).

- **Avoid mixing high-fat and high-carb foods.** One of the main causes of unwanted weight-gain is eating meals that have both large amounts of carbohydrates and fats. This combination is rarely seen in naturally occurring foods, but is quite common for humans: pizza, most sandwiches (such as burgers), meat and potatoes, spaghetti and meatballs, cookies, cakes, and candies. It is just too easy to over-consume such foods.

  By avoiding foods in the same meal that are simultaneously high in carbohydrates and fat, you will find it much easier to avoid over-consuming calories. This is done by simply reducing either the carbohydrates or fats in the same meal. For example, if your meal has a substantial amount of meat, cheese or other fatty foods, you would avoid high-starch foods, such as potatoes, rice or bread, or use them sparingly. If your meal has a substantial amount of high-starch foods, you would avoid animal products and other fatty foods, or use them sparingly.

- **Eat simply.** The more we process and mix foods, the harder it is to ovoid overconsuming calories. The body can more easily sense when it has had enough if the meal consists of simple combinations of foods that are naturally tasty and satisfying without strong spices. For example, high-quality fruit is typically tasty with no processing or cooking at all. Tender vegetables, such as romaine lettuce and baby spinach, can be used to create simple salads that are surprisingly tasty and satisfying. If the fruit is fresh and ripe, you might find that it is delicious and filling enough to make a meal in and of itself — even though fruits tend to be low in calories, compared to grains, potatoes and animal products. Or, fruit can the first course of meal. The second course can be a salad, or some steamed vegetables and a simple meat dish.

- **Listen to your Body.** All else being equal, the low-carb approach seems to produce faster results than the low-fat approach, but either one works. It is a matter of what is most appropriate for the individual at the time. For example, for someone who does not tolerate eating large amounts of animal fat and protein, or is concerned about the potential long-term issues of eating large amounts of animal products, the low-fat version would be best. On the other hand, for someone who feels the need for substantial amounts of meat or has issues with starchy foods, the low-carb approach would be more appropriate. Either way, the individual should make sure to get ample amounts of fresh fruit and vegetables.

How to Keep Your Brain Youthful

As with the rest of the body, the two key elements for promoting a healthy brain well into the latter years are exercise and nutrition.

Exercising the Brain

The same physical exercise that benefits the entire body, also benefits the brain. In addition, by simply using the brain, we stimulate the growth of new brain tissue and improve the efficiency of brain function. Engaging the brain in intellectually challenging activity increases the production of neurotransmitters and causes the brain cells to branch out and develop new connections, in essence, creating new brain tissue. This, in turn, prevents or delays the onset of degenerative brain diseases such as Alzheimer's disease, and allows patients to make a more complete recovery from strokes.

Curiosity, creativity, problem solving, the learning of new skills, and processing new information rejuvenates the brain so that it performs these activities faster and more efficiently.

The rule of thumb for brain regeneration is to do something new and different; use your mind and body in ways that you have never used them before. If you don't do crossword puzzles, do crossword puzzles. If you think you have two left feet, learn to dance, especially structured dancing that requires "learning steps." If you consider yourself to be mechanically retarded, fix something or build something. If you feel most comfortable with technical activities, try painting or poetry. If you feel more at home with art and poetry and feel that you can't memorize things, take a class in botany or anatomy. Do something that you find intriguing and perhaps a little scary.

Nourishing the Brain

Nutrition, like exercise, can profoundly affect the health of the brain and make a big difference in preventing degeneration and cognitive decline later in life. The main nutritional considerations are as follows:

- **The Right Fats.** Since the brain is a very fatty organ, the ingestion of adequate levels of the right fats is very important. Unsaturated fats are especially important, because they provide the ideal "fluidity" that is essential for proper transmission of signals that allow us to have clear thinking and emotional serenity. Polyunsaturated fats, such as the omega-3 and omega-6 fats, provide the most fluidity. Both are needed by the brain, but omega-3 fats are the ones that are generally in short supply in the civilized diet, while omega-6 are often excessive. Most of the omega-3 in the brain is in the form of DHA (decasohexanoic acid). The brain needs huge amounts of this fat for optimum health. The body makes it from other forms of omega-3 fats, but we can get it pre-made from certain foods such as cold-water fish, eggs and sea vegetation.

- **Antioxidants.** Antioxidants are substances that neutralize free radicals — highly reactive molecules that cause harmful oxidation of proteins, fats and DNA in the body. Since the brain is a very fatty organ, antioxidants are critically important for maintaining the long-term health of the brain. Furthermore, the fat that is most abundant in the brain also happens to be the one that is most sensitive to oxidation: DHA. This point is especially significant when we consider the high metabolic rate of brain cells, which means that they are constantly cranking out a substantial amount of free radicals.

- **Balance is Essential.** Both the fats and the antioxidants are important for brain health. With regard to supplementation, the emphasis is usually on the omega-3 fats, usually in the form of fish oil, because that is what produces the immediate noticeable results of clear thinking and lifting of depression. However, we must be mindful of the long-term consequences of increasing the levels of these highly sensitive fats. When fish oils are extracted from the fish and processed, they undergo oxidation. The fishy smell of omega-3 supplements is a clear sign that it has already undergone substantial oxidation, and is, therefore, toxic. Furthermore, once it enters the body, it will be quickly absorbed by the brain, which then has to tap into the body's limited antioxidant pool, to try to protect the ingested DHA from further oxidation. Therefore, it is best to get your omega-3 from whole foods whenever possible: fresh fish, eggs that have the rich orange yoke, fresh and raw nuts and seeds, especially flax seeds. If you must take an extracted omega-3 supplement, try to match the increase in omega-3 fats with a generous increase in antioxidants.

Facts on Mercury Dental Fillings

- "Silver" or amalgam dental fillings contain from 48-55 percent mercury, 33-35 percent silver, and various amounts of copper, tin, zinc, and other metals. Since mercury is the major component of the material, any representation of the material should include the word "mercury." Thus, we refer to them as mercury dental fillings.

- Mercury is a powerful poison. Published research has shown that mercury is more toxic than lead, cadmium, and even arsenic. Furthermore, there is no known toxic threshold for mercury vapor and world-renowned mercury toxicologists have stated that no amount of exposure to mercury vapor can be considered totally harmless.

- Scientific research has demonstrated that mercury, even in small amounts, can damage the brain, heart, lungs, liver, kidneys, thyroid gland, pituitary gland, adrenal gland, blood cells, enzymes and hormones, and suppress the body's immune system. Mercury has been shown to pass the placental membrane in pregnant women and cause permanent damage to the brain of the developing baby.

- Mercury is continually released from mercury dental fillings in the form of mercury vapor and abraded particles. This process is stimulated and can be increased as much as fifteen-fold by chewing, brushing, hot liquids, etc. The World Health Organization recently concluded that the daily intake of mercury from amalgam dental fillings exceeded the combined daily intake of mercury derived from air, water and food (including fish).

- The mercury vapor released from mercury dental fillings is absorbed very rapidly and thoroughly in your body, primarily by inhalation and swallowing.

- In human autopsy studies, it has been found that there is a direct correlation between the amount of mercury found in the brain and the number of mercury fillings in the teeth.

- Mercury causes normal intestinal flora to become mercury resistant and antibiotic resistant. Mercury resistant bacteria cause mercury in the intestinal tract to be converted back into vapor and recycled back into the body.

- Recent scientific research has shown high levels of mercury in the brains of individuals dead from Alzheimer's disease (AD). Other research is demonstrating mercury can cause similar pathological effects in the brain, as that seen in Lou Gehrig's Disease (ALS) and AD. Laboratory studies of spinal fluid from ALS and AD patients have confirmed that mercury inhibits key brain detoxification enzyme systems.

- The American Dental Association and various agencies of the U.S. Government still support the use of amalgam dental fillings. They claim they are safe based on 150 years of use and that there is no scientific evidence showing mercury exposure from dental fillings causes any known disease.

Is Your Cookware Safe?

If you are interested in becoming healthier and reducing the toxic burden on the body, here is a very simple, but very important action that you can take: Replace aluminum and Teflon cookware with stainless steel, ceramic or glass.

Facts about Aluminum

- Aluminum is toxic to the body.

- Aluminum toxicity has been linked to Alzheimer's type symptoms.

- The aluminum in the cookware and aluminum foil gets into the food. The longer you cook the food, the higher the aluminum content. The longer you leave those leftovers wrapped in aluminum foil, the more aluminum you will get when you finally eat it.

- Aluminum contamination is increased with foods that naturally react with metals, such as tomato sauce. If you cook a tomato-rich meal in an aluminum container and then let it sit for several hours, it will absorb significant amounts of aluminum. Individuals who eat such leftovers can get so ill they have to be rushed to the hospital.

Facts about Teflon

- Small pets such as birds have died from the fumes emitted from Teflon cookware in use.

- PFOA (perfluorooctanoic acid), a toxic chemical given off by Teflon, accumulates in the body and doesn't break down in the environment. This same chemical has been linked to cancer, liver damage, birth defects and immune-system suppression in animals.

- In the late 1990s', a family sued DuPont, claiming that the PFOA was contaminating their pasture and killing their cows. DuPont settled out of court.

- The EPA has accused DuPont of failing to notify the agency when two of five babies born to plant employees in 1981 had eye and face defects similar to those found in newborn rats exposed to PFOA.

- Every time you cook with Teflon, PFOA gets into the food you eat and the air you breathe.

The Gluten-Free Diet

By Rebecca A. Blessing, DC, MS, CNMT

Did you ever knead dough? Gluten is what gives dough its elasticity. It helps bread rise and gives it texture. Gluten is a protein that is found in wheat, barley and rye. Gluten is also found in other grains and their hybrids such as durum, spelt, kamut and triticale, which is a cross between wheat and rye.

According to the landmark study by Dr. Fasano at the University of Maryland, 1 out of 133 people in the United States have Celiac disease (CD). This is an autoimmune condition caused by eating gluten-containing grains, resulting in the destruction of the villi that are responsible for absorbing nutrients in the small intestines.

With CD, when gluten is ingested, it triggers a problem with the body's immune system, involving T-cells. In essence, the T-cells attack the inner lining of the digestive tract. The most obvious effect is atrophy of the villi (tiny finger projections on the wall of small intestine), resulting in severe malabsorption problems.

Symptoms of CD include fatigue, abdominal pain, depression, muscle, joint, or bone pain, and compromised immune function. According to the U.S. Food and Drug Administration (2005), CD has been linked to other disorders, such as type I diabetes, thyroid disease, Sjögren syndrome, Down syndrome, Turner syndrome and Williams syndrome, which is associated with neurologic disorders (such as lack of muscle coordination) and immunodeficiency syndromes.

The average length of time it takes for a symptomatic person to be diagnosed with celiac disease in the US is four years; this type of delay dramatically increases an individual's risk of developing autoimmune disorders, neurological problems, osteoporosis and even cancer.

In the past, CD was only diagnosed in children between the ages of 6 months to 18 months and was known as Celiac Sprue. Chronic diarrhea, failure to thrive, muscle wasting and abdominal bloating were common symptoms. Now, CD is being diagnosed in adults between the ages of 45-60.

Atypical Celiac Disease is the most common form. This form doesn't usually have any gastrointestinal symptoms but may show up as iron deficiency, infertility, dermatitis hepetiformis (DH), and tooth enamel deterioration. Because they don't typically present with gastrointestinal issues, these patients will usually go undiagnosed. A simple blood test and intestinal biopsies while accurate for celiac disease, miss the mark with patients with severe symptoms of what is called atypical celiac. These are the people whose blood test and biopsies are negative, still have severe gastrointestinal symptoms, autoimmune diseases, sleep disorders, and generalized or specific pain.

What is a Gluten-Free Diet?

First, gluten-free does not mean fat-free or calorie-free. A gluten free diet contains an abundance of carbohydrates and fats. With growing awareness of gluten sensitivity, gluten-free products today are now readily available. It is no longer difficult to stay gluten-free, with all of the wonderful tasty products on the market. But because of the idea of deprivation and psychologically dependent food issues, some individuals have a tendency to go way overboard and eat things that are not good for them. However, staying away from packaged food products and eating protein, carbohydrates and fats that are organic and prepared in your own kitchen will cut down on expense and will be more nutritious.

Our Practice

I have a 30 year-background in massage therapy combined with chiropractic, nutrition and health psychology. I see mainly patients with chronic musculoskeletal and autoimmune problems. I work in collaboration with an endocrinologist and a practitioner that specializes with chronic illnesses. We carefully examine history, blood work, as well as gene codes, if necessary.

I encourage a gluten-free life style for those that have had symptoms for years. For the first year, we eliminate soy and secondary grains such as; quinoa, amaranth and millet, because cross contamination can be high with these products in the United States. Once an individual has been gluten-free for awhile, we have found that eating secondary grains can return all symptoms that had once disappeared. Our patients seem to heal faster and it is sometimes easier to be all or nothing, keeping the guesswork to a minimum. However, if someone would like to reintroduce the restricted foods, we recommend one food at a time and self monitor for any adverse symptoms.

We have found that there is a big emotional attachment to food. There should be no judgment from a clinician if someone does not want to be gluten-free and has difficulty adhering to a gluten-free lifestyle. It is a personal choice to stay gluten-free or not. But when you see rashes and blisters heal that have been there for years, chronic constipation or diarrhea resolve, muscle and joint pain disappear, brain fog clear and sleep restore, it is truly remarkable.

Gluten-free is not for everyone, but for those who have major physical or psychological issues, the gluten-free diet might improve quality of life. Some see improvement right away, while other may require years to allow the body to repair the damage. It's really quite simple; if your health issues have been shown to be related to gluten, healing will happen only if gluten is totally removed from the diet.

Fasano, et al. (February 2003). A multi-center study on the sero-prevalence of celiac disease in the United States among both at risk and not at risk groups. *Archives of Internal Medicine.*
Food and Drug Administration (2005). Public Meeting: Gluten free labeling. http://www.fda.gov/Food/LabelingNutrition/FoodAllergensLabeling/GuidanceCompliance regulatory Information/ucm107204.htm
Green, P. et al. (2001, 2006). Characteristics of adult celiac disease in the USA: results of a national survey. *American Journal of Gastroenterology.*
Zipser, R. D., Patel, S., Yahya, K. Z., Baisch, D. W., & Monarch, E. (2003). Presentations of adult celiac disease in a nationwide patient support group. *Digestive Diseases and Sciences, 48*(4), 761-764.

Rebecca Blessing is a chiropractor and certified neuromuscular therapist. Her practice in Atlanta, GA includes nutritional counseling that supports a gluten free lifestyle.

The Seventh Day Adventists Health Plan

By Dante Tobias, LMT

Seventh-Day Adventism can be defined as a culture that promotes personal responsibility for one's health, by emphasizing the dietary and social laws in the Bible. The basic health principles were adopted during the mid 1800's, when Ellen G. White shared a vision she received regarding the need for health and temperance. The basic principles are expressed as 8 laws of health. They are commonly referred to as the "New Start" or God's Plan lifestyle: Nutrition, temperance, exercise, rest, water, trust in divine power, air, sunshine.

Dietary choices are based on the counsel in Leviticus 17:11 that "the life of the flesh is in the blood." Scientific research has proven that the human body is best served by a plant based diet of fruits, vegetables, seeds, nuts and grains. It has also been documented that our digestive systems, beginning with our teeth, are not designed to break down animal based products, and that we function better emotionally and socially when we limit our nutritional choices to plant foods. The Bible shows that the life span decreased drastically after a flesh diet was introduced.

I joined the Seventh-Day Adventist Denomination in 1969 after four years of service in the United States Marine Corps. My decision to join the Church has positively impacted my life mentally, spiritually, physically and socially.

As Adventists, we are encouraged to be vegetarians and vegans, exercise, drink plenty of water, and get adequate rest, not to smoke or drink, and to trust in Divine Power. It is recommended that potential food with a face, a mother or liver, should be considered harmful to our minds and bodies, and those foods that are healthy should be introduced into the stomach on a two-meal a day plan, with at least 4 to 5 hours between meals.

Not all members are on a plant based diet, but those who eat flesh avoid the unclean animals listed in Leviticus 11 (swine, dog, hare, camel, vulture, catfish, shark, lobster, shrimp, etc.) These are categorized as scavengers to keep the land, air and waters clean.

An article published in the November 2005 issue of National Geographic described three groups of people from around the world, whose members included a disproportionate number of centerians (people living over one hundred years). The people in this article were from Sardinia, Italy; Okinawa, Japan and Seventh-day Adventists from Loma Linda, California.

It was found that all of these "centenarians" had something in common; they all had a great love for the family and ate fresh foods that they grew in their own gardens. Two of the three groups, the Sardinians and Okinawans, are losing their longevity because they are changing their eating habits and adopting the western fast food and processed foods diets. The dietary and lifestyle concepts of the Seventh-day Adventists are still being urged upon its members and, by maintaining these concepts, they continue to live long and productive lives.

One woman living in Loma Linda, California, had just reached one hundred and renewed her driver's license. She had a vegan diet and a daily routine which included exercise each morning, lifting weights and riding her stationary bike before going out. Have you ever thought about living to be a hundred? Not only can you live this long, you can also enjoy a healthier life by following the example of this Seventh-day Adventist.

The principals described above, as practiced by SDA have served me well, as they would any health-conscious individual. It is my privilege to share them with you. It is my sincere belief that they will benefit you in your quest for wellness.

Rev. Dante Tobias is a massage therapist, health consultant and retired pastor in the Seventh-Day Adventist Church.

Fruitarian and Massage Therapist

By Anne Osborne, LMT

I have practiced as a Massage Therapist 14 years, and have been on a raw fruitarian diet for over 19 years. As a Massage Therapist, I find that my lifestyle and diet have had a great bearing on the treatments that I give. The fruit diet has bestowed upon me great energy. I have no less energy at 45 years of age than I did during my teenage years. Energy and zest for life, in my opinion, are not age-dependant. If one is living in a harmonious and natural way, there is no reason why one should not have an abundance of energy at any age.

The benefits of my fruit diet have been, to a certain extent, passed on to my massage clients. I feel that a natural diet enhances my instincts and intuition, which positively affects my massage practice, from being able to choose which oils are optimal for a particular client, to tuning in to the specific energy of a client. I feel that when one is on a natural diet, and eating according to instinct, one is best able to make instinctive choices in one's massage therapy.

In addition to adding vitality and vigor to my work, I also find that I have steady focus during a treatment, I often feel more energized *after* a massage, than before, even after a two hour intense sports or remedial massage.

I believe that therapists can potentially be exposed to all sorts of energies and emanations, whilst engaging with their clients. I feel that the stronger our own life-force, the better able we are to ground ourselves and keep ourselves fortified and protected during a therapy session.

Though a 100% fruitarian diet may not be for everyone, I feel that fruit has the *potential* to totally feed and nourish the body, mind, and soul in a most beautiful way — if the fruit is of high quality. In my opinion, a vital part of success on a fruit diet is access to great quality fruit, which is fully plant-ripened and is grown in healthy soil. I believe that fruit cannot optimally nourish us if it is not grown in rich, organic soil. And, if a fruit is grown with love and care, then we will also reap these energies when we consume the fruit. Also, in my experience, as the body is allowed to cleanse and rebalance itself, digestion and absorption of nutrients become more efficient. Therefore, the individual is more capable of thriving on fresh fruit.

Regarding supplementation, I think that the human body, when in its natural and healthy state, maintains a wonderful balance, and that supplements can adversely affect it. Therefore, as a rule, I do not take supplements. However I have supplemented with Vitamin B_{12} during pregnancy and the early stages of breastfeeding because, although I have never exhibited any B_{12} deficiency symptoms, I chose to supplement, because I was responsible for the health and life of another being.

Looking at the bigger picture, since I adopted a 100% fruit diet, I have developed a great awareness and appreciation for the interconnectedness of life. Beyond the realization that my own diet and lifestyle greatly influences my massage treatments, fruit eating is simply good for the Planet. More fruit-eating results in the planting of more trees, which clean the air, generate oxygen, enrich the soil and provide food and habitat for animals.

None-the-less, though the fruit diet satisfies my ethical and environmental values, if it did not also satisfy my health and nutritional requirements I would not have been able to thrive on this diet for over 19 years.

To conclude, fruit has blessed me with excellent health, and enhances my work as a Massage Therapist. For me, massage therapy and the raw diet are very harmonious companions.

Anne Osborne is a massage therapist, living in Queensland, Australia. She is the mother of two children and author of the book, *Fruitarianism, the Path to Paradise.*

Living Foods

By Marlene Webb

A key element of whole food nutrition is the consumption of living foods, especially tender young greens, along with other types of sprouts and seedlings. Such plants are in their formative or "biogenic" state, in which its life-generating and cell-renewal capacities are at maximum.

As each seed germinates, enzymes become active, triggering chemical reactions that release the seed's dormant storehouse of nutrition. These reactions break down the seed's complex proteins, carbohydrates and fats into simpler elements that are easier to digest.

The baby greens that we grow at Vonnie's Greens have a wealth of nutrients—first by activating the seeds' potent food supply, then by absorbing the soil's readily available minerals. This natural growing method insures that our crops are power-packed fresh young greens.

Sunlight stimulates the development of dark green chlorophyll, which has been nick-named "plant blood." It has also been called "liquid sunshine" because it converts the sun's energy into organic nutrients that we can eat. We also benefit from chlorophyll's exceptional detoxifying properties.

The tender greens grown by Vonnie's Greens are wheatgrass, sunflower sprouts and buckwheat lettuce. Wheatgrass is considered one of the most potent super foods. Most people juice it. Wheatgrass juice is the emerald-green liquid extracted from soil germinated young wheatgrass blades. It provides essential vitamins, minerals, amino acids, chlorophyll, enzymes and has an extremely high nutrient concentration. In fact, according to research by Charles F. Schnabel, Agricultural Chemist, The father of wheatgrass, 15 pounds of wheatgrass is equal in overall nutritional value to 350 pounds of ordinary garden vegetables. Wheatgrass offers an abundance of phytonutrients, requiring negligible energy to digest.

Grasses are packed with enzymes. Without enzymes, life is not possible. Enzymes are the spark of life. Fresh and raw foods, especially young greens, are rich in enzymes, some of which seem to provide health benefits when we ingest them.

Viiktoras Kulvinskas, the author of *Survival into the Twenty First Century,"* said, "Wheatgrass juice is the nectar of rejuvenation, the plasma of youth, the blood of all life. The elements that are missing in our body's cells, especially enzymes, vitamins, hormones, and nucleic acids can be obtained through this daily green sunlight transfusion."

One way to stay in balance and assure that your energy flow remains positive is to routinely enjoy baby greens, as well as young sweet wheatgrass. When we experience our connection to the grand universal energy source (the sun), we feel more alive, alert, and full of enthusiasm.

Marlene Webb is a massage therapist and cofounder of Vonnie's Greens, the first farm in the Southeast to produce wheatgrass and other young greens.

Study Guide

Here are some questions to help you further integrate the information in this book.

For best results:

¤ Answer each question so it serves *your* purpose.

¤ Understand your answer well enough to explain it to your client.

1. Briefly describe the three ways that the body uses nutrients.

2. What are macronutrients? Name the three main categories of macronutrients, and briefly describe the functions of each.

3. What are micronutrients? Name the three main categories of micronutrients.

4. What are enzymes?

5. What are hormones?

6. What are antioxidants?

7. Briefly describe how you would advise a client who is concerned about cholesterol.

8. What is plant fiber? What is soluble fiber? What is pectin? Briefly describe the health benefits of fiber.

9. It's time to play *Name that Nutrient!*

   ¤ Vitamin_____ is important for night vision.

   ¤ Vitamin_____ is important for hemoglobin production.

   ¤ Vitamin_____ is important for collagen production.

- Vitamin_____ promotes the absorption of Ca from the gut into the blood. Excessive amounts can also pull Ca out of bones.

- Vitamin_____ is an antioxidant. It is beneficial for the heart and prostate.

- Vitamin_____ is one of our clotting factors.

- The minerals, _____ and _____ help relieve insomnia and nervousness.

- The mineral, _____, helps the heart muscle to relax.

- The mineral, _____, is part of the *glucose tolerance factor*.

- The mineral, _____, is important for the thyroid gland.

- The minerals, _____ and _____ are important for the integrity of tendons and ligaments.

- The mineral, _____, is an important antioxidant.

- The mineral, _____, promotes liver detoxification and healthy skin, hair and nails.

- The mineral, _____, promotes wound healing and healthy prostate. A deficiency can cause body odor.

- The term _____ includes a broad category of nutrients derived from plants. These nutrients include flavonoids and carotenoids.

10. What sort of bread would you recommend for a client with digestive issues or wheat sensitivities? (Hint, make sure you advise them to eat bread in moderation.)

11. What would you tell a client who asks you about soy? (Hint: benefits and drawbacks).

12. Briefly describe the major nutritional blessing or possible medicinal value provided by the following foods: carrots, beets, dandelion greens, celery, broccoli, kale, apples, blueberries, red or purple grapes, kiwi, watermelon, walnuts, pumpkin seeds, flax seeds, sesame seeds.

13. What are the benefits of fermented foods? What are some examples of fermented foods?

14. _____ digestion is the process of chewing up food, mixing it with digestive juices and propelling it along, through muscular contraction called _____.

15. _____ digestion is the process of breaking down large food Molecules, through the action of enzymes.

16. Name the parts of the alimentary canal. Name the accessory organs of the digestive system.

17. Briefly describe the digestion that occurs in the mouth, stomach, small intestine and large intestine.

18. What are fermentative and putrefactive bacteria? How do they impact our health?

19. Briefly describe the functions of the pancreas, liver and gall bladder.

20. What is the composition of amalgam dental fillings? What are the health risks associated with mercury?

21. Briefly describe the three major pollutants found in municipal water.

22. What are the criteria for designating a given food as "organically grown?"

23. Describe the nutritional and ecological advantages of eating organically grown foods.

24. Briefly describe the low-Carb Diet. Briefly describe various examples of this dietary approach.

25. Briefly describe the low-fats Diet. Briefly describe various examples of this dietary approach.

26. What are the possible advantages and disadvantages/challenges of a vegetarian diet? What is a vegan diet?

27. What are the possible advantages and disadvantages/challenges of a raw food diet?

28. Briefly describe the fruit-based diet.

29. Briefly describe general adaptation syndrome (GAS).

30. What does the immune system do for us? Make up a list of things that can be done to boost the immune system. How does massage affect the immune system?

31. What are antibiotics? Briefly describe their advantages and disadvantages.

32. What are vaccinations? Briefly describe their advantages and disadvantages.

33. What is an allergy? What are some things that can be done to help allergies?

34. Briefly describe fibromyalgia syndrome.

35. What is hypoglycemia, and briefly describe the causes.

36. What is diabetes mellitus? Briefly describe type I and type II diabetes and their possible causes. What suggestions would you make for a client with diabetes mellitus?

37. What are the symptoms of yeast overgrowth? What are the causes of yeast overgrowth? What would you suggest to a client who has a yeast issue?

38. Regarding acid/alkaline balance:

    ¤ The _____ content of a given food is the main factor that determines whether it has an acidic or alkaline reaction in the blood.

    ¤ Name the major acid and alkaline-forming minerals.

    ¤ Which foods are acid forming and which are alkalizing?

39. The ideal ratio of acid-forming to alkaline-forming foods in the diet is _____% alkaline and _____% acid forming.

40. What are the signs and symptoms of excess acidity in the body?

41. How do excess acidity, caffeine and sodium influence your client's response to massage?

42. How would supplemental K, Ca, Mg benefit your client's response to massage?

Endnotes and References

1. Mattila, PT (1999). Dietary xylitol in the prevention of experimental osteoporosis: Beneficial effects on bone resorption, structure and biomechanics. Dissertation, Institute of Dentistry, University of Oulu.

2. Curi, R. Alvarez,M. Bazotte, RB. Botion LM. Godov, JL. Brach, A. Effect of Stevia rebaudiana on glucose tolerance in normal adult humans. Brazil J Med Res. 1986;19(6):771-4.

3. Bray GA. Bray GA. Fructose: pure, white, and deadly? Fructose, by any other name, is a health hazard. J Diabetes Sci Technol. 2010 Jul 1;4(4):1003-7.PMID: 20663467.

4. Bosetti C, Gallus S, Talamini R, Montella M, Franceschi S, Negri E, La Vecchia C. Artificial Sweetners and Risk of Gastric, Pancreatic and Endometrial cancers in Italy. Cancer Epidemiol Biomarkers Prev. 2009 Aug;18(8):2235-8.

5. Wu HZ, Guo L, Mak YF, Liu N, Poon WT, Chan YW, Cai Z. Proteomics investigation on aristolochic acid nephropathy: a case study on rat kidney tissues. Anal Bioanal Chem. December 2010.

6. Mann SW, Yuschak MM, Amyes SJ, Aughton P, Finn JP. Food Chem Toxicol. 2000;38 Suppl 2:S91-7.PMID:

7. Saffritti, M. Belpoggi, E. Manservigi, M. Lauriola, M. Faconi, L. Bua, L. Aspartame administered in feed, beginning prenatally through life span, induces cancers of the liver and lung in male Swiss mice. American Journal of Industrial medicine. 2010 Dec;53(12):1197-206.

8. The Feingold Association. Pure Facts. April 2005. Vol. 29, No. 3.

9. Simopoulos, A. P. 1999. American Journal of Clinical Nutrition. Essential Fatty Acids in Health and Disease. 70. (3) 560-569).

10. Fernstrum, J. 2001. American Journal of Clinical Nutrition. Can Nutrient Supplements Modify Brain Function? 71. (3) 1669-1673.

11. Tuomilehto J, Lindstrom J, Eriksson JG, Valle TT, Hamalainen H, Hanne-Parikka P, Keinanen-Kiukaanniemi S, Laakso M, Louheranta A, Rastas M, Salminen V, Uusitupa M. New England Jounal of Medicine Med. Prevention of type 2 diabetes mellitus by changes in lifestyle among subjects with impaired glucose tolerance. 344:1343–1350, 2001

12. Blaylock, Russell L. Health and Nutrition Secrets that can Save Your Life. Albuquerque, NM. Health Press, 2006. 293-294.

13. Ascherio, A. Willet, W.C. Health Effects of Trans Fatty Acids. American Journal of Clinical Nutrition. 66 (4 supp.) 10065-10S.

14. Ofori, B. Rey, E. Bérard, A. Risk of Congenital Anomalies in Pregnant Users of Statin Drugs   Br J Clin Pharmacol. 2007 October; 64(4): 496–509. Published online 2007

15. Parrett, Owens, S. Why I Am A Vegetarian. On-line essay.

16. Stanton. R, Crowe T. Risks of a high-protein diet outweigh the benefits. Nature. 2006, Feb 13:440(7086:868.

17. Robbins, John. Healthy at a Hundred. Pg 110-121. New York, NY. Balantine Books, 2006.

18. Cordain, Loren. The Paleo Diet. Pg. 20-37. New York. John Wiley and Sons. 2002.

19. Bulhões, A.C.; Goldani, H.A.S.; Oliveira, F.S.; Matte, U.S.; Mazzuca, R.B.; Silveira, T.R. Correlation between lactose absorption and the C/T-13910 and G/A-22018 mutations of the lactase-phlorizin hydrolase (LCT) gene in adult-type hypolactasia. Brazilian Journal of Medical and Biological Research 40 (11): 1441–6.

20. Sission, Mark, The Primal Blue Print. Primal Blueprint Inc. 2009. P 1-8

21. Campbell, T. Colin. The China Study. Pg. 43-68. Benbella Books, 2006.

22. Cordain, Loren. The Paleo Diet. Pg. 40, 67, 101. New York. John Wiley and Sons. 2002.

23. From the South Beach Diet Website.

24. Horne, Ross. Improving on Pritikin. Pgs 119-138. Avalon Beach, Australia. 1988.

25. Fuhrman, Joel. Do Primitive People Live Longer? From Dr Fuhrman's website.

26. Iburg KM, Bronnum-Hansen H, Bjerregaard P. Health expectancy in Greenland. Scand J Public Health 2001;29(1):5-12. Choinere R. Mortality among the Baffin Inuit in the mid-80s. Arctive Med Res 1992;51 (2):87-93.

27. Stirban A, Negrean M, Götting C, Uribarri J, Gawlowski T, Stratmann B, Kleesiek K, Koschinsky T, Vlassara H, Tschoepe D. Dietary advanced glycation endproducts and oxidative stress: in vivo effects on endothelial function and adipokines. Annals of N Y Academy of Sciences. 2008 Apr;1126:276-9.

28. Graham, D. N. The 80/10/10 Diet. Pgs 29-50. Decatur GA. FoodnSport Press, 2006.

29. Robbins, John. Healthy at a Hundred. Pg 41. New York, NY. Balantine Books, 2006.

30. Artemis P. Simopoulos, MD, FACN. Omega-3 Fatty Acids in Inflammation and Autoimmune Diseases. Journal of the American College of Nutrition, Vol. 21, No. 6, 495-505 (2002)

31. Eggleston DW. The Interrelationship of Stress and Degenerative Diseases. J Prosthet Dent. 1980 Nov;44(5):541-4.

32. Shah SK, Gecy GT. Prednisone-induced osteoporosis: an overlooked and undertreated adverse effect. Journal of the American Osteopath Assoc. 2006 Nov; 106(11):653-7.

33. Hegsted DM. Calcium and Osteoporosis. Journal of Nutrition. 116 (1986): 2316-2319.

34. Birgisdottir BE, Hill JP, Thorsson AV, Thorsdottir I. Lower consumption of cow milk protein A1 beta-casein at 2 years of age, rather than consumption among 11- to 14-year-old adolescents, may explain the lower incidence of type 1 diabetes in Iceland than in Scandinavia. Ann Nutr Metab. 2006;50(3):177-83.

35. Blaylock, Russell L. Health and Nutrition Secrets that can Save Your Life. 180. Albuquerque, NM. Health Press, 20006.

36. Hancock CR, Han DH, Chen M, Terada S, Yasuda T, Wright DC, Holloszy JO. High-fat diets cause insulin resistance despite an increase in muscle mitochondria. Proc Natl Acad Sci U S A. 2008 Jun 3;105(22):7815-20.

37. SH Holt, JC Miller and P Petocz. An insulin index of foods: the insulin demand generated by 1000-kJ portions of common foods. American Journal of Clinical Nutrition. 66. (1997) 1264.

38. Graham, D. N. The 80/10/10 Diet. 29-35. Decatur GA. FoodnSport Press, 2006.

39. Colin A, Reggers J, et al. Lipids, depression and suicide. Encophale 2003; 29: 49-58.

40. Sagducu K, Dokucu ME, et al. Omega-3 fatty acids decreased irritability of patients with bipolar disorder in an add-on, open label study. Nutrition Journal (2005); 4:6.

41. Blaylock, Russell L. Health and Nutrition Secrets that can Save Your Life. 356. Albuquerque, NM. Health Press, 2006.

42. D'Adamo, Peter. Eat Right 4 Your Type. New York, NY. C.P. Putman's Sons, 1996.

43. D'Adamo, Peter. Live Right 4 Your Type. New York, NY. C.P. Putman's Sons, 1998.

44. Thie NMR. Prasad, N, Major PW. Evaluation of Glucosamine Sulfate Compared to Ibuprofen for the Treatment of Temporomandibular Joint Osteoarthritis: A Randomized Double Blind Controlled 3 Month Clinical Trial. J Rheumatol 2001;28:1347-55)

45. Ho C, Kauwell GP, Bailey LB. Practitioners' guide to meeting the Vitamin B-12 recommended dietary allowance for people aged 51 years and older. J Am Diet Assoc. 1999;99(6):725-727.

46. Buettner, Dan. The Blue Zone. Washington, D.C. National Geographic Society, 2008.

47. (Sherman, JD. 1996 Chlorpyrifos (Dursban)-associated birth defects: report of four cases. Arch. Env. Health 51(1): 5-8).

48. Selye, Hans. The Stress of Life. New York: McGraw-Hill, 1956.

49. Bracha HS; Ralston, TC; Matsukawa, JM; Williams, AE; Bracha, AS (2004). "Does "Fight or Flight" Need Updating?". *Psychosomatics* 45 (5): 448–9. doi:10.1176/appi.psy.45.5.448. PMID 15345792. Retrieved 2010-10-04. "Walter Cannon's original formulation of the term for the human response to threat, 'fight or flight,' was coined exactly 75 years ago, in 1929."

50. Wolfe AR, Arroyo C, Tedders SH, Li Y, Dai Q, Zhang J. Epub 2010 Nov 23. Dietary protein and protein-rich food in relation to severely depressed mood: A 10 year follow-up of a national cohort. Neuropsychopharmacol Biol Psychiatry. 2011 Jan 15;35(1):232-8.

51. Bonnefoy M, Drai J, Kostka T. [Antioxidants to slow aging, facts and perspectives]. Presse Med. 2002 Jul 27;31(25):1174-84.

52. Dybing, E. Development and implementation of the IPCS conceptual framework for evaluating mode of action of chemical carcinogens. Toxicol. 181-182:121-125 (2002).32

53. Ledochowski M, Widner B, Bair H, Probst T, Fuchs D. Fructose- and Sorbitol-Reduced Diet Improves Mood and Gastrointestinal Disturbances in Fructose Malabsorbers. Scand J Gastroenterol. 2000 Oct;35(10):1048-52.

54. John P. Reganold, Preston K. Andrews, Jennifer R. Reeve, Lynne Carpenter-Boggs, Christopher W. Schadt, J. Richard Alldredge, Carolyn F. Ross, Neal M. Davies, and Jizhong Zhou, Fruit and Soil Quality of Organic and Conventional Strawberry Agroecosystems. Plos ONE, September 2010, Vol. 5, Issue 9, e123456.

55. Environmental Protection Agency's 1994-95 report: Conventional Pesticides Applied to Agricultural Crops.

56. Esselstyn, Caldwell, B. Prevent and Reverse Heart Disease. 31-32. Every Books. New York. 2007.

57. Vogel, Robert, A. Clinical Cardiology. June 1999. Brachial Artery Ultrasound: A Noninvasive Tool in Assessment of Triglyceride Rich Lipoproteins.

58. Ilona Staprans; Xian-Mang Pan; Joseph H. Rapp; Kenneth R. Feingold. Oxidized. Cholesterol in the Diet Accelerates the Development of Aortic Atherosclerosis in Cholesterol-Fed Rabbits Arteriosclerosis, Thrombosis, and Vascular Biology. 1998;18:977-983.).

59. Albert MJ, Mathan VI, Baker SJ. Vitamin B_{12} synthesis by human small intestinal bacteria. Nature. 1980; 283 (Feb 21):781-2.

60. Watanabe F, Takenaka S, Katsura H, Masumder SA, Abe K, Tamura Y, Nakano Y. Dried green and purple lavers (Nori) contain substantial amounts of biologically active Vitamin B_{12} but less of dietary iodine relative to other edible seaweeds. J Agric Food Chem. 1999 Jun;47(6):2341-3.

61. Osborne, A. Fruitarianism, the Path to Paradise. Queensland, Australia. Anne Osborne, 2009.

62. Graham, D. N. The 80/10/10 Diet. Pg 127. Decatur GA. FoodnSport Press, 2006.

63. Olié E, Picot MC, Guillaume S, Abbar M, Courtet P. Measurement of total serum cholesterol in the evaluation of suicidal risk. J Affect Disord. 2011 Apr 25.

64. Sang-Jun Lee, Ha-Yull Chung, In-Kyung Lee, Seung-Uk Oh and Ick-Dong Yoo. Phenolics with Inhibitory Activity on Mouse Brain Monoamine Oxidase (MAO)from Whole Parts of Artemisia vulgaris L (Mugwort). Food Sci. Biotechnol. Vol. 9, No. 3, pp. 179-182.

65. Aviram M, Dornfeld L, Rosenblat M, et al. Pomegranate juice consumption reduces oxidative stress, atherogenic modifications to LDL, and platelet aggregation. Am J Clin Nutr. 2000 May;71(5):1062-76.

66. Lyon P, Cohen M, Quintner J. An Evolutionary Stress-Response Hypothesis for Chronic Widespread Pain (Fibromyalgia Syndrome). Pain Med. 2011 Jun 21. doi: 10.1111/j.1526-4637.2011.01168.

67. Bennett RM, Cook DM, Clark SR, Burckhardt CS, Campbell SM: Hypothalamic-pituitary-insulin-like growth factor-I axis dysfunction in patients with fibromyalgia. *J.Rheumatol.* 1997, 24:1384-1389.

68. Strickland PL, Deakin JF, Percival C, Dixon J, Gater RA, Goldberg DP. Bio-social origins of depression in the community. Interactions between social adversity, cortisol and serotonin neurotransmission.

69. Denison, Barbara MSN, ARNP, HNC, QTTT/P. Touch the Pain Away: New Research on Therapeutic Touch and Persons With Fibromyalgia Syndrome. Holistic Nursing Practice: May/June 2004 - Volume 18 - Issue 3 - p 142-150.

70. Albsi. M Stress and Addiction. Biological and Physychological Mechanisms. Academic Press. 2007. P 25.

71. Sinha, R. Chronic Stress, Drug and Vulnerability to Addiction. Ann NY Acad Sci. Oct 2008; 1141: 105-130.

72. Armstrong, D.J. Meenagh, G.K. Lee, A.S.H. Curren E.S. Finch, M.B. Vitamin D Deficiency is Associated with Depression and Fibromyalgia. Clinical Rheumatology. Volume 26, Number 4, 551-554.

73. Forastiere F, Pistelli R, Sestini P, et at. Consumption of Vitamin C in Fresh Fruit and Wheezing Symptoms in Chidren. SIDRIA Collective Group. Thorax 2000:55(4): 283-8

74. Furhman, J. Fasting and Eating for Health. St. Martin;s Press. 1995. P. 101-3.

75. Donpunha W, Kukongviriyapan U, Sompamit K, Pakongviriyan V, Pannangech P. Protective Effect of Ascorbic Acid on Cadmium-induced Hypertension and vascular Dysfunction in Mice. Miometals. 2011 Feb:24(1) 105-15.

76. Abeywardenia MY. Patten, GS. Role of Omega 3 longchain Polyunsaturated Fatty Acids in Reducing Cardio-Metabolic Risk Factors. Endocr Immun Metab Disorder Drug Targets. 2011 June 8. PMMID: 21651471.

77. Nunez-Cordoba JM, Martinez-Gonzalez MA. Antioxidant Vitamins and Cardiovascular Disease. Curr Top Med Chem. 2011, April 21.

78. Schliess F, von Dahl S, Haussinger D. Insulin Resistance Induced by Loop Diuretics and Hyperosmolarity in Perfused Rat Liver. Biol Chem. 2001 July; 382(7):1063-9.

79. Holt H, Miller JC, Petocz P. Insulin Index of Foods: the insulin demand generated by 100kj portions of common foods. Am J Cli Nutri. 1997. 66:1264-1267.

80. Koyyalamundi SR. Jeong SC. Cho KY, Pang G. Vitamin B12 in the active corrinoid produced in cultivated white button mushrooms (Agaricus bisporus). J Agric Food Chem. 2009 July 22;57(14):6327-33.

81. Milton, K (2003). "Micronutrient intakes of wild primates: are humans different?" Comparative Biochemistry and Physiology. 136 (1): 47–59.

82. Levine M, Dhariwal KR, Washko PW, Butler JD, Welch RW, WangYH, Bergsten P. Ascorbic acid and in situ kinetics: a new approach to vitamin requirements Am J Clin Nutr December 1991 54: 1157S-1162S.

83. McKinlay JB, McKinlay SM. "The questionable contribution of medical measures to the decline of mortality in the United States in the twentieth century". Milbank Mem Fund Q Health Soc. 1977 Summer; 55(3): 405-28.

84. *Boffey, P.M. Polio: Salk Challenges Safety of Sabin's Live-Virus Vaccine. Science 1 April 1977: Vol. 196 no. 4285 pp. 35-36.*

85. Steinmetz KA, et al. Raw Vegetables and cancer. J Am Dietary Association. 1996 (10)1027-39.

86. Haag M. Essential fatty acids and the brain Can J Psychiatry 2003;48(3):195-203.

87. Mortensen EL; Michaelsen KF; Sanders SA; Reinisch JM. The association between duration of breast-feeding and adult intelligence. JAMA 2002;287(18):2365-2371.

88. Helland IB, Smith L, Saarem K, et al. Maternal supplementation with very-long-chain n-3 fatty acids during pregnancy and lactation augments children's IQ at 4 years of age. Pediatrics 2003;111(1):e39-40.

89. Horrocks LA, Yeo YK. Health benefits of docosahexaenoic acid (DHA). Pharamcol Res 1999;40(3):211-225.

90. Turner N, Else PL, Hulbert AJ. Docosahexarnoic acid (DHA) content of membranes determines molecular activity of the sodium pump: implication for disease states and metabolism. Naturwissenschaften 2003;90(11):521-523.

91. Eaton SB, Konner M, Paleolithic Nutrition: A consideration of its nature and current implications. New England Journal of Medicine 1985, Jan 31;312(5):283-9.

92. Milton K. Huntergather diets; a different perspective. American Journal of Clinic Nutrition 2000. 71:665.

93. Milton K., Demmend M. Digestive and passage kinetics of chimpanzees fed high fiber and low fiber diets and comparison with human data. Journal of Nutrition 1988;118:1

94. Milton K. Hypothesis to explain the role of meat eating in human evolution. Evolutionary Anthropology 1999; 8:11.

95. Kiehm TG, Anderson JW, Ward K. Beneficial effects of a high carbohydrate, high fiber diet on hyperglycemic diabetic men. American Journal of Clinical Nutrition. August 1976 29: 895.

96. Anderson JW, Ward K. High-carbohydrate, high-fiber diets for insulin-treated men with diabetes mellitus Am J Clin Nutr November 1979 32: 2312-2321.

97. A. S. Wiener, J. Moor-jankowski and E. B. Gordon. Blood groups of apes and monkeys. II. The A-B-O blood groups, secretor and lewis types of

apes. American Journal of Physical Anthropology. Volume 21, Issue 3, pages 271–281, September 1963.

98. Jäger A.K., Saaby L. Flavonoids and the CNS. Molecules 2011, *16*, 1471-1485.

99. Kouchakoff P. The influence of food on the blood formula of man. 1st International Congress of Microbiology II. Paris (France): Masson & Cie; 1930. p. 490–3.

100. Pottenger F. The effect of heat-processed foods and metabolized vitamin D milk on the entofacial structures of experimental animals. Am J Orthod Oral Surg 1946;32:467–85.

101. Holden C. et al, Royal College of Nursing. Nutrition and Child Health, p. 59. Elsevier Health Sciences, 2000.

102. Tomkins P. Bird C. The Secret Life of Plants.

103. http://www.biodynamics.com/biodynamics. Biodynamic farming is a system developed by Austrian scientist and philosopher, Rudolf Steiner, in the early twentieth century. It produces foods that are even more nutritious then organically produced foods. I have personally noted a significant difference (in look and taste) between organic and biodynamic vegetables. The best yogurt I have tasted was a brand called Seven Stars, which was made from biodynamically produced milk.

104. Natural Hygiene is a system of health and healing based on the principle that the body is self-healing and self-maintaining, if it is given its natural foods, rest, sunshine, clean air and clean water. http://naturalhygienesociety.org/present.html.

INDEX

Acid forming minerals, 45
Algae, 80
Alkaline forming minerals, 45, 46
Ammonia, 62
Antioxidants, 8
Aspartame, 19, 20
B vitamins, 37, 38
Calcium, 43
Calories, 93, 94, 98
Carbohydrates, 7, 13-21
Carotenoids, 47
Chemical digestion, 54
Chlorine, 65
Cholesterol, 31, 32, 33
Chromium, 44
Cleansing & Elimination, 59
Coconut oil, 33
Colonic irrigation, 60, 61
Dental Fillings, 65-66
DHA, 27
Diabetes, 182-185
Digestion, 49-57
Enema, 60
Enzymes, 8
EPA, 27
Essential Fatty Acids, 26, 27
Fermentative bacteria, 56, 57
Fiber, 17, 18
Flavonoids, 46
Flax seeds, 73
Fluoride, 65
Fructose, 14

Galactose, 14
Gallbladder, 53
Glucose, 14
Glycogen, 17
Hepatic Portal System, 53, 54
Hiatal Hernia, 51
High Fructose Corn syrup, 19
High-density lipoproteins, 31
Hormones, 9
Hydrochloric acid, 51
Intestinal Bacteria, 56, 57
Iodine, 44
Iron, 44
Lactose, 15
Large Intestine, 52, 56
Lipids, 21-33
Liver, 53, 61-62
Low density lipoproteins, 31
Lymphatic System, 64, 164, 165
Macronutrients, 7
Magnesium, 43
Maltose, 15
Manganese, 44
Margarine and Shortening, 28
Mechanical digestion, 54
Mercury, 65-66, 75
Metabolism, 9
Methylcobolamin, 40
Microminerals, 44
Micronutrients, 7
Minerals, 42
Molybdenum, 44

Monounsaturated fatty acid, 24
Mucus, 51
Neotame, 20
Nickel, 44
Omega-3 fatty acids, 26
Omega-6 fatty acids, 26
Palm oil, 33
Pancreas, 52, 53
Partially hydrogenated oils, 28, 29
Pepsin, 51
pH, 45
Phospholipids, 30
Phosphorus, 44
Phytonutrients, 46
Polyunsaturated fatty acids, 24
Potassium, 43
Probiotic Supplements, 57
Protein Requirements, 36
Proteins, 33-36
Putrefactive bacteria, 56
Refined Sugar, 18
Saccharin, 19
Saturated fats, 23
Selenium, 44
Sesame seeds, 74
Small Intestine, 51, 56
Sodium, 43
sodium fluoride, 65
Sorbitol, 19
Starch, 16, 17

Steroids, 31
Stevia, 19
Stomach, 50, 51
Sucralose, 19
Sucrose, 15
Sugar Addiction, 20, 21
Sugars, 14
Sulfur, 44
Sweeteners, 18
Toxins, 9
Trans Fats, 29, 30
Triglycerides, 23
Unsaturated fatty acids, 23
Urea, 62, 63
Uric Acid, 62, 63
Vaccinations, 178, 179
Vitamins, 46
Vitamin B_{12}, 40
Vitamin C, 40-43
Vitamin D, 42
Vitamin E, 42
Vitamin K, 42
Vitamins, 37, 38
Walnuts, 73
Water, 10, 11, 64, 65
Weight Loss, 191-196, 225, 226
Whole food, 6
Xylitol, 18
Yeast, 188, 189
Zinc, 44

About the Author

Dr. Scarfalloto began his career as a health professional by graduating from The Swedish Institute of Massage in New York City in 1978, where he also taught Anatomy and Physiology and Swedish Massage.

He worked as a massage therapist for several years, until he received his Doctor of Chiropractic Degree at Life College in 1984. He maintains a chiropractic practice, specializing in low-force spinal adjusting, muscle balancing, nutrition and techniques for promoting the health of the integral organs.

Dr. Scarfalloto teaches Anatomy & Physiology and Nutrition at ASHA School of Massage, where he designed the Anatomy & Physiology and Nutrition programs. His other teaching interests include two seminars called *Visceral Technique*, and *Muscle Testing for Body Therapists*.

In addition to his chiropractic practice and teaching, Dr. Scarfalloto has also published three other books, called *The Dance of Opposites, Cultivating Inner Harmony* and *The Edge of Time*.

Made in the USA
Charleston, SC
01 June 2014